RETIRE RICH!

Winning Strategies for Higher Retirement Income

Stephen Gadsden

B.A., M.A., C.F.P.

 **McGraw-Hill Ryerson**

Toronto Montreal New York Burr Ridge Bangkok Bogotá Caracas
Lisbon London Madrid Mexico City Milan New Delhi Seoul
Singapore Sydney Taipei

McGraw-Hill
Ryerson Limited

A Subsidiary of The McGraw·Hill Companies

Care has been taken to trace ownership of copyright material contained in this text; however, the publisher will welcome any information that enables them to rectify any reference or credit for subsequent editions.

The material in this publication is provided for information purposes only. Laws, regulations and procedures are constantly changing, and the examples given are intended to be general guidelines only. This book is sold with the understanding that neither the authors nor the publisher is engaged in rendering professional advice. It is recommended that legal, accounting, tax, and other advice or assistance be obtained before acting on any information contained in this book. Personal services of a competent professional should be sought.

ISBN: 0-07-560158-3

1 2 3 4 5 6 7 8 9 0 TRI 7 6 5 4 3 2 1 0 9 8
Printed and bound in Canada.

Canadian Cataloguing in Publication Data

Gadsden, Stephen
    Retire rich: winning strategies for higher retirement income

Previously published under title: The Authoritative Canadian guide to understanding retirement options.

Includes index.
ISBN 0-07-560158-3

1. Retirement income – Canada – Planning. 2. Retirement – Canada. 3. Finance, Personal – Canada. I. Title. II. Title. Authoritative Canadian guide to understanding retirement options.

HG179.G334 1998   332.024'01   C98-932803-1

Publisher: **Joan Homewood**
Editorial Co-ordinator: **Catherine Leek**
Production Coordinator: **Susanne Penny**
Editor: **Tita Zierer**
Electronic Page Composition: **Pages Design**
Cover Design: **Dianna Little**

To my wife and friend,
Eileen Rose

About the Author

Stephen Gadsden is recognized as one of Canada's leading financial authorities on personal finance and investment. He has published more than 150 articles on personal finance and has published nine books on estate, investment and retirement planning. He has been a frequent guest on radio and television across Canada and he has been profiled in many of today's major newspapers, including *The Calgary Herald, The Financial Post, The Globe and Mail, The Toronto Star* and *The Vancouver Sun.* Mr. Gadsden is also contributing editor to *Microsoft Money 98, Canadian Edition.*

Mr. Gadsden is a branch manager and senior financial advisor at The Equion Group, Toronto, and he offers financial advice on estate, investment and retirement planning. Mr. Gadsden also provides one of Canada's finest investment portfolio repair services.

In addition to helping his clients achieve financial security, Mr. Gadsden conducts personal finance seminars and workshops for associations, banks, trusts, public & private corporations, government and special interest groups located across the country.

To arrange your own personal financial review or financial seminar, you can reach Mr. Gadsden by dialing 416-495-9339 or 1-800-591-7568 or by E-mail at **gadsden@yesic.com.** Visit Mr. Gadsden's advisor web page at **http://www.equion.com.**

Mr. Gadsden is a *Chartered Financial Planner* and graduate of the Canadian Institute of Financial Planning (CIFP), the Investment Funds Institute of Canada (IFIC) and the Canadian Securities Institute (CSI), Toronto. He is also a *Certified Financial Planner* and member of the Canadian Association of Financial Planners (CAFP), The Financial Planners Standards Council of Canada (FPSCC) and the Canadian Association of Insurance and Financial Advisors (CAIFA).

Other Books by Stephen Gadsden

The Canadian Guide to Investing for Life
ISBN 0-07-552820-7 $18.99

The Canadian Mutual Funds Handbook, Third Edition, Fully Revised
ISBN 0-07-560155-9 (3rd ed.) $18.99

The New Heir's Guide to Managing Your Inheritance
ISBN 0-07-552772-3 $21.99

Contents

Preface: THE IMPORTANCE OF STARTING NOW ix

Chapter One: RETIREMENT UNDER FIRE 1

Chapter Two: SIX KEYS TO RETIREMENT WEALTH 13

Chapter Three: EFFECTIVE STRATEGIES TO
ACCUMULATE WEALTH 49

Chapter Four: HOW TO PLAN YOUR RETIREMENT
FINANCES..83

Chapter Five: TODAY'S RETIREMENT RESOURCES....97

Chapter Six: TWELVE SUPER INCOME
STRATEGIES...125

Chapter Seven: REAL LIFE INVESTING—
FOUR CASE STUDIES...........................153

Chapter Eight: PLANNING FOR WHEN YOU'RE
GONE...169

Chapter Nine: THIRTY HINTS FOR RETIREMENT
RICHES 187

Appendix I: Retirement Planning Resources 187
    Health Issues..197
    Insurance Issues 200
    Financial Planning & Investment Issues...........................201
    Pensions 202

Appendix II: Revenue Canada Taxation & TIPS 203

Appendix III: Samples of Important Estate Planning
                      Documents 210
     Estate Planning Worksheet 210
     Will 216
     Living Will 224
     General Power of Attorney 226
     Power of Attorney for Personal Care 231
     Continuing Power of Attorney 233

Appendix IV: Sources for Further Reading............................235

Appendix V: How to Find an Excellent Retirement
                      Advisor 237

Index 241

The Importance of Starting Now

A March 1998 *Gallup Poll* conducted by Deloitte and Touche, Toronto, revealed the unnerving fact that 59 per cent of people polled admitted that their net worth probably would amount to less than $250,000 by the time they retire. This surprising statistic comes at a time when past sources of financial security, such as the Canada Pension Plan (CPP) and Old Age Security (OAS), are on the chopping block, employment remains a dream for about 2.5 million Canadians, and traditional long-term job security has been replaced by longer hours and decreased pay. No matter where you look, traditional sources of financial security have given way to a new lean and mean Canadian reality. Those people who can adjust to this climate will succeed, while those who cannot adjust will find the achievement of financial security more difficult than ever.

At a time when Canadians should be more concerned than ever with retirement planning they are in fact contributing far less to registered retirement savings plans (RRSP) than ever before. Almost 20 per cent of the *Gallup Poll* respondents said they had never contributed to an RRSP, while 50 per cent said they had contributed less than their maximum allowable amount. It makes you wonder just how many people will be able to afford to retire at all. The situation is exacerbated further by the fact that newly released data from *Statistics Canada* show Canadians are living longer than ever before – about 78.6 years.

Retire Rich!: Winning Strategies for Higher Retirement Income has been written to provide you with the advice you need to insure that you will enjoy your retirement years with dignity, financial security, self-respect and the knowledge that you've accomplished a job well done. This book is designed to give you all the tools you need to get you to a level of financial security easier and faster than you could on your own.

But, do not be deceived by the title. You can retire rich. But the onus to do so rests squarely on your shoulders.

The fact of the matter is that all of us need to plan for our future to one degree or another. And this is my point. Just how much planning does one have to undergo to assure a prosperous financial future? Do I need a complete financial plan? Or do I only need a financial tune-up? What if the rules of the game change tomorrow? Do I need to revise my retirement program? If so, what do I need to revise and by how much? These and many more questions like them affect us every day of our lives. My book *Retire Rich! Winning Strategies to Higher Retirement Income* has been written to help you answer these questions and keep you on track to a positive and self-fulfilling financial future. *Bona fortuna.*

Stephen Gadsden
Certified Financial Planner
Aurora, Ontario

December 1998

CHAPTER ONE

RETIREMENT UNDER FIRE

When it comes to funding their retirement years, one of the biggest problems Canadians have had to deal with is *government*. For decades, federal fiscal and monetary policy and, to a lesser extent, provincial policy, have exerted a huge influence on the way Canadians managed their financial affairs. In the past, fiscal policy in the form of high taxation hindered the ability of Canadians to save and invest for their financial future. At its worst, unbearably high taxation discouraged legions of income earners to save at all, preferring to live well now at the expense of financial security down the road. Decades of questionable monetary policy also had its impact by creating volatile boom-bust economic cycles that caused havoc for Canadians across the country. As a consequence of a series of poorly designed federal budgets and government-spending policies, Canadians suffered years of financial constraint and instability. The result of such fiscal and monetary ineptitude was an insufferable period of high inflation, high borrowing costs and the launch of such punitive tax grabs as the goods and services tax (GST) and provincial sales tax (PST).

One of the areas that has had the largest impact on the way Canadians save and invest for their future, however, has been the gradual revamping of Canada's public and private pension system. Undertaken first by the Macdonald Commission in 1985, the federal government began its first steps towards what was to become a complete restructuring of Canada's entire pension system. Under the guise of making what was labeled a diverse and complicated pension system into a more equitable, cost-efficient model, Ottawa began to systematically undo its financial commitment to Canadians. The result was a series of changes that would save our government billions of dollars, but shift the financial shortfall back to Canadian taxpayers.

THE FAILURE OF CANADA'S PENSION SYSTEM

For the first time in history our federal government is faced with the fact that a major percentage of today's population will retire within a comparatively short period of time. Numerous demographic studies have shown that the bulk of working Canadians today were born as a result of the great "baby boom" that occurred immediately after World War II. According to recent statistics, an unprecedented proportion of Canada's population will reach 65 years of age—in many cases the age for mandatory retirement—by the year 2031. Only 9.7 per cent of Canada's total population had reached age 65 in 1961. By 2031, a full 23.9 per cent of Canadians will be 65 years of age or older. If you factor the predicted population of 30 million people into the equation, about 7.2 million Canadians will be retired. Factor in the probability that an additional 20 per cent of the population will be below 18 years of age and you'll discover that for every person who is actively employed, about one person will be either retired or as yet be ineligible for full-time work. This means that between government and taxpayers, a full 44 per cent of the population will have to be supported under today's current pension system! According to government pundits, this is unacceptable. This is because, as more and more Canadians retire from the work force, there will be a corresponding decrease in the size of the labour pool. A decrease in the labour pool means less tax revenues that can be used to fund pension handouts. In retrospect, it's no wonder that our federal government is determined to get out of the retirement funding business.

The trend towards an aging population isn't the only one facing our government. According to *Statistics Canada,* Canadians are living longer—78.6 years in fact. Projected longevity will increase to 81 years by 2031. This means that current pension resources in the form of the CPP, OAS and the proposed Seniors Benefit programme will have to be increased dramatically if Canadians are to continue to receive publicly funded retirement benefits. The cost of doing so, unfortunately, may outweigh the long-term benefits of these social programmes. Based on the numbers, government actuaries assert that funding of the CPP, for example, must increase substantially to ensure that we "baby boomers" have access to this social assistance plan by the time we retire. But don't look to government coffers to do so. The cash required will come directly from the pockets of Canadian taxpayers. Here's how government will accomplish its task.

RESTRUCTURING THE CANADA PENSION PLAN

We all know about our government's concern for the future viability of the CPP. With the 1996 budget, the federal government launched a marketing campaign explaining that our CPP was headed for financial difficulty. Later the same year, a much-touted federal task force in the form of a national forum trooped across Canada gathering responses from taxpayers as to how to best fix the CPP so that it might continue to supplement future incomes of retired Canadians. The federal government released the results of its research and recommended strategies that it said would rescue the CPP from financial collapse. According to government actuaries, the CPP would run out of money sometime during the early part of the second millenium. Without an immediate increase in CPP contributions, they said, the plan would have to be wound up.

When the CPP was first implemented in 1966, the plan's funding was based on what is known as a "pay-as-you-go" formula, where employed Canadians contributed a percentage of their income to the plan. Actuarial studies in 1965 showed that CPP premiums could be set at a comparatively low rate once the plan was implemented. This was based on the observation that, during the 1960s, Canada was enjoying a wave of economic expansion and a rapidly expanding work force. This economic expansion, coupled with increasing numbers of employed Canadians, guaranteed that CPP contributions would continue to outpace benefits paid over time. With the advent of the 1980s, however, a gradual economic shift occurred. For the first time in two decades, Canada's economic expansion and employment peaked. In addition, where inflation had remained comparatively benign through the 1960s and 1970s, the 1980s brought dramatically increased inflation and an actual loss in real wage growth. The end result for the CPP was a drop in the amount of capital inflow to the plan. As this situation worsened through the 1980s, government increased contribution rates in an attempt to shore up funding for the plan. In the government's 1996 budget, it recognized that if it continued to raise contribution rates Canadians would eventually pay 14.2 per cent of their income to fund the CPP by 2030.

According to the current Liberal government, the Canada Pension Plan's restructuring will ensure its survival well into the second millenium. To do so, however, Canadians must realize that simply raising contribution rates will serve only to extend the life of the CPP for a few years, not solve the structural weaknesses of the plan. To be effective, any proposed solution must account not only for the consequences of declining economic and employment growth, but other important factors as well. First, demographic changes over the next several years will result in far fewer Canadians contributing to the plan. Second, a major segment of Canada's working population will retire at almost the same time. Third, as Canada's health and social system improves and the benefits of more sophisticated medical research and improved nutritional knowledge are enjoyed by the general population, the longevity of Canadians will improve substantially and eventually will result in more Canadians drawing benefits from the CPP for longer periods of time. Fourth, economic growth in Canada is predicted to continue to slow over the next decade and this will have a negative impact on the amount of money CPP deductions will generate from an already shrinking segment of Canada's employed.

On February 14, 1997 the Liberal government introduced and eventually passed proposals they believed would allow the CPP to retain its function as a supplementary income plan for retired Canadians. According to these proposals, there will be no changes for current CPP recipients or for individuals who have turned age 65 by the end of 1997. Traditional retirement benefit age restrictions of between 60 and 70 years remain in place and full indexing of CPP benefits will continue for all recipients. The down side, however, was to increase the cost of CPP contributions and reduce benefits. CPP contributions are to rise from the 1997 rate of 5.85 per cent to 9.9 per cent by 2003. Based on actuarial studies, once this so-called *steady-state* rate has increased to its 9.9 per cent ceiling, no further increases will be necessary.

In a bid to reduce costs by 9.3 per cent by the year 2030, the government intends to tighten and streamline administration procedures to reduce work hours, improve processing and verification, and reduce CPP overpayments. But, it will also change certain aspects of benefits currently available under the plan. First, determining your benefit will be based on the average of pensionable earnings over the last five years, rather than three; depending on your income, this may reduce CPP benefits you receive at retirement. Second, to receive CPP benefits under the plan's disability provision you will have to have made CPP contributions in four of the last six years; if not, disability benefits will not be available. Third, disability benefits will be based on the maximum pensionable earnings at the time your disability occurs and will be indexed to age 65. Fourth, combined survivor and disability benefits will be reduced in many cases to the higher of the two benefits plus 60 per cent of the lower benefit to a maximum disability ceiling. No longer will qualifying taxpayers receive two separate flat dollar amounts. Fifth, the CPP lump sum death benefit has been reduced from 10 per cent of annual maximum pensionable earnings or $3,580 for 1997 to a maximum of $2,500 in 1998 and beyond. All of these changes will mean less dollars in the pockets of taxpayers.

Restructuring the CPP, though, doesn't end here. Other important issues have yet to be addressed and, based on past experience, it is quite likely that other changes to the CPP will end up costing you even more in lost income either in the form of higher contributions, income tax or the gradual erosion of CPP benefits. The government is hard at work defining new rules to reduce partial CPP pension amounts as well as implementing mandatory CPP income splitting between spouses on marriage breakdown. The government is also looking at a reduction in survivor benefits for working widows and widowers as well as raising the maximum limit of pensionable earnings on which taxpayers calculate CPP contribution levels. An interesting debate surrounds whether to continue simultaneous payment of CPP benefits and unemployment benefits, which currently allows anyone who draws CPP benefits to also draw up to 44 weeks of unemployment payments upon formal retirement from the work force.

THE SENIORS BENEFIT—NOW YOU SEE IT...

Old Age Security (OAS) and other supplementary pension benefits such as the Guaranteed Income Supplement (GIS) and Spouse's Allowance/Widowed Spouse's Allowance (SPA) are also being restructured. The reasons given for restructuring are exactly the same as those given for the CPP. The difference is, however, that Old Age Security is being dismantled entirely and is to be replaced by what is known as the *Seniors Benefit.* While opinions differ as to how much the new Seniors Benefit will affect Canadians, most observers contend that the Seniors Benefit will mean a reduction in retirement benefits for most Canadian taxpayers. Here are the highlights of these changes and how they will affect you.

CPP benefits are paid directly by taxpayers. According to the old "pay-as-you-go" formula, contributions made by working Canadians are supposed to pay for benefits received. This formula no longer works as a result of a shrinking labour pool, an aging population and slowing economic growth. OAS, the GIS and SPA are paid out of the general revenues of the federal government, including taxation. Rather than increase taxation as a means of funding OAS and related programmes, government believes it far more prudent to dump the Old Age Security benefit, the GIS and SPA altogether, and replace them with the Seniors Benefit. According to this new programme, say government officials, the Seniors Benefit will prevent abuse currently found in the old benefit system by reducing benefits to higher income pensioners and fully protecting lower income recipients. Overall, the new Seniors Benefit will give higher benefits to those individuals who really need them. No longer will OAS be seen as the right of taxpayers who have simply reached their sixty-fifth birthdays.

The new Seniors Benefit will be implemented fully in 2001.[1] Anyone receiving OAS, GIS and SPA or who reached age 60 by December 31, 1995 will remain unaffected by this new benefit system. The government states that 75 per cent of seniors will be better off under the Seniors Benefit, while nine out of ten senior women will be better off than they are today. The SPA will remain as it is but recipients will enjoy an annual increase of $120. The Seniors Benefit payment will be based on the combined incomes of married couples and benefit payments will be received separately. Those receiving GIS benefits will also receive an annual increase of $120. Benefits will be received tax-free. Finally, benefits

---

1. In July 1998, Minister of Finance, Paul Martin, put the implementation of the Seniors Benefit on hold, citing a booming economy as the reason for doing so. At that time, however, it was not clear whether the Liberals were going to shelve the proposal temporarily or throw it out. It is my opinion that the Liberals will reintroduce the Seniors Benefit once political opposition has cooled to tolerable levels. I therefore have left my discussion the way it is for future reference.

provided under the Seniors Benefit will be fully indexed to inflation right up to the maximum threshold of $52,000 for individuals and $78,000 for couples before benefits are lost entirely.

What the government doesn't tell you is that, while benefits are tax-free, the Seniors Benefit actually imposes a very high combined income tax rate and a similarly high claw-back rate. Second, the age and pension tax credits will be eliminated once the Seniors Benefit is implemented in 2001. Third, it seems rather unfair that high income Canadians, who often pay punitively high amounts of income tax, will lose all seniors benefits. However for those showing little other income the Seniors Benefit is quite generous. This fact will provoke Canadian taxpayers to reduce the amount of other income they receive as much as they possibly can. Actuaries believe that the new Seniors Benefit will cost government only $68.1 billion as opposed to $77.3 billion currently projected for the present pension system by 2030. This will only work under ideal conditions. Where Canadians are encouraged to show less taxable income in order to reap the rewards of the new Seniors Benefit, will these projected savings really bear fruit? If not, we are no further ahead with this system than with the one we have in place today. If costs do in fact increase to eventually nullify the desired target for the year 2030, who will end up paying for it? Taxpayers, of course!

REGISTERED RETIREMENT SAVINGS PLANS (RRSPs)

RRSPs have been one of the principal ways Canadians have been able to build their retirement nest eggs. For every dollar you contribute to your plan, you save income tax equal to your marginal tax rate. In addition, earnings generated inside your RRSP grow on a tax-deferred basis until retirement, after which money may be withdrawn at lower levels of tax. Subject to a predetermined formula, income earners can contribute up to $13,500 per year. So, someone who is paying federal tax at 29 per cent and Ontario tax at 40 per cent, for example, could save as much as $5,481 ($13,500 x 40.6%) each year he or she contributes the maximum amount allowable to an RRSP. This is a substantial tax saving and, where money inside of an RRSP is allowed to compound for 10 years or more, becomes one of the most powerful ways of accumulating retirement capital. Originally, RRSP contributions were set at 20 per cent of your *net qualifying earned income* (gross annual income less CPP and UI contributions). Your maximum allowable RRSP contributions were fixed according to a predetermined schedule as shown in Figure 1.1.

Changes to the Old RRSP Rules

By 1996, however, the federal government realized that such generous RRSP contribution limits were in fact costing it billions of dollars a year in lost tax revenues. Ottawa subsequently changed those ceilings so that future RRSP contribution limits would now be restricted to $13,500 a year until the year 2003. Only in 2004 would RRSP contribution limits again be allowed to increase and eventually be indexed to what is known as the *average industrial wage,* commencing in 2006. Government also lowered the percentage of net qualifying earned income allowed from 20 per cent to just 18 per cent. These two changes dramatically reduced the amount of capital Canadians could accumulate in their RRSPs.

Figure 1.1

Original Money Purchase Limits and Current RRSP Contribution Limits

Year	Original Money Purchase Limit $	Original Current RRSP Contribution Limit $
1991	12,500	11,500
1992	12,500	12,500
1993	13,500	12,500
1994	14,500	13,500
1995	15,500	14,500
1996	Indexed	15,500
1997	Indexed	Indexed

To illustrate this point, assume you paid income tax at a combined marginal rate of 40 per cent and could have contributed your RRSP maximum under pre-1996 RRSP rules for 1996 through 2001. Your combined tax savings would have amounted to $31,000 for those five tax years. If your combined $77,500 RRSP investment were allowed to compound at 10 per cent per year for 20 years, your RRSP would have grown to $521,381.25. Under the revised rules of 1996, your total RRSP contributions would have amounted to $67,500, resulting in a combined tax saving of just $27,000. The end-value of your RRSP nest egg would be $454,106.25, for a retirement capital shortfall of $67,275. If, however, your net earned income did not allow you to contribute your maximum RRSP amount, Revenue Canada still wins. This is because your percentage of qualifying earned income has dropped from 20 per cent to 18 per cent. So, on $50,000 of earned income, your RRSP contribution would amount to $10,000 under the old rules and only $9,000 under the 18 per cent rule. If you paid tax at a marginal rate of 42 per cent, Revenue Canada would get an additional $420 each year. Multiply this figure by 8 million taxpayers and the tally amounts to a cool $3.4 billion tax grab! This is a great deal for the federal government, but a poor one for you and I.

The government also changed the rules concerning RRSP contribution *carry-forward* provisions. In 1991 taxpayers were allowed to carry-forward unused RRSP contribution amounts for up to seven years. This concept was introduced to provide more flexibility for contributors, especially taxpayers who had moderate to low incomes or who were self-employed. In the March 6, 1996 budget, carry-forward limits were dropped. This meant that taxpayers had the option to carry-forward accumulated RRSP contribution amounts indefinitely. While increased flexibility was probably the goal of legislators, being able to carry-forward unused contributions indefinitely actually resulted in a decrease in the amount of money flowing into RRSPs. As of January 1, 1997, unused RRSP contribution room amounted to a whopping $132.3 billion. To put things in perspective, this dollar figure accounts for almost 75 per cent of the $179.3 billion of contributions available to Canadian taxpayers for 1996. This huge accumulation of unused contributions occurred because there was even less of an obligation on the part of taxpayers to make contributions on a regular basis.

In addition to this discipline problem, delaying RRSP contributions meant a corresponding loss in tax-deferred compounding of assets held inside an RRSP. As well, overly large lump sum RRSP contributions can sometimes push a taxpayer's taxable income level down by one or more tax brackets, making the tax-effectiveness of the RRSP contribution less so than if a taxpayer made regular annual contributions. Where a taxpayer retired and received a severance package, making a one-time catch-up contribution could trigger *alternative minimum tax* (AMT)—an item which was introduced to ensure taxpayers who received large retirement settlements would pay a minimum amount of income tax (rescinded for 1998 and subsequent years). The pre-1991 "use it or lose it" rule, while restrictive, did force Canadians to contribute to their financial future in an effective manner. Today, this important incentive is gone.

Prior to 1995, Canadians were allowed to make a *one-time RRSP over-contribution* of $8000. While not tax deductible, this over-contribution amount could be carried forward to a year when further RRSP deductions could be claimed. The real beauty behind an over-contribution was that money inside of the RRSP could continue to compound on a tax-deferred basis until removed. If given a minimum of 10 years to grow, an $8,000 over-contribution to an RRSP could grow virtually free of income tax. If you had over-contributed this amount at the beginning of 1990 and earned 10 per cent per year for the next 20 years, you would have been able to increase your retirement nest egg by $53,820. Extend this period to 30 years and your over-contribution would have grown to $139,592.22! Unfortunately, the Federal Budget of February 26, 1995 reduced the over-contribution amount to just $2,000, where it remains to this day. While not a significant tax reducing strategy, an RRSP over-contribution of $8,000 allowed your money to grow on a very efficient, tax-deferred basis which could add tens of thousands of dollars to the value of your retirement nest egg.

Pension revisions continued throughout 1995 and 1996. A major tax grab occurred again in 1995 when the federal government disallowed further rollovers of retirement allowances into RRSPs. Under the old rules, a taxpayer who was retiring could roll over the proceeds of his or her retiring allowance up to certain prescribed limits, which in the major-ity of cases would amount to huge tax savings. The new rules stopped further rollovers of retirement allowance benefits directly to an RRSP. Now taxpayers can only contribute up to $2,000 for each year or part year of employment service before 1996. A further $1,500 per year was allowed for every year a taxpayer wasn't a member of, or had money invested in, a registered pension plan (RPP) or deferred profit sharing plan (DPSP) prior to 1989. Any employment service earned after 1995 would be ineligible for a direct RRSP rollover. As you can imagine, someone who had worked for 30 years and had never con-tributed to an RPP or DPSP could have rolled over up to $60,000 directly into an RRSP without tax. Considering the vast number of Canadians who will be leaving the work force over the next 30 years, this legislative change was a masterful stroke of genius. Imagine, almost 7.2 million boomers retiring in the next 25 to 30 years, many of whom will have received substantial retiring allowances. What's particularly surprising here is that Canadians allowed the federal government to get away with it!

To illustrate one consequence of this rule change, let's assume that you're age 60 and just received a $30,000 retiring allowance from your employer for whom you worked 15 years. According to the old rollover formula you could have protected your retiring allowance by rolling it directly into an RRSP. If you had left it there until age 71 and it earned 10 per cent per year, your retiring allowance would have grown to $77,812.27. When converted to an income stream, this capital would have generated an additional minimum retirement income of $6,100! Under the new rules, though, you received $30,000, paid tax of $12,180 (using the 1998 revised Ontario tax rate of 40 per cent), leaving a balance of $17,820 to invest outside of an RRSP. If we ignore the fact that you probably paid higher tax on your other income during the year in which you received your $30,000, and you earned no dividends on your $17,820 investment, your nest egg would have amounted to just $45,079.24 under exactly the same conditions as the RRSP. This is a big difference and quite a penalty for those of us looking to maximize our retirement savings over the coming years.

Another notable change occurred on March 6, 1996 when Minister of Finance, Paul Martin, lowered the year in which all registered assets, such as RRSPs, Life Income Retirement Accounts (LIRAs) and deferred annuities, had to be converted to income generating vehicles. In the case of RRSPs, for example, pensioners now have to convert them to either registered retirement income funds (RRIF) or registered annuities (RA) by the end of the year in which they turn age 69. The old age limit was 71 years. The rationale here was a simple tax grab by both Ottawa and the provinces. Today, more and more Canadians work well beyond what was once considered to be the unofficial retirement age of 65. Government knows that this trend will continue upwards as the baby boom generation continues to age. As a result of a lower conversion age, many Canadians will be forced to receive additional retirement income earlier and thus pay a greater amount of income tax than they would have under the old age 71 rule.

Furthermore, considering that many Canadians still have qualifying earned income on which to make tax-deductible RRSP contributions, the lowering of the age limit to 69 years effectively quashes two full years of RRSP contributions. If you were lucky enough to be able to contribute your maximum of $13,500 for each of those two years, you would have lost about $12,000 in tax savings. What the Liberals also don't tell you is that you have likewise lost one of the most important features of RRSPs, namely, tax-deferred compounding of earnings. With a potential 7.2 million taxpayers falling into this catch basin over the next few decades, it doesn't take a lot to appreciate that, with this one simple legislative change, federal and provincial governments have once again sucked up billions of precious tax dollars from taxpayers!

Less obvious tax grabs are found in changes made to private pensions such as *defined benefit* and *defined contribution pension plans.* With the freezing of contribution amounts to RRSPs and defined contribution plans such as money purchase plans in the March, 1996 budget, many higher income Canadians lost out as a result of lost contributions, tax savings and lower levels of tax-deferred, compound growth. This is because indexing allowed taxpayers to stay with, and occasionally exceed, the long-term corrosive effects of inflation. However, with contribution limits frozen since 1996, these high-income earners continue to pay taxes at the highest marginal rate and continue to be exposed to the effects of inflation. With less money in their pockets, they have an even harder time trying to reach their retirement goals. Members of defined benefit registered pension plans (RPP) found that the maximum pension amount of $1,722 per year of employment service was frozen again until 2004 as a result of the Liberal's 1996 budget. Originally, in 1976, members of defined benefit RPPs could earn up to 2 per cent of earnings, to a maximum of $1,722, per year of employment service. It was due to be indexed to inflation in 1991 and again in 1996. This indexing of RPP contribution amounts would have brought a badly eroded pension contribution system up to date, allowing plan members to build sufficient retirement capital in the face of long-term inflation. The federal government has promised to implement inflation indexing in 2005.

RETIREMENT PLANNING AND THE IMPACT OF PENSION REFORM

When you consider the many changes government has made to the pension system during the last decade, it's easy to see where these reforms will lead Canadians. Thirty-two years ago few taxpayers suspected that the treasured Canada Pension Plan would find itself in serious financial difficulty early in the second millenium. Fewer Canadians still would have dared believe that Old Age Security, the Guaranteed Income Supplement and Spouse's Allowance would also be candidates for the fiscal chopping block. Difficult as it may be to comprehend, pension reform is today's reality. The government is committed to the revision of our public pension system and, short of a general uprising by the electorate, will not be dissuaded from its task. So, with no acceptable alternative at hand, Canadians should prepare for the worst and acknowledge once and for all that they will no longer enjoy the level of financial assistance governments offered pensioners in the past. For the first time since the CPP was implemented in 1966, the financial future of Canadians has been uncoupled as a result of both federal and provincial agendas. Canadian taxpayers will have to assume more and more responsibility for their future financial welfare. Our financial success in retirement will depend entirely on how quickly we accept this new financial reality and how well we adapt to it.

The future doesn't look good. As mentioned in the preface to this book, just 41 per cent of Canadians polled stated that they would have more than $250,000 of accumulated assets by the time they retired. This means that a full 59 per cent expect to enter their retirement years depending on some form of government-sponsored pension or income supplement. As remarkable as this fact is, it is particularly troubling to note that the major source of retirement income on which these individuals will depend, will be proceeds from employer-sponsored registered pension plans, not from liquid assets such as individual RRSPs, accumulated investments or cash. When you consider that almost 60 per cent of the 7.2 million Canadians who will be retiring over the next three decades will have less than $250,000 of retirement assets to live on, this situation has far reaching ramifications for society in general. The prospect of having one of every three Canadians retired from the work force is a challenge. Having three out of every five retirees in financial distress is frightening.

If you think I am being "alarmist," think about what the future holds for those of us who have yet to prepare financially for our retirement. Results of an Angus Reid Group poll conducted in July, 1998 show that the majority of Canadians contacted believe that their financial situation has deteriorated since 1989.[2] Of the 1,515 adults surveyed, 54 per cent said their financial circumstances had declined. Only 15 per cent stated that their financial situation had improved, while 31 per cent believed their circumstances remained the same. The most cited reason for this unfortunate state of affairs was the difficulty experienced by Canadians in handling their personal finances—in other words, to make ends meet. What this poll doesn't emphasize, however, is the fact that the group that has felt the greatest deterioration in financial circumstances—those who earned up to $60,000 per year—also represents the majority of Canada's working population. If people cannot improve their financial situation while employed and earning $60,000 per year, what chance do these individuals have to enter their retirement years with dignity and financial security? And, if this isn't enough, what will happen to the children of such families? Will they be able to break out of their parents' experience and improve their lot?

Canadians are living much longer thanks to improvements in nutrition, sanitation, health care and medical advances. One in four Canadians age 50 years today can expect to live to at least age 90. How will society cope if a large proportion of retired Canadians have to depend on some form of government-sponsored benefit for long periods of time? Will the government raise taxes or implement higher contribution rates to the CPP? If so, just how much money are Canadians able to contribute to assist those people who are unable to look after themselves?

What can be done about it? Obviously, government is willing to do only so much. As I mentioned earlier in this chapter, the responsibility for our future financial security has been placed squarely back on our shoulders. It's up to the individual. Retirement planning, while considered more a luxury 10 or 15 years ago, should now become a major priority for Canadians who are concerned about their financial future. The big question, today, is *how to go about arranging our personal finances in a way that makes the most efficient use of what savings we can muster to build sufficient retirement capital as quickly as we can.* As you will see in the next chapter, the financial success we enjoy in our retirement will depend almost exclusively on how we define the obstacles to our financial success and what strategies we are prepared to implement now to ensure a prosperous and secure financial future.

---

2. Cited in *The Globe and Mail*, August 4, 1998, p. A7.

CHAPTER TWO

SIX KEYS TO RETIREMENT WEALTH

M any people who make the commitment to build a secure financial future are surprised at how difficult it really can be to begin the financial planning process. This is due to a number of factors. First and foremost, human nature being what it is, people have always preferred to take the path of least resistance when it comes to decision making. This is especially true when it comes to making big decisions, such as providing for one's financial future. Think about it. If you had the choice of spending all of your hard-earned money each month, secure in the knowledge that the government would look after you when you are too old to work, would you bother to sock away money for your retirement? Your answer would likely be a resounding no! We have to ignite the *desire* to achieve financial success. Without the cultivation of this desire, most people remain stuck where they are.

Another factor is the need to develop a new *attitude* towards successful money management. Poor habits, such as not budgeting, not saving systematically, and not paying off debt on a timely basis, can be hard to overcome, especially if these habits have become ingrained over the years. No amount of desire alone will eradicate these and other poor money skills. This is why good financial planners will always probe to see just how deep a person's personal commitment to financial success really is and how much effort will be pledged by an individual to achieve it. To be successful at the money game, you have to be totally committed to money management excellence and be committed to it over the short, medium and long term. To do this, you have to adopt an attitude that is commensurate with the task at hand and carry it through until you have achieved your goal.

An equally important factor is having the *determination* to achieve your financial goal. Having the desire and attitude to achieve financial success will orient you to the task at hand. It is raw determination, however, that will propel you forward. In my own financial planning practice, I have seen people with the best intentions fail in their journey to financial independence simply because the desire to do so wasn't reinforced by the energizing capacity of determination. The road to financial success is not a smooth one. It is fraught with countless twists and turns and filled with obstacles of every kind. It is your determination to succeed that will help you overcome these obstacles and make your journey a success.

PLANNING FOR RETIREMENT

It's one thing to have the desire, attitude and determination to achieve a financially secure retirement and another to know where to begin. This is because no one's financial situation is the same. The rules of the game will be different for someone who has just graduated from university and is looking for his or her first job as compared to a middle-aged married couple with two young children. Similarly, a bachelor who has reached his fiftieth birthday will have conditions and needs quite different from a young single parent, widow or widower. In this regard, retirement planning is not a fixed set of rules that can be applied to every financial situation. Retirement planning is the process of assessing your present financial situation and altering the rules whenever required to enhance the pursuit and eventual achievement of your financial goals.

THE IMPORTANCE OF NET WORTH

Financial planning professionals know the value of net worth. This is because knowing what financial circumstances you face today is the starting point of every retirement plan. Before you can begin a journey, you have to know what resources you have at hand. When it comes to retirement planning, completing a *net worth statement* is the most effective way of doing so.

As you can see from Figure 2.1, a net worth statement is an organizational tool that provides you with an accurate summary of where you are today and what you have at your disposal in your quest for retirement security. When completed properly, your net worth statement will give you a comprehensive snapshot of your current financial situation. It will outline the income resources you currently enjoy, how you spend them, and when. It will list your assets, such as your home, personal property and investments, and the particulars of each. The net worth statement outlines your personal liabilities, such as credit card balances, mortgage, lines of credit and other personal debt. It will also highlight your insurance portfolio, providing details as to the amount of protection you have for yourself and your dependents.

The real importance of having completed a net worth statement, however, is that it can highlight both the strengths and weaknesses of your financial circumstances. By so doing, your net worth statement provides the foundation on which to develop a financial programme that is effective, manageable, and is an accurate representation of where you are today and what tools you have to enlist to ensure your future financial security.

Figure 2.1
Net Worth Statement

	PERSONAL AND FAMILY DATA	

1. NAME/AGE

	Title	Preferred First Name	Middle Name or Initial	Last Name	Birthdate	Social Insurance Number
Client						
Spouse						

2. MAILING ADDRESS

Street Address	
City	Province Postal Code
Home Phone ( )	

3. EMPLOYMENT DATA

	Occupation	Employer	Work Phone
Client			
Spouse			

4. CHILDREN

Name	Birthdate	Social Insurance Number	Marital Status	Living at Home?	Annual Support You Provide

5. OTHER PERSONS FOR WHOM YOU PROVIDE SUPPORT

Name	Relationship	Age	Annual Support You Provide

Figure 2.1
Net Worth Statement (*Continued*)

PERSONAL AND FAMILY DATA	

6. FINANCIAL ADVISORS

	Name	Firm Name and Address	Phone	How Frequently Consulted?
Lawyer				
Accountant				
Bank Manager				
Investment Advisor/Broker/ Agent				
Life Insurance Agent/Broker				
Property and Casualty Insurance Agent/Broker				
Others				

Figure 2.1
Net Worth Statement (*Continued*)

PERSONAL AND FAMILY DATA	

7. EDUCATION FUNDING

List below children, grandchildren, or others for whom you plan to fund university, post-secondary or private schooling costs.

Name					
Relationship to Client					
Age					
Current Grade Level					
Pre-University Private: Years of Private School Remaining					
Current Annual Costs	$	$	$	$	$
University/Post-secondary and Post-graduate: No. of Years Remaining					
Current Annual Costs	$	$	$	$	$
Current Value of Child's Assets	$	$	$	$	$
Annual Income Earned on Child's Assets	$	$	$	$	$
Describe Other Funds or Plans to Fund Costs					

Figure 2.1
Net Worth Statement (*Continued*)

ASSETS
Market Value as at

	Ownership				
	Client	Spouse	Joint*	Community*	Total
PERSONAL ASSETS					
Principal Residence	$	$	$	$	$
Other Personal Residences					
Household Furnishings					
Jewellery					
Vehicles and Boats					
Other Personal Assets					
Subtotal					
CASH AND CASH EQUIVALENTS					
Chequing & Savings Accounts					
Money Market Accounts and Funds					
Guaranteed Investment Certificates					
Canada Savings Bonds					
Other Liquid Assets (such as Treasury Bills)					
Subtotal					
LIFE INSURANCE CASH VALUE					
RETIREMENT ASSETS					
Registered Retirement Savings Plans (RRSPs) (LIRAs)					
Registered Retirement Income Funds (RRIFs)					
Life Income Funds (LIFs)					
Registered Pension Plans (RPPs)					
Corporate Pension and Profit Sharing Plans					
Corporate Savings or Stock Purchase Plans					
Tax-deferred Annuities					
Other Retirement Assets					
Subtotal					

*In most common-law provinces, jointly-held assets are "joint". However, in Quebec, jointly-held assets are "community" unless an agreement is entered into between the spouses to make them "joint".

Figure 2.1
Net Worth Statement (*Continued*)

ASSETS Market Value as at	

	Ownership				
	Client	Spouse	Joint*	Community*	Total
CLOSELY-HELD BUSINESSES (Net Value) Professional Practice	$	$	$	$	$
Manufacturing or Retail					
Farm					
Other Closely-held Business(es)					
Subtotal					
FIXED INCOME INVESTMENTS					
Notes Receivable					
Mortgages Receivable					
Mutual Funds					
Taxable Bonds and Bond Funds					
Other Fixed-income Investments					
Subtotal					
EQUITY INVESTMENTS Convertible Bonds					
Shares Publicly Traded					
Stocks Not Publicly Traded					
Other Equity Investments					
Subtotal					

Figure 2.1
Net Worth Statement (*Continued*)

ASSETS Market Value as at	

	Ownership				Total
	Client	Spouse	Joint*	Community*	

REAL ESTATE
  Commercial and Residential
  Rental Property
	$	$	$	$	$

Undeveloped Land					
Other Real Estate					
Subtotal					

HARD ASSETS
  Gold, Silver and Other Hard
  Assets					

Art, Gems and Collections					
Subtotal					

OTHER DIRECT INVESTMENTS
  (including Agricultural, Research
  and Development, Exploratory Oil
  and Gas Drilling and Equipment
  Leasing Limited Partnerships)					

TOTAL ASSETS	$	$	$	$	$

*In most common-law provinces, jointly-held assets are "joint". However, in Quebec, jointly-held assets are "community" unless an agreement is entered into between the spouses to make them "joint".

Figure 2.1
Net Worth Statement (*Continued*)

LIABILITIES
As at

Personal Liabilities	Client	Spouse	Joint*	Community*	Total
Mortgage on Principal Residence	$	$	$	$	$
Other Personal Mortgages					
Credit Cards and Charge Accounts					
Automobile Loans					
Other Instalment Debt					
Bank Loans					
Loans from Individuals					
Loans from Closely-held Businesses					
Other Loans					
Subtotal					
Investment And Business Liabilities					
Investment Mortgages	$	$	$	$	$
Bank Loans					
Loans from Individuals					
Loans from Closely-held Businesses					
Other Loans					
Limited Partnership Debt					
Brokerage Margin Loans					
Subtotal					
TOTAL LIABILITIES	$	$	$	$	$

*In most common-law provinces, jointly-held assets are "joint". However, in Quebec, jointly-held assets are "community" unless an agreement is entered into between the spouses to make them "joint".

Figure 2.1
Net Worth Statement (*Continued*)

CASH RECEIPTS For the Period / / to / /	

Cash Receipts	Current 19
GROSS SALARY AND BONUSES	
Client	$
Spouse	
NET INCOME FROM UNINCORPORATED BUSINESS	
Client	
Spouse	
OTHER EARNED INCOME	
Client	
Spouse	
PENSION INCOME	
Client	
Spouse	
INTEREST INCOME	
DIVIDEND INCOME	
NET CASH FLOW FROM RENT AND ROYALTY INCOME [real estate equipment leasing, oil and gas]	
OTHER [partnership distributions, repayments of advances to private companies]	
OTHER CASH RECEIPTS	
Sale of Assets	
Alimony and Child Support	
Trust Distributions and Recurring Gifts	
TOTAL CASH RECEIPTS	$

Figure 2.1
Net Worth Statement (*Continued*)

CASH EXPENDITURES For the Period / / to / /	

Cash Expenditures	19
DEDUCTIONS FROM PAY	$
CPP/QPP	
UI Contributions	
Federal and Provincial Income Tax	
Company Pension	
Other	
Subtotal	
HOUSING	
Mortgage Payment or Rent	
Utilities	
Housing Maintenance	
Property Insurance	
Property Taxes	
Home Furnishings	
Subtotal	
FOOD AND HOUSEHOLD	
Groceries	
Household Supplies	
Subtotal	
CLOTHING	
Clothing Purchases	
Cleaning	
Subtotal	
TRANSPORTATION	
Automobile Payments	
Automobile Insurance	
Fuel, Repairs and Parking	
Public Transit	
Subtotal	
Subtotal this page	$

Figure 2.1

Net Worth Statement (*Continued*)

CASH EXPENDITURES For the Period / / to / /	

Cash Expenditures (Continued)	19
Subtotal, previous page	$
INSURANCE	
Life Insurance	
Disability Insurance	
Medical/Dental Insurance	
Additional Property/Liability Insurance	
Subtotal	
ENTERTAINMENT/RECREATION	
Vacation and Travel	
Vacation Home	
Meals Out and Other Entertainment	
Clubs and Other Recreation	
Subtotal	
CONTRIBUTIONS/CHARITIES	
DEBT REPAYMENT	
Credit Cards and Outstanding Bills	
Instalment Debt	
Other Debt	
Subtotal	
ESTIMATED TAX PAYMENTS	
MISCELLANEOUS EXPENSES	
Education Expenses	
Domestic Help and Day Care	
Alimony and Child Support Paid	
Business and Professional Expenses	
Other Miscellaneous	
Subtotal	
TOTAL CASH EXPENDITURES	$

Figure 2.1
Net Worth Statement (*Continued*)

ANNUAL CASH FLOW ANALYSIS FORM	

Summary	19
(1) Total Cash Receipts	$
(2) Total Expenditures	
(3) Cash Available after Living Expenses (1) - (2)	$
(4) Existing Savings and Investment Commitments, e.g., Limited Partnership Payments and RRSPs, CSBs	( )
	( )
	( )
	( )
	( )
	( )
	( )
	( )
	( )
(5) Net Annual Cash Flow (Available for Additional Savings and Investments) (3) - (4)	$

Figure 2.1
Net Worth Statement (*Continued*)

LIFE INSURANCE POLICIES SCHEDULE					

	Policy 1	Policy 2	Policy 3	Policy 4	Policy 5
Name of Insured					
Policy Holder					
Policy Number					
Issue Age					
Insurance Company					
Beneficiary					
a. Face Value	$	$	$	$	$
b. Accumulated Dividends	$	$	$	$	$
c. Cash Surrender Value (CSV)	$	$	$	$	$
d. Policy Loans	$	$	$	$	$
e. Net Coverage (a.+b.-d.)	$	$	$	$	$
f. Net Cash Value (b.+c.-d.)	$	$	$	$	$
g. Approx. Annual Dividend	$	$	$	$	$
h. Approx. Annual CSV Increase	$	$	$	$	$
i. Annual Premium	$	$	$	$	$
j. Net Cost of Insurance (i.-g.-h.)	$	$	$	$	$
Type of Policy[1]					

PLANNER USE ONLY					
Cost per Thousand					
Rating (e.g., Best's, Stone & Cox)					

PLEASE LIST SIGNIFICANT OR UNUSUAL RIDERS ON THE ABOVE POLICIES

Policy Number	Description of Rider

[1]Universal Life = UL; Ordinary Life = OL; Term = T; Group Term = GT; Term to 100 = T100

Figure 2.1
Net Worth Statement (*Continued*)

	DISABILITY INSURANCE POLICIES SCHEDULE			

	Policy 1	Policy 2	Policy 3	Policy 4
Name of Insured				
Policy Number				
Insurance Company				
Issue Date				
Definition of Disability: Income replacement				
Cannot perform "own" occupation				
Cannot perform "any" occupation				
Combination of above based on a time period				
Waiting Period: Accident				
Sickness				
Maximum Benefit Period: Accident				
Sickness				
Cost-of-living Rider? Pre-disability				
During Claim				
Face Amount Update (Pre-claim)?				
Waiver of Premium?				
Non-cancellable and Guaranteed Renewable?				
Monthly Benefit—Total Disability: Accident	$	$	$	$
Sickness	$	$	$	$
Partial Disability Benefit: Accident	$	$	$	$
	$	$	$	$
Qualification Period?	days	days	days	days
Indexing of Pre-claim Income?				
Annual Premium	$	$	$	$

PLEASE LIST SIGNIFICANT OR UNUSUAL RIDERS ON THE ABOVE POLICIES

Policy Number	Description of Rider

Figure 2.1

Net Worth Statement (*Continued*)

DISABILITY INSURANCE POLICIES SCHEDULE	

PLANNER USE ONLY				
Rating of Insurer:				
Cost per $100 of basic monthly benefit				
If permanently disabled today, amount of benefit that would be received in lifetime (to actuarial expectancy)				
Cost per $1,000 thereof				

NET WORTH AND RETIREMENT PLANNING

There are several important items found in your net worth statement that you need to evaluate because of their impact on your long-term retirement plan. They are:

- your marital status & dependents
- your present age and health
- employment or career path
- kinds of accumulated assets
- liabilities and circumstances of each
- gross income, type and frequency
- monthly expenditures or distribution of income
- regular savings and investment capacity
- disability and life insurance
- estate considerations.

Each one of these items has long-term ramifications for your retirement. A married couple, for instance, will often enjoy two incomes and will be able to save and invest for their retirement faster than just one individual. Having dependents, however, will cost you more, making the prospect of saving and investing for your retirement all that more difficult. Age and health will affect your retirement plan too. A younger person has longer to accumulate capital, and someone in good health has obvious advantages over someone who is bedridden or restricted as to the kind of work he or she can do. Your career or employment will dictate how much income you will enjoy over the years. Someone who is highly skilled and whose skills are in high demand will be able to plan for his or her retirement more easily than someone whose employment or career path is being impacted regularly by boom-bust economic cycles or whose skills are less sophisticated and worth less.

The amount and kind of assets you have accumulated so far in life will have far-reaching implications for your retirement plan. This is because your assets can grow over time and could make your job of accumulating sufficient retirement capital a relatively painless task. As you will see in the next section of this chapter, how successful you will be in this regard will depend exclusively on what kind of assets you have now.

The Impact of Debt

What you owe today will detract from your ability to save and invest tomorrow. This is because, for every dollar you owe, it takes as much as double that amount of debt to repay it. If you pay income tax at a combined federal and provincial rate of 40 per cent, for example, you have to earn $1.67 *before income tax* to repay one dollar of debt. If you pay tax at, say, 50 per cent, you need $2 to repay one dollar of debt. So, where you owe $10,000 and you pay income tax at 40 per cent, you have to earn $16,667 to repay your debt—and this is before interest that your lender charges on your debt!

Another feature is the kind of debt you have. Credit card debt can be repaid without penalty other than interest. A mortgage or car lease, to the contrary, is locked-in and inflexible. Where debt is illiquid or inflexible, such debt can cost you a bundle in terms of future savings and investment potential. This is because you will incur interest charges and carry certain debts longer than necessary, even if you had the cash available to retire them. As you will see later, time is an important factor for anyone looking to accumulate a retirement nest egg. The longer it takes to rid yourself of debt, the longer and harder it will be to save sufficiently for your retirement.

A net worth statement will also portray the amount, type and frequency of income you enjoy. While a majority of Canadian taxpayers are paid by salary today, a growing segment of Canadian income earners have multiple sources of income. You could be a salaried employee and run a business on the side. Or, you could have investment income, pension income from a previous employer, income from a foreign country such as England or the U.S., or be the lucky recipient of income from a trust set up by a parent or grandparent. What the "cash receipts" section of your net worth statement will tell you is how much income comes from which resource and how long such income will continue. Knowing how much income you have before income tax and inflation will give you a good idea of what renewable financial resources you have at hand and how much of these income resources can be directed to your long-term accumulation programme.

Knowing your income and how you dispose of it monthly will give you a good picture of how well you manage your income. It will underscore your money management skills and weaknesses, and what you have to do to correct them. You will be able to understand how you allocate your income and identify where and under which circumstances such distributions have to be altered to reach your long-term retirement goals. In particular, your monthly budget will tell you how much you are saving and investing regularly and how much more you may have to put aside to reach your retirement goal.

Some people have a tendency to not save at all. Sometimes people save too much. The ideal guideline is to save a minimum 10 per cent of your after-tax income and invest it for your future. This basic rule, of course, will change according to your age and other circumstances as noted above. Where you are 25 years old and have an inflation-adjusted financial target of $1 million at age 65, for example, you would have to save $216.42 per month, if you earned eight per cent, compounded annually, and increased your monthly deposits by 3 per cent per year. Based on the 10 per cent rule, you would have to have an after-tax income of $25,970.40. A person of the same age who wants to retire at age 55, however, would have to save $523.30 per month. This increased monthly saving is equivalent to 24.2 per cent of your after-tax income, a figure that, today, would not be possible for many Canadians. Knowing how much you can save and invest on a regular basis to achieve a specific long-term goal is a particularly important feature that can be derived from a net worth statement.

Insuring Your Assets

Outlining what disability insurance you own will give you a bird's-eye view of what protection you have should you become disabled and unable to continue to work. The last thing you want to fall prey to is a disruption of your long-term financial goals. Disability insurance or income protection insurance, as it is otherwise called, is one easy way of ensuring that your financial plan continues unabated. It is a relatively easy task to note what income you need to sustain your lifestyle and what amount of disability insurance you require to assure your present and future income. The same goes for life insurance. Life insurance is really for the living, that is, for your dependents and relatives. Your net worth statement tells you what your survivors have at their disposal should you pass on prematurely. If you have debt you have to have enough life coverage to pay this debt. Since you no longer have employment income, you also have to calculate just how much money would have to be invested to provide your dependents with this lost income. The net worth statement will go a long way to providing you with the solution.

Finally, knowing your net worth, that is what you're worth after debts have been paid, will give you a good idea as to the value of your estate.

Knowing what you have left after federal and provincial income tax, probate fees and legal costs will help you design and implement strategies that will keep these liabilities under tight control.

HOW TO CONSTRUCT YOUR CAPITAL ACCUMULATION PLAN

Every good financial plan has to make use of a net worth statement. This is because a net worth statement gives you both an overview of your present financial circumstances and illustrates your financial strengths and weaknesses. It is your financial inventory that you use to construct your financial plan. The major components of a financial plan are the:

- designation and allocation of assets you have earmarked for investment
- capital you have committed to regular retirement savings
- length of time you have to achieve your retirement goal
- inflation management
- tax management
- long-term plan maintenance.

How you deal with each component and weave them together into one homogeneous financial plan will determine the ultimate success of your retirement capital accumulation programme. Here are some ideas to consider when building your financial plan.

Long-Term Capital and Effective Asset Allocation

Sometimes, knowing what you have to invest can be a problem. Some investments that you already have may not be suitable for a long-term investment programme. In this regard, you have to be prepared to make the right choices to ensure you have sufficient short-term assets and don't disrupt the integrity of your long-term plan.

Obviously, RRSPs represent a long-term commitment on your part. Real estate, however, can be a potential source of difficulty. This is because people treat real estate differently. Some people treat their home as part of their retirement nest egg. They have no intention of keeping it and will sell their home prior to retiring. They often move to warmer climates and rent, using the sale proceeds as their retirement nest egg. Individuals with families often plan to sell their larger family home once their offspring have grown and left the nest. These "empty nesters" usually purchase a smaller home and use the remaining proceeds realized by the sale of their family home to help fund their retirement. Other homeowners will keep their property, preferring to live out their lives relatively undisturbed.

The family cottage is treated in much the same way as the family home. Some cottage owners see their property as an investment to be sold when the time is right. Other individuals will sell their home and refurbish and inhabit what had once been their summer residence. Still other cottage owners want to keep their properties in the family to pass on to subsequent generations.

Many Canadians own other property such as a second home, apartment building or commercial property. These real estate assets are investments. However, just as a cottage can mean different things to different people, investment properties too have to be carefully considered. Sometimes investment properties can be good sources of retirement funds because of rental income, but in many instances these kinds of real estate are highly illiquid and often require a great deal of effort, expense and time to sell. Once sold, however, the proceeds from the sale can provide a good financial buffer for your retirement.

When deciding on what you need to fund your eventual retirement, a lot of care and consideration has to be taken when thinking about real estate and the equity you will have built up over time. Should you use the projected future value of your real estate assets as part and parcel of your retirement accumulation formula? Your decision will depend on many circumstances such as the health of real estate markets, costs and income tax.

A business interest doesn't normally qualify as an asset that can be committed to a long-term money accumulation programme. This is because such interests have been contracted to generate equity in the form of cash flow. Franchises are a good example of this kind of equity and anyone who is familiar with franchise agreements in Canada knows that there is no assurance that you will have built any real equity into your franchise operation, other than regular cash flow. So, your use of such business interests as part of your future retirement nest egg will depend exclusively on your franchise agreement and the value you think will build in your business over time.

Figuring mortgages that you hold as part of your retirement assets can be problematic, too. This is because a mortgage is a repayment of interest charged and original principal. As a depleting asset, what you have now is good cash flow for the duration of the mortgage term. Your decision to include this investment in your retirement calculations will depend on what you do with your cash flow. If you reinvest it in a portfolio of mutual funds, for example, you could easily include such funds as part of your accumulated retirement capital. If, on the other hand, you use your cash flow to fund your lifestyle, it's not suitable to think of your mortgage as a retirement asset.

Notes held could be business or family related or collateral loans and could be of long- or short-term duration. In most cases, notes held are not liquid and are drawn from financial resources known as operating capital. As such, notes held are not generally viewed as potential retirement assets.

"Personal assets" have obvious advantages because their value can be contested for estate planning purposes. They cannot, however, be considered retirement assets. Such things as furniture and personal belongings are necessities of life. It is important to note here, too, that such assets are, like mortgages, depreciating commodities.

Determining Your Retirement Needs

Once you have decided which assets can be allocated to the investment category, you now have to determine how much of your investment assets should be allocated to your long-term retirement goal. This is probably the easiest part of preparing a long-term retirement accumulation plan. Examine your net worth statement's cash expenditure section and calculate what it costs you to live each month. You should have a financial reserve that is a minimum of three times your monthly expenditures, including regular savings. Depending on your comfort zone and financial circumstances, the amount you hold as a reserve, however, could be up to six times your monthly expenditures. Most financial planners will recommend you keep your financial reserve in liquid securities, such as 30-90 day term deposits, Canada Savings Bonds (CSBs), money market mutual funds, banker's acceptances and Government of Canada treasury bills. More aggressive people, with the need for substantial yet liquid financial reserves, will often use short-term corporate and government bonds of less than three years' duration. Many so-called short-term investments that offer high liquidity require minimums of $50,000 and up so care must be taken when selecting short-term investments.

Here's an example. Fred needed about $5,000 per month to maintain his lifestyle. This included regular long-term savings of $800 per month. He did not feel comfortable with the minimum three-month cash reserve and decided to allocate $30,000 of his accrued assets to a short-term, emergency reserve. He chose to distribute his cash in three blocks: $10,000 to highly liquid CSBs, $10,000 into a 90-day term deposit and $10,000 into a quality no-load money market mutual fund. He can cash his Canada Savings Bonds any time and, if he waits until the last business day of the month, he will retain the entire previous month's interest as well. Fred chose a money market mutual fund that will provide cash to him within 48 hours of his redemption request, and, he followed up with a 90-day term deposit that, for a small adjustment in the interest payable, could be accessed on any regular business day. By structuring his short-term reserve in this way, Fred maximized capital liquidity through the use of CSBs, liquidity and better returns through his money market mutual fund, and a superior rate of return using a 90-day term deposit.

Allocating your other accrued investment assets will depend on a number of important factors, all of which will be determined by your current familial and financial circumstances. Before deciding as to what capital will be directed to your retirement accumulation plan, you have to account for future capital expenditures. You may want to have some money available to reduce your mortgage at renewal time, or, you may wish to set some money aside to purchase another automobile. If you have children, an education savings plan is often a priority and, in view of the new, attractive rules for Registered Education Savings Plans (RESP), lump sum investments make more sense now than ever before.

As of 1998, RESPs have been given a boost as a result of the new *Canada Education Savings Grant* (CESG). Enacted in February, 1998, the CESG allows a lifetime maximum contribution of $42,000 to be made to a child's RESP. Based on an annual maximum contribution of $4,000, the federal government now credits 20 per cent of the first $2,000 contribution made to an RESP or $400 per plan per year. This amount is added to the amount already contributed to the RESP.

Sometimes, other priorities will suddenly appear that you hadn't factored into your financial planning equation. A death of a parent or dear friend who lives out of province requires a large capital expenditure for travel, or your daughter asks you to help with a down payment for her first home. Oh yes, speaking of daughters, you would not be popular if you didn't have the cash to pay for her wedding! These and seemingly countless other costs have to be accounted for before putting the remainder of your investment assets to work for your retirement. Once you have cleared the decks, so to speak, you're now in a position to consider building your retirement portfolio.

Investment Suitability and Risk-Reward

The most important challenges any investor will face are *investment suitability* and *risk-reward.* This is because these two characteristics will impact on the long-term success of an investment portfolio more than all other factors combined.

Investment suitability is just what it says—investing in a way that is suitable to an investor's knowledge, experience, goals and financial skills. Your ability and willingness to choose investments that are suitable to your present personal and financial circumstances will go a long way to provide you with the kind of investment portfolio you'll need to build your retirement nest egg. For example, some people prefer to allow a professional investment advisor to make investment decisions for them; other individuals prefer to make all investment decisions themselves. When it comes to choosing particular kinds of investments, such as mutual funds and individual bonds or stocks, some investors are particularly aggressive and want, and are comfortable with, securities that rise and fall in value. Other investors have a low tolerance for changes in value of their capital and choose investments with little volatility. Still other investors prefer investments that are moderately volatile and, while comfortable with some value fluctuation, will not enjoy too much additional investment volatility.

Choosing investments that are suitable to your goals is another feature of investment suitability. You would hardly invest in treasury bills or 90-day term deposits when trying to build capital for your retirement. We know from experience that these and other similar securities do not provide enough growth for such a long-term goal. This is similarly the case for speculative stocks that rise and fall dramatically in value. These kinds of securities often lose money and are not suitable as long-term retirement investments. Your ability to understand your choice of investments in light of stock market activity, fiscal and monetary policy, foreign exchange and many other factors that affect securities prices will also impact on the overall success of your investment portfolio. Occasionally investors panic and sell out of an investment as a result of not knowing why a security does what it does; such action often sabotages what was otherwise a good investment that would have produced generous results over time. Choosing suitable investments means building a portfolio that is a direct extension of you as a person, your risk tolerance, your goals and your investment skills. Too often novice investors simply make uninformed investment decisions, which cost them and their capital dearly.

Risk-reward, to the contrary, is the *measure of an investor's anticipated rate of return relative to the amount of risk of capital loss he or she is willing to assume to earn that return over time.* Your ability to choose investments that you are comfortable with and provide you with the rates of return you wish is an item that will go a long way to ensure you build your retirement nest egg efficiently and quickly. You should be prepared to understand what the concept of investment risk is and how it can help determine the kinds of investments you can include in your portfolio. Risk is, for most people, the possibility of loss in capital value. Studies in post-modern portfolio theory have shown that the amount of pleasure and relief that comes as a result of earning a profit on invested capital is far less than the amount of discomfort and fear generated by an equivalent loss in value of original invested capital. In other words, investors react more significantly to a loss in value than to an equivalent gain or profit. This being the case, it is incumbent on every investor to ensure that the exposure to risk is at least equal to the rate of return he or she expects from the investment. If post-modern portfolio theory is correct, you should be prepared to purchase investments that provide you with the highest possible return with the lowest possible risk. You should avoid falling into the trap of simply trying to earn the highest returns you can. This has been an age-old problem and has caused a lot of grief for novice and experienced investors alike. To truly succeed at the investment game you have to determine the level of risk with which you are comfortable and then choose those securities that reflect your tolerance for risk. Only then will you be ready to invest profitably for the long term.

The Critical Importance of Regular Savings and Investment

One of the biggest mistakes people make when building capital for retirement is not saving and investing regularly. Every year people are encouraged to invest in RRSPs throughout the year rather than wait until year-end. There are three reasons for this. First, saving and contributing a small amount of money each month is much easier to accomplish than saving irregularly and making a larger lump sum RRSP contribution prior to the annual deadline. As we noted in the preface to this book, Canadians do not save and invest for the future as well as they could. Systematic saving and investment is a sure fire means of overcoming this problem. Second, saving and investing on a regular, usually monthly, basis has been proven to be far more effective when it comes to the time-value of money. Countless RRSP studies have shown that making timely investments now, rather than year-end ones, will provide significantly higher results over the long term. By saving and investing regularly, you make more efficient use of investment compounding over time. Third, if you invest in common stocks or common stock mutual funds, making regular contributions to your investment portfolio will allow your capital to take advantage of the normal and constant variation in value of such equity securities. This concept is known as *dollar cost averaging* and, while attempts have been made to debunk this idea by the media, it remains one of the best ways to average out the cost of purchasing equity securities. I have discussed this concept in detail in Chapter Three of this book.

After having had the pleasure of participating in one of the longest stock market upswings in North American history, it's a tough sell to try and downplay the importance of investment rates of return. Some investors, I know, have more than doubled the value of their investments in just a few years. Some mutual funds, for example, have been absolute superstars, earning their shareholders tens of thousands of dollars over the last four years. But, the truth of the matter is that the average historical return for North American stock markets has been about 11 per cent per year. This contrasts dramatically with the 20 to 30 per cent annual returns that many North American investors have enjoyed since 1992. However, a gross return of 11 per cent per year is nothing to sneeze at.

In fact, when perceived over the long term, say 20 years or more, an 11 per cent rate of return is more than acceptable as shown in Figure 2.2.

Things begin to look even better if you add a few dollars each month. Let's first add $100 monthly to our lump sum, followed by $150, $200 and $300. If we added $100 per month to our $25,000 original lump sum under exactly the same circumstances as given in Figure 2.2, our $201,557.79 would have grown to $283,118.51, representing an increase of 41 per cent or $81,560.92.

Increase your regular, monthly contributions by $50 and the end-value of your nest egg jumps to $323,898.87. But, it's your lucky day and your boss decides that you are a great employee and, to show his appreciation, gives you a raise thereby increasing your monthly savings and investment capability to $200. In this instance, your nest egg would have grown to a tantalizing $364,679.24. Increase your monthly savings and investment to $300, and your retirement nest egg now becomes a whopping $446,239.96!

Figure 2.2

The Future Value of a One-Time Investment of $25,000

Year	Investment $	Total Investment $	Total Value $
1	25,000	25,000	27,750.00
2	0	25,000	30,802.50
3	0	25,000	34,190.78
4	0	25,000	37,951.76
5	0	25,000	42,126.45
6	0	25,000	46,760.36
7	0	25,000	51,904.00
8	0	25,000	57,613.44
9	0	25,000	63,950.92
10	0	25,000	70,985.52
11	0	25,000	78,793.93
12	0	25,000	87,461.26
13	0	25,000	97,082.00
14	0	25,000	107,761.02
15	0	25,000	119,614.74
16	0	25,000	132,772.36
17	0	25,000	147,377.32
18	0	25,000	163,588.82
19	0	25,000	181,583.59
20	0	25,000	201,557.79

Based on a one-time investment of $25,000. Saved at an Interest Rate of 11%. Over 20 years.

From this somewhat simplistic illustration, it is easy to see and appreciate the fact that regular, systematic savings and investment can
significantly enhance the value of your retirement nest egg. It is important
to note that systematic savings and investment, however, works best over
a long period of time. Unless you have a substantial amount of money to
invest at the beginning of your investment time line, it is often best to
consider regular savings and investment for periods of 10 years and more.

Time, Not Timing, is Your Best Ally

The problem with trying to build retirement capital over the long term
is that it doesn't provide a lot of immediate or ongoing gratification. To
be honest, accumulating capital over a long-time horizon can be just a
long grind. It's often only after you've managed to build a large lump
sum that you begin to feel as if there may be financial freedom at the end
of the tunnel. But, there are other dangers that can impact on your long-
term savings and investment programme. The first is the power of time.

One of the greatest enemies you will face when it comes to building
adequate retirement assets is time itself. This is because time, once lost,
can never be recovered. We live in a linear world, where space provides
our context for living and time propels us forward. When it comes to
accumulating retirement capital, having more time in which to save and
invest can make a dramatic difference now and for your future. Here's why.

Let's return to our $25,000 illustration in Figure 2.2 above. We've
seen how a moderate lump sum earning 11 per cent per year can grow to
a substantial amount after 20-year period. What would happen if we
extended our investment horizon by just a paltry five years?

By simply adding nothing to your nest egg and allowing it to grow for
another five years earning 11 per cent per year, your retirement nest egg
would have increased in value by almost 69 per cent or $138,078.81 as
shown in Figure 2.3. But, wait another five years and your nest egg
would have grown to $572,307.41. Put off retiring for five more years
and, like magic, your one-time investment of $25,000 would now be
worth almost $1 million—$964,371.28 to be exact! If you've never had
the opportunity to think that you could retire rich, you can see now that,
depending on your investment time horizon, being wealthy, living in
Bermuda and playing golf is not such a far-fetched dream after all.

Hold your horses, you say! What if you don't have $25,000 to invest
today for your retirement? You are 30 years of age, married, with bills to
pay and children to raise. What happens if all you can muster now is
$275 per month? If we go back to our long-term saving projections, the
amount of capital you would have accumulated by the time you retire at,
say, age 60 years, will still amount to a sizeable $695,277.57. If you think

Figure 2.3
The Value of Time

Year	Investment $	Total Investment $	Total Value $
1	25,000	25,000	27,750.00
2	0	25,000	30,802.50
3	0	25,000	34,190.78
4	0	25,000	37,951.76
5	0	25,000	42,126.45
6	0	25,000	46,760.36
7	0	25,000	51,904.00
8	0	25,000	57,613.44
9	0	25,000	63,950.92
10	0	25,000	70,985.52
11	0	25,000	78,793.93
12	0	25,000	87,461.26
13	0	25,000	97,082.00
14	0	25,000	107,761.02
15	0	25,000	119,614.74
16	0	25,000	132,772.36
17	0	25,000	147,377.32
18	0	25,000	163,588.82
19	0	25,000	181,583.59
20	0	25,000	201,557.79
21	0	25,000	223,729.15
22	0	25,000	248,339.35
23	0	25,000	275,656.68
24	0	25,000	305,978.91
25	0	25,000	339,636.60

Based on a one time investment of $25,000. Saved at an Interest Rate of 11%. Over 25 years.

back to the fact that a vast majority of Canadians age 50 years or older have less than $250,000 in assets accumulated for retirement, you are obviously much better off than you might first think. Your retirement prospects suddenly become much brighter if you decided to save and invest for another five years and retire instead at age 65. In this case, your retirement nest egg would have grown dramatically to $1,193,339.90!

The relevance of time can be appreciated, once more, if we combined our $25,000 lump sum with regular, monthly deposits. If we invested $25,000 and added $275 monthly for 30 years, earning 11 per cent per year, the value of our investment would be a whopping $1,267,584.98. Continue saving and investing for another five years and the value of your retirement nest egg would have grown to a remarkable $2,157,711.18!

When saving for your retirement, time is your ally and the earlier you begin to save and invest towards that goal the easier the prospect becomes. To reinforce the point, I have outlined in Figure 2.4 what you would have to save and invest on a monthly basis over decreasing time periods. As you can see, the more time you have to save and invest, the easier the task becomes.

Figure 2.4

The Importance of Starting When You're Young

Starting Age	Period	Monthly Savings @ 11%	End Value
20 Years	45 Years	$ 100	$1,242,533.35
35 Years	30 Years	$ 496	$1,243,169.32
45 Years	20 Years	$1,535	$1,241,116.46

INFLATION — THE INVISIBLE ENEMY

Getting started early is an important factor in any long-term savings and investment strategy. The sooner you begin, the easier the job becomes. Sometimes, though, people forget that there are factors that will make the task of saving and investing for retirement more difficult than ever. Inflation is one such factor. We've all heard about inflation. We've read about it in the papers, heard about it on the radio, and witnessed its power through television. But, inflation is the most overlooked factor when it comes to managing our money. This is because inflation is an invisible enemy. Simply put, *inflation increases prices without adding value to goods sold.* In less technical terms, inflation increases our living costs without increasing our current standard of living.

Here's a simple but accurate example. Let's say you have $100 to spend each month. In the first year, you can buy 100 food items valued at $1 each. One year later, you discover that the same $100 will purchase only 97 items. In the third year, you find that you can only purchase 94 items, and so on. This decrease in purchasing power is due to the fact that the cost of your original 100 items has increased by three per cent. If you had only $100 to spend and the cost of those items increased by three per cent, the cost to you has also increased to $103. This means, of course, that you can only purchase 97 items with the same $100 in year two. In year three, you can only afford to purchase 94 items. Has there been any value added to the items you originally purchased each year? No. Inflation simply results in higher costs and adds no intrinsic value to those items. A 675-gram loaf of bread accomplishes the same thing no matter when you buy it. Even if the cost of a loaf of bread has increased, there is no increase in intrinsic value to your stomach. It just costs more to satiate that hungry beast.

What causes inflation? It will depend on which economic theory you deem correct. But, when all is said and done, inflation is the consequence of supply and demand. Prices gradually inflate because the capacity of an economy to produce is finite, while consumer demand can be infinite. Price inflation occurs when the demand for goods outstrips the ability of an economy to produce them. This increasing scarcity of produced goods raises prices for those goods. This situation leads to a gradual increase in the cost of living, as the effects of price inflation seep through the economy. Consumers realize their purchasing power is decreasing and, in turn, demand wage increases to offset inflation. This trend inevitably becomes a price-wage inflation spiral that, if unchecked, eventually undermines the essential integrity of an economy and a country's currency. "Oh, don't go there to spend your vacation, everything costs too much!" Sound familiar? This example is the result of inflationary pressures wrought by a booming tourist economy—too many tourists, too much money. "Hey, let's make even more money by raising prices. After these tourists arrive, they'll have no choice but to pay!"

So, how does inflation affect a long-term savings and investment programme? This is the difference between what economists call the *present and future value of money*. Today, in Canada, a dollar is a dollar. It purchases a fixed number of goods. But, will today's dollar buy the same number of goods 20 years down the line? Following our first example above, the answer is no. Here are a few illustrations of how even moderate inflation can corrode the future value of your savings and investment programme. We saw how $25,000 grows to $201,557.79, if your capital earned an average 11 per cent each year for 20 years. But how much will that money be really worth?

This phenomenon is what economists call the *future value* of money. The result is simply the consequence of a standard compounding formula. The *present value* of money, however, is far more accurate. This is because it accounts for the long-term effects of the corrosive power of inflation. Inflation reduces value. It also reduces the value of money. If annual inflation is one per cent, for example, the value of our $201,557.79 must be measured in terms of what this lump sum could purchase 20 years from now. So, instead of being worth what it is to us today, its real purchasing power 20 years from now is not $201,557.79, but $164,855.51! The calculations are as follows.

The Long-Term Effects of 1% Annual Inflation

As shown in Figure 2.5, where inflation is just one per cent per year, the real purchasing power of your retirement nest egg in 20 years will have been reduced by 18 per cent or $36,702.28. Unfortunately, the long-term inflation rate here in Canada has been between three and four per cent, increasing to 12.3 per cent for a short period during the heady days of 1981-1982. Today, inflation is hovering around 1.5 per cent. Using just one per cent as our long-term inflation factor, let's see what the real value of our $201,557.79 would be 20 years hence.

Figure 2.5
The Long-Term Effects of 1% Annual Inflation

Period	Opening Balance $	Closing Balance $
1	201,557.79	199.542.21
2	199,542.21	197,546.79
3	197,546.79	195,571.32
4	195,571.32	193,615.61
5	193,615.61	191,679.45
6	191,679.45	189,762.66
7	189,762.66	187,865.03
8	187,865.03	185,986.38
9	185,986.38	184,126.52
10	184,126.52	182,285.25
11	182,285.25	180,462.40
12	180,462.40	178,657.78
13	178,657.78	176,871.20
14	176,871.20	175,102.49
15	175,102.49	173,351.46
16	173,351.46	171,617.95
17	171,617.95	169,901.77
18	169,901.77	168,202.75
19	168,202.75	166,520.72
20	166,520.72	164,855.51
Total		**164,855.51**

The Long-Term Effects of 3.5% Annual Inflation

As you can see from Figure 2.6, the long-term effects of inflation can be devastating, reducing your nest egg by $102,714.80 or over half! How can you protect your retirement accumulation programme from the ravages of long-term inflation? The solution is twofold. You can gradually increase the amount of money you commit to your savings and investment programme each year or ensure that your annual investment rate of return will be high enough to compensate and still get you to where you want to be financially at retirement.

I will show you how these two solutions work, how to implement them and what the end results can be in Chapter Three of this book.

The importance of this segment is to recognize that the real value of your retirement nest egg can be attacked by factors that you initially may not recognize and that a solution to offset inflation will only enhance the success of your retirement accumulation strategy.

Figure 2.6
The Long-Term Effects of 3.5% Annual Inflation

Period	Opening Balance $	Closing Balance $
1	201,557.79	194,503.27
2	194,503.27	187,695.65
3	187,695.65	181,126.31
4	181,126.31	174,786.88
5	174,786.88	168,669.34
6	168,669.34	162,765.92
7	162,765.92	157,069.11
8	157,069.11	151,571.69
9	151,571.69	146,266.68
10	146,266.68	141,147.35
11	141,147.35	136,207.19
12	136,207.19	131,439.94
13	131,439.94	126,839.54
14	126,839.54	122,400.16
15	122,400.16	118,116.15
16	118,116.15	113,982.09
17	113,982.09	109,992.71
18	109,992.71	106,142.97
19	106,142.97	102,427.96
20	102,427.96	98,842.99
Total		**98.842.99**

TAXATION—THE GRIM HARVEST

Another danger that you face when trying to design a good capital accumulation programme is taxation. Of approximately 20 million tax filers in 1995, 14,026,670 Canadians paid a total of $93.82 billion to federal and provincial treasuries. This huge tax windfall excludes sales tax, goods and services tax, excise tax and import and export duties. Translated into individual terms, depending on your gross annual income and where you live in Canada, you can lose more than 50 per cent of your income to taxes each year.

As might be expected, accumulating a retirement nest egg, income tax can be a major hurdle. This is because income tax takes valuable capital away that might otherwise compound and grow over term. For example, let's assume that you are a resident of British Columbia and have an annual taxable income of $53,000. As a taxpayer, you pay taxes at a combined federal and provincial rate of 40.3 per cent. So, out of the $53,000 you report on your tax return, you face a potential tax liability of $21,359! While there will normally be tax credits that will help ease the pain, you are trying to reduce whatever taxes have been levied at 40.3 per cent per year. If you had been able to invest this $21,359 for your retirement 20 years down the road, you would have accumulated a whopping $172,202.91 at 11 per cent earnings per year!

The Future of Tax Payable

As Figure 2.7 shows, the future value of tax payable could have had a tremendous impact on your retirement savings. Particularly hard to digest is the fact that this lost earnings potential is the result of income tax ($21,359) paid for just one year based on an annual income of $53,000. Imagine how easy the task of saving adequate retirement capital would be if you were allowed to save and invest this tax liability for five years. Imagine how wealthy you'd be if you didn't have to pay income tax at all! Unfortunately, reality being what it is, Canadians pay, and will continue to pay, an inordinate amount of tax every year. With our national debt exceeding $630 billion, and escalating annually, the chances of a significant reversal in tax payable will not arrive any time soon.

Figure 2.7

The Future Value of Tax Payable For One Year

Year	Investment $	Total Investment $	Total Value $
1	21,359	21,359	23,708.49
2	0	21,359	26,316.42
3	0	21,359	29,211.23
4	0	21,359	32,424.47
5	0	21,359	35,991.16
6	0	21,359	39,950.18
7	0	21,359	44,344.70
8	0	21,359	49,222.62
9	0	21,359	54,637.11
10	0	21,359	60,647.19
11	0	21,359	67,318.38
12	0	21,359	74,723.41
13	0	21,359	82,942.98
14	0	21,359	92,066.71
15	0	21,359	102,194.05
16	0	21,359	113,435.39
17	0	21,359	125,913.29
18	0	21,359	139,763.75
19	0	21,359	155,137.76
20	0	21,359	172,202.91

Based on a one time investment of $21,359. Saved at an Interest Rate of 11%. Over 20 years.

But, income tax can hit our saving and investment strategy in other ways, too. If we return to Figure 2.4 outlined earlier, our 20-year old, who now pays tax at the same 40.3 per cent rate, would have to allocate $168 instead of $100 per month before income tax to reach his or her capital goal. If this individual was calculating a $100 monthly savings and investment programme based on pre-tax dollars, the real monthly amount allocated to his capital goal would be just $59.70 ($100 less 40.3 per cent). Over a 45-year period, his or her accumulated retirement nest egg would be worth $748,271.67, well below the original end-value of $1.24 million. When calculating how much capital you are prepared to allocate to your long-term retirement accumulation programme, make sure you are using after-tax dollars. This means you are using money that you have left in your hand, after Revenue Canada has taken its share.

Income tax also affects the long-term earnings potential of your savings and investment strategy by reducing the amount of earnings that will compound inside of your investments. If your investments are non-registered, that is, other than RRSPs and similar tax-deferred savings plans, any earnings in the form of reinvested interest, dividends or capital gain dividends will be taxed at your marginal tax rate. While investors normally do not pay these accrued taxes directly from investment earnings, taxes still are payable from other resources, which, if left alone, could be earmarked for future savings and investment as well. In our example of a person with a taxable income of $53,000, interest earnings would be taxed at 40.3 per cent, dividends from shares of Canadian corporations, 26.5 per cent, and taxable capital gains at 30.23 per cent. So, where part of your total 11 per cent annual investment return is comprised of 6 per cent interest dividends per year, your real rate of return after a 40.3 per cent tax bill is just 8.6 per cent (6 less 40.3 per cent plus 5 per cent). After 20 years, a $25,000 investment would have grown to only $130,177.68. Where an investment generates Canadian dividends and capital gain dividends, the results are a little better because of more favourable tax treatment. Where the entire 11 per cent annual growth of your investment is comprised of reinvested compound interest, your net after-tax return would be 6.6 per cent or $89,760.26 after 20 years!

You would hope that this is the last that we hear of the government tax grab. Unfortunately, the grim harvest has yet to run its course. Even if you paid 40.3 per cent tax on your investment earnings each year, the value of your capital would still continue to grow. In this context, a full 59.7 per cent of your earnings remain to compound each year. It is this additional growth in value, however, that is once again taxed at your combined federal and provincial tax rate when you retire and begin to draw an income from your nest egg. Where a chunk of your nest egg is in the form of an RRSP or registered pension plan income, you pay income tax at your full marginal rate once you begin to access your plan. This is because your capital was allowed to compound on a tax-deferred basis as long as you kept the money in your registered plan.

THE FINAL DEPRESSING TALLY

As individual sources of frustration, inflation and taxation alone can be tough customers with which to deal. Consider the far-reaching consequences where these two problems combine. If we return to our $25,000 investment example, which, under normal circumstances would earn 11 per cent interest per year, the end result is altered dramatically as a 3.5 per cent inflation rate and a 40.3 per cent marginal tax rate are factored into the equation. Instead of reaping the rewards of a $201,557.79 retirement nest egg, the *net after-tax present value of your nest egg* would be a paltry $45,770.49! An annual rate of return of 3.07 per cent has been calculated by simply deducting 40.3 per cent of 11 per cent and then deducting an additional 3.5 per cent to account for inflation (approximate values only).

The combined impact of inflation and taxation on our original $25,000 investment is shown in Figure 2.8 A paltry $45,770.49 is a far

Figure 2.8

The Combined Impact of Inflation and Taxation

Year	Investment $	Total Investment $	Total Value $
1	25,000	25,000	25,767.50
2	0	25,000	26,558.56
3	0	25,000	27,373.91
4	0	25,000	28,214.29
5	0	25,000	29,080.47
6	0	25,000	29,973.24
7	0	25,000	30,893.42
8	0	25,000	31,841.84
9	0	25,000	32,819.39
10	0	25,000	33,826.94
11	0	25,000	34,865.43
12	0	25,000	35,935.80
13	0	25,000	37,039.03
14	0	25,000	38,176.13
15	0	25,000	39,348.13
16	0	25,000	40,556.12
17	0	25,000	41,801.20
18	0	25,000	43,084.49
19	0	25,000	44,407.19
20	0	25,000	45,770.49

Based on a one time investment of $25,000. Saved at an Interest Rate of 3.07%. Over 20 years.

cry from the original $201,557.79 nest egg we thought we had. Things become even worse if the amount of time you have to accumulate money for your retirement is shorter than 20 years or your regular savings schedule is interrupted through disability or unemployment. The situation doesn't get any better if your investments fail to produce the returns you need to achieve your retirement goal or the amount of capital you can initially allocate to your long-term savings and investment strategy is less than the $25,000 base amount we have used throughout this chapter.

PLAN MAINTENANCE—THE OTHER LONG-TERM COMMITMENT

The other major stumbling block to a successful retirement accumulation plan is change. Unfortunately, today, the pace of change is hard and fast. As part of an expanding and increasingly complicated global village, Canadians are affected by changes that occur around the world. The softening of the Japanese economy and the Pacific Rim, for example, can push down the value of our currency, making imports and travel outside of Canada expensive propositions. Economic slowdowns faced by our Asian trading partners can cause recessions in our resource sectors, resulting in higher unemployment and deteriorating corporate earnings. Lower corporate earnings in turn affect stock market prices, sowing economic instability through flagging capital markets and investor reluctance.

Government can add to this sea of change by virtue of its control of fiscal and monetary policy. Taxation can become an insurmountable problem and can sap much of the vitality out of our economy. Interest rate policy and a restricted money supply can cause economic hardship and consumer uncertainty as well as inhibit the willingness of foreign investors to bring much needed capital to our shores. A lack of capital availability causes government to raise revenues through the use of such punitive tax grabs as the GST and PST. These and many other related factors continue to impact on our ability to manage our financial affairs and our ability to save and invest for our financial future.

Being able to stand firm and focussed in your resolve to achieve a financially secure retirement through good and bad is the real measure of your commitment to the task. Too often Canadians make the important step to develop and implement a good financial plan, but ultimately fail to achieve their retirement goal. This occurs because many individuals forget that building a secure financial future requires an incredible amount of input and maintenance. Twenty years ago, for example, very few Canadians would have thought that the CPP would find itself in financial difficulty. Fewer Canadians still would have believed that the federal government would be prepared to trash most of our social benefit programmes as a result of fiscal and monetary restraints. If government decided to do just that, how many Canadians facing retirement would in fact have been able to do so, and survive? The answer, of course, would depend on just how well you managed your long-term savings and investment programme and how well you maintained your long-term focus.

Being able to build sufficient capital assets for your retirement is a long-term proposition. Being willing to commit yourself to the task at hand by adjusting and maintaining your capital accumulation programme in the face of such a barrage of continuous change will be the ultimate measure of your future financial success.

CHAPTER THREE

EFFECTIVE STRATEGIES TO ACCUMULATE WEALTH

Making a commitment to build your retirement nest egg is one thing. Knowing how to do it is another. This chapter has been designed to provide you with the tools necessary to get you organized fast. It makes no pretensions to be an exhaustive treatment of investment theory or the many kinds of securities available. But, what this chapter will do is provide a systematic enunciation of the steps you have to take to build an investment portfolio that is right for you now. Once you've implemented your basic investment strategy, you can then take the time necessary to learn and grow with your portfolio. Here are the items you need to understand to get your retirement accumulation plan on track.

TODAY'S INVESTMENT RESOURCES

Canada's investment industry has virtually exploded over the last few years. This is because of the return of favourable economic conditions, low consumer interest rates, flourishing stock markets, increased investment capital and changing population demographics. This dramatic expansion of Canada's investment community has given rise to a huge increase in the number and variety of investments. Fortunately for first-time investors, many of these "new" investment products are just variations of more traditional investment types. Once you have a grasp of these more traditional investments, you have a good foundation from which to launch out and examine other investment alternatives.

All investment vehicles share one important feature. This feature is called *risk-reward*. As outlined earlier in Chapter Two, *risk-reward is the measure of an investor's anticipated rate of return in light of the amount of risk of loss of capital he or she is willing to assume to earn that return over time.* In other words, if you want to earn high rates of return on your investments, you have to be prepared for a greater potential for the loss in value of your original invested capital. When thinking about investing, you first have to understand that not all investments are alike from the standpoint of risk-reward. You should be aware of the amount of risk each security incurs in order to earn a certain rate of return. My "Risk-Reward Investment Pyramid" in Figure 3.1 will give you a bird's eye view of where the seven major investment classes stand with regard to the principle of risk-reward.

Figure 3.1
The Risk-Reward Investment Pyramid:
A Comparison of Investment Classes

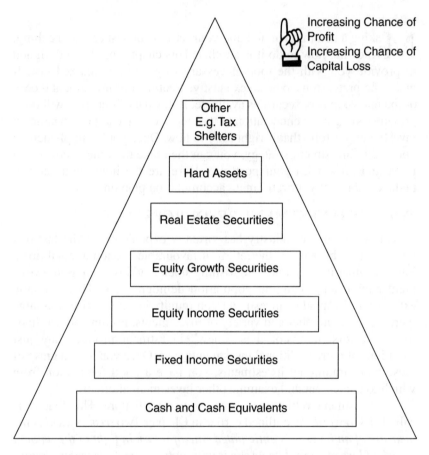

Increasing Chance of Profit
Increasing Chance of Capital Loss

Other E.g. Tax Shelters

Hard Assets

Real Estate Securities

Equity Growth Securities

Equity Income Securities

Fixed Income Securities

Cash and Cash Equivalents

Cash and cash equivalents are the safest investments of all. This is because, in most cases, your capital is essentially guaranteed from loss, regardless of what goes on in the economy. Typical securities that fall under this investment class are Canada Savings Bonds, cash, chequing and savings accounts, Guaranteed Investment Certificates (GICs), Government of Canada treasury bills, money market accounts and short-term deposits. When analyzing these securities, you should consider the following items first. You should examine the health of the financial institution that is offering the security and the strength of the insurer involved (bank, insurance company or government agency). The investment term of the security or maturity date, costs and penalties associated with the product will have a big impact on your investment returns and should be considered carefully. A security's compounding frequency (daily, weekly, monthly, semi-annually or annually) and yield to maturity (its total value on the day the security matures) will also be important issues that affect your investment results. These kinds of securities depend on federal monetary policy and consumer interest rates. They can provide double-digit returns during periods of exceptionally high inflation, however, under normal circumstances, cash and cash equivalents offer the lowest returns of all available investments.

Fixed income securities are comprised of corporate bonds, corporate debentures, Government of Canada bonds, mortgage-based securities, municipal bonds, notes receivable, and provincial bonds. Important factors you should consider before investing in these securities are the current yield or amount of interest earned per year. You should also be aware of the investment horizon or maturity term (short-term—0-2 years, medium-term—3-10 years, long-term—11+ years) and quality rating given to all bonds and debentures. Understanding traditional investment characteristics of bonds and debentures is also important, for example, call or redemption features, conversion features, and extendable and retractable features. Such investment characteristics as the investment grade and early repayment features associated with mortgage-backed securities will also impact on the end-result of your investments.

Fixed income securities, in particular bonds, offer good interest earnings during periods of high rates, as well as additional capital growth during periods of declining interest rates. But, while cash and cash equivalents can guarantee the original value of your capital, often fixed income securities will not. This is because bonds have fixed interest rates and, where market interest rates fluctuate, will result in a market value that is either higher or lower than what you originally paid for your bond. This is why the fixed income investment class is designated more risky than cash and cash equivalents. Fixed income securities are usually purchased by individuals who are looking for low risk investments that pay a high level of interest income and offer the potential for additional capital growth in the form of capital gains. Investors who hold bonds, first mortgages or secured debentures have first crack at an issuer's assets should that issuer fail or ultimately wind up its operations.

Preferred stocks are typically referred to as *equity income securities.* Unlike the previous two investment classes, the value of capital invested in equity income securities is never guaranteed. A company looking for capital to expand its business but doesn't want to give shareholders voting rights usually issues preferred stock. Investors who purchase preferred shares are usually looking for high investment income, but lower overall risk of loss to their capital. An additional advantage to a company issuing preferred stock is that dividends generated by preferred stock are from after-tax profits earned by the issuing company. Therefore, in years where no profits are earned, the company is under no obligation to pay dividends. The advantage to investors is that dividends paid by distinctly Canadian companies are subject to favourable tax treatment by Revenue Canada. Investors who are looking to invest in preferred stock should make special note of the kind of company offering the stock, its financial situation, future direction and prospects for growth. Investors should also be aware of any kind of special characteristics a preferred stock issue may have, for example, whether a stock is a quality one, convertible to a common share, and redeemable or retractable. Preferred stock holders have second claim to a company's assets, after bond, debenture and mortgage holders.

Equity growth securities is the fourth of seven asset classes and includes such vehicles as publicly traded common shares and common stock mutual funds. This class includes a huge variety of securities and, while all are referred to as common stock, they can in fact vary dramatically from one another. Common stockholders have last claim against an issuing company's assets in the event the company declares bankruptcy, merges with another or simply ceases operations. This makes common stocks more risky than the previous three classes. Investors who want superior long-term, capital growth choose common stocks. Some common stocks pay income dividends but many others do not. Companies who do pay dividends on their common shares are usually utility companies and large corporations that prefer to distribute profits on a regular basis. Companies whose shares do not pay dividends are usually growth-oriented and reinvest whatever profits they earn to strengthen the company's balance sheet. When purchasing common stocks, or, for that matter, common stock mutual funds, be aware that a company that consistently pays regular, reasonably-sized dividends indicates a healthy company that is often a good long-term investment. When evaluating equity securities, you should examine any professional ratings of the stock or mutual fund in question, where the company stands in relation to its respective industry, the dividend yield, its marketability or liquidity and the nature of your voting rights, where applicable.

Real estate securities are those tied to residential and commercial properties and anyone who purchased a real estate property in 1988 knows about the risks and rewards of real estate investment. That year marked a peak in real estate pricing which subsequently dropped in value for almost 10 long years. After the inflationary bubble burst in 1988, undeveloped land dropped 50 per cent in value, while estate homes plunged 40 per cent. Vacation properties dropped as did residential rental property and commercial properties, such as office buildings, shopping centres and warehouses. Even so-called diversified real estate mutual funds took a thrashing, some to the point where they were forced to liquidate their assets and close their doors. This occurred because there had been an unprecedented amount of real estate speculation during the heady 1980s that drove prices into the stratosphere, virtually doubling property values in most of Canada's major urban centres.

In situations like these, real estate can be a risky undertaking, especially if you invest in it at the peak of a real estate cycle. In Canada, today, real estate boom-bust cycles can last anywhere from 10 to 20 years. So, as a real estate investor, you could have a long, long wait before being in a position where you could sell your investment. But what makes most real estate investments particularly risky is their essential lack of liquidity. Unlike a Canada Savings Bond or a money market mutual fund, you can't simply dial up your broker and say "sell." Real estate securities of all kinds take a great deal of time to liquidate. This characteristic can be exacerbated by long periods of stagnant market activity and large property inventories.

However, when inflation is rising and the economy is growing, real estate can be a great investment, even with its essential lack of liquidity. When the supply of property is falling, real estate prices will move upwards, sometimes over just a few short years. Where you've invested in an income-producing property, such as an apartment, duplex, rental house, commercial/industrial complex or warehouse, you can have good cash flow in the form of rental income as well as capital appreciation. A lot of care, though, should be exercised before you buy into real estate. You should examine your investment's location, occupancy rate and potential cash flow, the developer's track record, the nature of any guarantees and financing as well as investment liquidity. By doing so, you have a pretty good shot at knowing what you have as a potential investment and the prospects for investment return.

Hard assets include such items as gold, silver, platinum and other precious metals, gems and jewelry, art, antiques, coin collections and other collectibles. These assets are considered high risk. This is because they provide neither investment income nor good liquidity. They are usually purchased to provide safe havens for capital during periods of economic and political uncertainty, high inflation and excessive stock market volatility. When dealing with hard assets, authenticity is one of the biggest issues with which you have to deal. Other risks are associated with changing public demand for such assets, variable appreciation values and portability of the assets you own. The issue of gold is a perfect example of the kinds of risk associated with investing in hard assets. Gold production, gold prices and gold speculation came to a crashing halt when, in 1997, the Canadian junior mining company, *Bre-X,* was discovered to be a fraud. Not only did the price of gold fall from $U.S. 358 to $U.S. 277 in less than a year, but just about every other kind of metal fell in price as well. Even towards the end of 1998, the price of gold was still hovering around $U.S. 300 per troy ounce. What really beat up the price of gold was the unloading of gold reserves by several central banks, including those of Australia, Belgium, Germany and Switzerland.

The seventh and last asset class of *other investments* is the most risky of all. This asset class is comprised primarily of limited partnerships (LPs). These LPs can be in the form of Canadian film production, oil and gas, equipment leasing, farming, mutual funds and real estate. LPs normally provide investors with a blend of income, tax deferral and tax savings. Depending on the LP, you may receive more tax benefits in the early years, but have increased income later. Sometimes, in the case of mining LPs, you may receive no income at all, but have significant tax benefits. On rare occasion an LP will have an option to convert to an open-end mutual fund.

You should note, however, that LPs vary in quality and should be examined as if there were no tax benefits attached. Second, only individuals who have healthy cash assets and cash flow should look to LPs. They are often not liquid. Third, the world of LPs is not as diversified as other investments such as mutual funds. They focus on one investment only. Fourth, LPs are often subject to changes in tax law and you can be left with a poor investment should government, in particular, Revenue Canada, decide to shut down your LP investment. You should take care to ensure that the LP is compatible with your risk profile.

BUILDING YOUR INVESTMENT PORTFOLIO

The principal reason why people invest their capital is to earn a superior rate of return. The more money a person makes through his or her investments, the happier he or she usually is. The amount of risk an individual is willing to accept to earn that superior return, however, will vary widely. This is because risk tolerance is a subjective matter and is evaluated differently by people. No amount of investment theory will change a person's penchant for risk. Fortunately, though, years of investment experience have produced certain rules that, when consistently applied, will help make your risk tolerance level more meaningful and make you aware of the kinds of investments that are most suitable for you.

ASK YOURSELF SOME TOUGH QUESTIONS

The following questions will give you insight as to how you react to and treat investing generally. These questions won't solve the relation of risk and reward. What they will do is give you some important parameters to help guide your choice of suitable investments.

- How much time are you willing to spend each month managing your investments?
- Do you wish to control investment decision-making? If not, how do you intend to delegate the management of your capital?
- How large of a financial loss would you be willing to suffer and how would it impact your current financial situation? $1,000? $5,000? $10,000? $25,000? More?
- Is your spouse part of the investment decision-making process?
- How concerned would your spouse be if your investments suffered a loss?
- In which investments do you think you have expertise that would enable you to make decisions without assistance?
- Are there areas that you would like to invest in but lack the necessary experience?
- Do you hold investments you are reluctant or unwilling to sell? If so, which ones and why?
- Are there investments you would not buy? If so, which ones and why?
- Name two or three of your best and worst investments you've made thus far.

Personal Financial Goals

Personal financial goals are like a compass that you use to first determine the direction in which you wish to travel and then use to keep yourself on track. Financial goal setting is also an important aspect of determining where you fit within the risk-reward equation. In most cases, long-term financial goals such as building retirement capital will encourage you to invest more aggressively than might be the case for shorter- or medium-term goals. This, of course, will depend on your age, too. But, an investment horizon of 10 years or longer is usually sufficient to allow all but the most conservative person to invest in securities that offer higher return potential and incur higher short-term capital risk. This is because investors normally grow with their investments and the longer they invest the more comfortable they become. Research has shown that an individual's risk tolerance level generally increases in proportion to the increase in that person's investment knowledge. Other factors, such as a person's understanding of economic forces and how they impact on investments, increased capital liquidity, awareness of the impact of income tax and increasing net worth also determine the level of risk-reward an investor is willing to tolerate over time.

ASSET ALLOCATION

Once you've determined how you feel about investment risk and have set your sights on securities with which you are comfortable, you should now be in a position to start thinking about how you would like to allocate your money and future savings to achieve your long-term retirement goal. Before going out and actually purchasing securities, though, you will have to refine your thinking to include those investment characteristics you think would best assist you in achieving your goal. There is no one correct answer. This is because people will define their tolerance for risk and reward differently and will link their risk tolerance to different short-, medium- and long-term financial goals. This is why there are several important characteristics or features of investment management which, when combined differently, will provide an almost infinite number of unique investment portfolios. These characteristics are as follows:

- capital growth
- capital preservation
- investment control
- investment income
- investment liquidity
- portfolio performance
- protection from inflation
- tax reduction and deferral.

To determine those investment characteristics that are most important to you today, number them one through eight. Choose your first three investment characteristics and build your portfolio according to them.

Dozens of investment authors have grappled with the theory of portfolio construction and the allocation of investment capital. Their theories, while written from different perspectives, all work from the idea that *maximizing investment rates of return while simultaneously reducing risk to its minimum is the goal of asset allocation.* Also called diversification, asset allocation ensures that you do not place all of your investment capital in just a few investments. No one investment, or even a few investments, will grow your capital all of the time. Asset allocation attempts to obviate this problem. How successful you are in this endeavour will depend on how you've allocated your capital in accordance with the principles of good diversification, personal risk tolerance and investment characteristics you deem important for your portfolio.

Allocation According to Asset Classes

The first step in actually designing your investment portfolio is to designate which asset classes you wish to include as part of your long-term investment strategy. If we return to Figure 3.1 at the beginning of this chapter, you have seven choices. Few investors would be foolish enough to use just one asset class. Most investors would use at least two or three classes. Depending on your level of sophistication, you may wish to include several asset classes in your portfolio. For someone who is trying to accumulate capital for their retirement and can tolerate a much higher level of risk, a portfolio comprised principally of equity growth securities, real estate and hard assets would be appropriate. Another person who has a high penchant for risk, has a great deal of investment experience and has a high annual tax liability might also include a limited partnership to help shelter current and future income, thereby leaving more after-tax capital to allocate to his or her retirement nest egg.

Novice or conservative investors would probably look to a blend of fixed and equity income asset classes, preferring to build their retirement nest eggs through the compounding power of reinvested investment income. These individuals would likely have larger cash reserves in the form of cash and cash equivalents, if only because they are not as knowledgeable about the benefits of other asset classes or have low risk tolerance levels.

Other more seasoned investors, who are looking to build retirement capital, but have average risk tolerance, would likely have a blend of fixed and equity income asset classes, coupled with a moderate percentage of money allocated to the equity growth class.

The asset classes you choose coupled with the percentage of capital you allocate to each asset class is the first step towards building an appropriate long-term investment portfolio. Unfortunately, there are no hard and fast rules as to how or what to include in an investment portfolio. This is because no two investors perceive risk and reward in exactly the same manner and no two investors share exactly the same personal and financial circumstances. To help you along, I have designed five portfolios that correlate our seven asset classes with five typical risk-reward scenarios. You can choose from these five *portfolio archetypes* to help arrange your assets. Your final asset allocation, of course, will ultimately be your own. The column ratings for each portfolio are compared with Government of Canada treasury bills, which are the most risk-averse investments money can buy. Values are based on a maximum of 10 basis points and the legend is given below.

The Capital Preservation and Income Portfolio

This portfolio, as depicted in Figure 3.2, is designed for risk-averse investors who want the opportunity for superior growth but do not want their capital to rise or fall in value to any great degree. Only 10 per cent of invested capital has been allocated to the equity-growth class and the portfolio does not depend on long-term capital gain to any extent. This portfolio focuses on the preservation of original invested capital as well as on long-term capital appreciation through the use of cash equivalents, fixed income and equity-income asset classes. The major source of growth for this portfolio is by way of compounding interest and dividend dividends.

The High Income Portfolio

The high income portfolio as shown in Figure 3.3 is comprised of 10 per cent securities from the cash equivalent asset class, 50 per cent from the fixed income asset class, 30 per cent from the equity income class and 10 per cent from the equity growth asset class. This portfolio is designed for the risk-averse investor who does not want to expose his or her invested capital to too much short-term volatility but wants the potential for higher returns. This portfolio has a growth advantage over the first one because only a small portion of capital has been allocated to low risk cash equivalents. The difference of 20 per cent has been invested in fixed income securities, providing investors with potentially higher returns through the compounding of reinvested interest and dividend dividends.

The Moderate Growth and Income Portfolio

With this portfolio comes a major shift away from fixed and equity income asset classes to the equity growth asset class. Now, 25 per cent of capital has been allocated to equity securities while the fixed and equity income capital weighting has been reduced from 80 to 55 per cent. This portfolio, as depicted in Figure 3.4, is an ideal archetype for investors who are willing to assume more variation in capital value, but who are not yet comfortable with the more aggressive volatility associated with the pure equity growth asset class. Its growth potential is based on a blend of compounding interest, dividend dividends and capital gains.

The High Growth Portfolio

The high growth portfolio represents breaking out into the world of pure growth. As you can see from the asset allocation model shown in Figure 3.5, the cash and cash equivalent component has been dropped entirely, while the fixed and equity income asset classes have been whittled back substantially. A full 70 per cent of available investment capital has been allocated to the equity growth class. You may have noted in the previous portfolio that the equity growth component was divided into two sub-classes—growth and international growth. In the high growth portfolio a third sub-class has been added called aggressive growth. These sub-classes refer to progressively higher risk securities within the equity growth asset class. For example, *Bell Canada Enterprises* (BCE) is an example of a domestic growth security, while *International Business Machines* (IBM) is an example of an international growth security. *Diamet Minerals,* which is a junior mining company, would be a good example of an aggressive growth security. This high growth portfolio is designed for more aggressive investors who can stomach much higher short-term variation in the value of their capital in return for superior growth potential over the long term. The features of this portfolio should be carefully compared to the previous three portfolios.

The Aggressive Growth Portfolio

Figure 3.6 represents the last of our five portfolio archetypes. This portfolio has jettisoned the cash and cash equivalent and fixed income asset classes entirely. A full 90 per cent of invested capital has been allocated to the equity growth asset class, while only 10 per cent has been allocated to the equity income class. As it suggests, this portfolio is for the aggressive investor who can handle much more variability in the value of his or her capital. The aggressive investor is devoted to earning the highest rate of return on capital possible and is willing to close his or her eyes to the prospect of losing capital value over the short and mid term.

Asset Allocation According to Security Types

Using asset allocation models are great tools when trying to figure out how to organize your capital. But you cannot simply put your capital into classes of assets. You have to purchase individual securities that pertain to each asset class you wish to include in your portfolio. This section of the chapter selects and defines some of the more popular security types found in each of the first five asset classes given in Figure 3.1. I have taken a great deal of time to isolate those securities you should seriously consider as components of your retirement accumulation portfolio. I have outlined these individual securities to provide the basics for further research. You can conduct other research on your own or with your financial advisor.

Cash and Cash Equivalents

Technically speaking, cash and cash equivalents are called *money market securities*. This is because securities that are found in this asset class are *highly liquid*, of short-term duration and have little or no risk to capital. When choosing securities from this asset class, you should avoid concentrating capital in just one kind of security. Be aware as well, that your average rate of return from this asset class will seldom be great, and, when it is, will never be for extended periods of time. The investment horizon of cash and cash equivalents is up to one calendar year duration, no more.

Figure 3.2
The Capital Preservation and Income Portfolio

Portfolio Features						
Income	Growth	Volatility	Capital Risk	Liquidity	Tax Savings	Diversified
8	3	3	3	10	3	3

Treasury Bills						
10	1	1	1	10	1	1

30.0% – Cash
40.0% – Fixed
20.0% – Eq. Inc.
10.0% – Eq. Gth.

Figure 3.3
The High Income Portfolio

Portfolio Features						
Income	Growth	Volatility	Capital Risk	Liquidity	Tax Savings	Diversified
10	4	5	4	8	4	4

Treasury Bills						
10	1	1	1	10	1	1

10.0% – Cash
50.0% – Fixed
30.0% – Eq. Inc.
10.0% – Eq. Gth.

Legend

Income	= capacity of the portfolio to produce reinvested investment income
Growth	= capacity of the portfolio to grow by capital appreciation or capital gain
Volatility	= amount of variability in value of original invested capital
Capital Risk	= overall risk of loss of original capital
Liquidity	= measure of access an investor has to his or her money

Figure 3.4
The Moderate Growth and Income Portfolio

Portfolio Features						
Income	Growth	Volatility	Capital Risk	Liquidity	Tax Savings	Diversified
6	5	6	5	6	5	6

Treasury Bills						
10	1	1	1	10	1	1

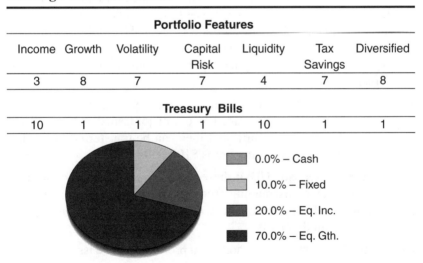

10.0% – Cash
25.0% – Fixed
30.0% – Eq. Inc.
35.0% – Eq. Gth.

Figure 3.5
The High Growth Portfolio

Portfolio Features						
Income	Growth	Volatility	Capital Risk	Liquidity	Tax Savings	Diversified
3	8	7	7	4	7	8

Treasury Bills						
10	1	1	1	10	1	1

0.0% – Cash
10.0% – Fixed
20.0% – Eq. Inc.
70.0% – Eq. Gth.

Legend continued

Tax Savings = ability of the portfolio to grow after tax each year
Diversified = amount of investment diversification each portfolio can provide to protect the value of investor capital
Treasury Bills = no risk security

Figure 3.6

The Aggressive Growth Portfolio

Portfolio Features						
Income	Growth	Volatility	Capital Risk	Liquidity	Tax Savings	Diversified
2	9	9	9	2	9	9

Treasury Bills						
10	1	1	1	10	1	1

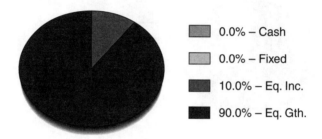

- 0.0% – Cash
- 0.0% – Fixed
- 10.0% – Eq. Inc.
- 90.0% – Eq. Gth.

Treasury Bills (T-bills): highly liquid debt securities (under one year in duration) offered for sale and guaranteed by our federal government in amounts of $1,000, $5,000, $25,000, $100,000 and $1 million. T-bills are sold at a discount and are redeemed at 100%. The difference between the discount and the redemption price represents your earnings and is taxed as interest.

Bearer Deposit Notes (BDNs): these securities are similar to T-bills except they are sold and guaranteed by our major Canadian banks. They cannot be sold prior to maturity but they can be transferred to another owner. The minimum issue amount is $100,000.

Certificates of Deposit (CDs): these securities are issued by our chartered banks in amounts ranging from $5,000 to $1 million. They are usually not cashable before maturity (30 days to five years) and are not transferable to another party.

Commercial Paper: this is a short-term promissory note issued by quality companies for up to one year in duration. Commercial paper is secured by the normally high credit of the issuing firm and is sold in minimum amounts of $50,000.

Finance Paper: a security issued by finance companies which is similar to commercial paper, except that it is secured by accounts receivable by the issuing company.

Other less common short-term securities are banker's acceptances, repurchase agreements and swapped deposits.

Fixed Income Securities

This asset class is comprised exclusively of interest-driven and interest-producing securities. The most common forms of fixed income securities are bonds, debentures, strips, mortgages and mortgage-backed securities. They are all interest-sensitive and will fluctuate in value as market interest rates fluctuate. In the case of bonds, where interest rates rise, their market or redemption value will fall. Where interest rates fall, however, bonds will increase in market value. If the market value of your bond is greater than the original value of the capital invested, called the bond's face value, the difference is a profit in the form of a tax-preferred capital gain. It's important to remember that fixed income securities can be quite complicated, depending on the type of security purchased. You have to know about such items as current yield, yield-to-maturity, extendible and retractable bonds, election and conversion options, prohibitions of prior liens and negative pledge provisions. The main thing to remember, however, is that fixed income securities often provide better returns than cash and cash equivalents with little additional risk.

Canada Savings Bonds (CSBs): these securities have been around since 1946 and comprise 25 per cent of all non-marketable (i.e., non-transferable) securities issued in Canada. They are risk-free as they are issued by the federal government and guaranteed by its general credit worthiness and power of taxation. This is one major reason for their continued popularity. They can be cashed at the end of every month prior to maturity without penalty and can be purchased annually towards the end of October. CSBs can be purchased as "R" bonds and "C" bonds; the former type pay out accrued interest, while the latter allow interest to compound until cashed or until maturity. CSBs have had varying terms to maturity, the conditions of which will be stated in each issue. Sometimes CSBs are allocated to cash and cash equivalent securities.

Government of Canada Bonds: these are marketable bonds and are transferable to other prospective owners. They can be purchased as a new issue from government through registered stock brokers and they can be bought and sold on a secondary basis or "bond market." These bonds are usually available in amounts between $1,000 and $1 million. Government of Canada Bonds are issued for short-, medium- and long-term maturity periods. Short-term bonds are available for terms up to three years in duration, medium term bonds from three to 10 years, and long-term bonds for periods of beyond 10 years. These bonds are often purchased by major institutions such as banks, corporations, stock brokerages and trust companies.

You can purchase smaller denominations of these bonds but they are more suitable for individuals with larger sums of capital.

Provincial Bonds: these bonds are more readily available to investors than Government of Canada bonds because almost every province issues them in attractive denominations of $500, $1,000, $5,000, $10,000 and $25,000 or more. These bonds work exactly like other forms of debt securities. You are lending your capital to a provincial government, which guarantees the value of your principal. In return, you receive an attractive rate of interest, which is paid to you over the life of your bond. On maturity, the province repays your original principal. The government has used your money to finance special capital projects that it might not have been able to finance with resources currently on hand.

Municipal Debentures (Serial Bond): these are based on the same principles as federal and provincial bonds. The difference is twofold. First, interest rates paid are usually higher. Second, most municipal debentures have a definite capital repayment schedule so that a portion of your principal is paid back, plus accrued interest each year, until the entire original amount has been repaid.

First Mortgage Bonds: these bonds are corporate bonds and represent the highest security a company can issue. Your capital is secured by both the current assets of the company and its future earnings. In the event of corporate bankruptcy or termination of activity, you are repaid first.

Debentures: these securities are unsecured bonds. They involve higher risk to your capital, but they usually pay a higher rate of return for that extra risk. In the event of liquidation of the issuing company, you are only paid after all current corporate liabilities and first mortgage bond owners. There are two kinds of debentures: corporate and subordinated. Corporate debentures are attractive alternatives to bonds. Subordinated debentures are just as the title suggests—an additional debenture level that is second to a first issue.

Foreign Bonds: as opposed to domestic bonds which are bonds issued in the currency and country of origin, foreign bonds, including Eurobonds, are issued in the currency and country other than those of the issuer. They can provide additional diversification without having to go to the trouble of actually participating directly in the foreign market. They can also provide you with a hedge against variable interest rates and the dollar here at home.

Strip Bonds: these securities are regular coupon bonds that have had their respective interest coupons removed and cashed by a stockbrokerage. The residual bond, which is measured in terms of its face value or original invested capital, is then sold at less than the face value. Your return is measured as the difference between the discounted value and its face value over a specified period of time.

Mortgage Backed Securities (MBS): these are certificates of ownership in a pool of the Canada Mortgage and Housing Corporation (CMHC) approved first mortgages. As a federal crown corporation, the CMHC guarantees the conditions of your capital investment. What you receive is a blend of capital plus accrued interest over a specified, usually five-year, time period. MBSs pay a rate that is competitive with GICs. They differ from GICs because the latter only pay interest, not principal, and MBSs offer some liquidity through a small but available secondary market.

Other securities that may be suitable for individual investors include collateral trust bonds, equipment trust bonds, corporate notes, warrant bonds or debentures and real estate bonds.

Equity Income Securities

Equity income securities are about as volatile as many fixed income securities, except that, where income generated by fixed income securities is fully taxable interest, equity income securities often provide above-average yields as a result of the favourable tax treatment of dividends generated by distinctly Canadian corporations. However, care must be given to which preferred shares you choose from this asset class. There are several different kinds of preferred shares that react differently to specific economic factors such as fluctuating interest rates, common share valuation and share availability. Preferred shares can also have special characteristics such as cumulative and non-cumulative features and callable and non-callable features, each of which will further complicate your choice of securities. Equity income securities can offer superior after-tax returns to fixed income securities and, depending on the security purchased, may result in additional and sometimes handsome profits in the form of tax-preferred capital gains.

Preferred Shares: these securities offer a level of capital safety between bond investors and common shareholders, and provide a decent income dividend that can be reinvested or paid out at a preferred rate of income tax. After tax returns (yields) on many preferred shares have either equaled or outpaced returns generated by cash equivalents and fixed income securities making them attractive investments to many investors.

Straight Preferred Shares: these shares pay a fixed income dividend and will trade based on their respective yields. They are more attractive than common shares because of their comparatively high dividends, liquidity and lower short-term share-price volatility. There are several potential drawbacks to owning this kind of preferred share. First, the issuing company is not obligated to continue to pay dividends to you. Second, a fixed dividend will never go up in pay out. Third, you have no maturity date like most bonds. Fourth, you have ownership in the issuing company but you usually have no voting rights as do common shareholders. Fifth, these shares can offer only limited growth potential, depending on the number of shares available and the buy-back price offered by the issuer.

Convertible Preferred Shares: these shares allow you to convert to a different class of share, usually common shares. The advantage of this kind of preferred share is that investors can convert to common shares at any time for a predetermined price for a fixed period of time. If your common shares rise in value, such a conversion would result in an attractive capital gain for the preferred shareholder. If you decide to stick with the convertible preferred shares, your income yield is often higher than with dividends paid by common shares. There are also drawbacks to preferred shares. First, they normally produce a yield that is below the yields provided by straight preferred shares. Second, if its respective common share declines in value, so will the price of the convertible preferred share, making the latter more volatile than the straight preferred variety. Third, conversion from preferred to common shares may result in an odd number of shares which will be more costly and difficult to sell when the need arises. Fourth, where conversion is not undertaken, convertible preferred shares revert to straight preferred shares. Finally, issuers of such shares can force a conversion whether investors want to or not.

Retractable Preferred Shares: these shares allow investors to force the issuing company to buy back the preferred share at a specific time at a specified price. You would force a repurchase if the price you paid for retractable preferred share had a higher market value than the retraction price. Under this circumstance, you could earn a handsome profit in the form of a capital gain. This kind of preferred share provides some price stability as it moves towards a nearby retraction date in an increasing interest rate environment. But beware. These shares lose their retraction option if not exercised and convert to a straight preferred share. If interest rates are rising, this could mean a decline in value.

Variable (Floating Rate) Preferred Shares: this security offers a "floating dividend rate" which rises and falls as a consequence of rising and falling interest rates. Where interest rates are expected to rise, this kind of preferred share is worth considering. It is probably one of the least attractive preferred share options should interest rates begin to decline. Many of these kinds of preferred shares do not enjoy an appreciation in their respective share price during periods of declining interest rates.

Other preferred share options are preferred shares with warrants and participating preferred shares, foreign-pay preferred shares and class "A" preferred shares.

Equity Growth Securities

As the title suggests, these securities are devoted solely to growth. Any income that may occur is really the result of a distribution of a portion of a company's profits. These dividends are voluntary and in no way form part of an obligation on the part of a company to do so regularly. Common shares offer much higher risk to your capital, but the potential for high returns is also part of the equation. In fact, of the three asset classes discussed so far, securities found in the equity growth class have the highest return potential of all.

Aside from great growth potential, common shares also have excellent tax deferral in the form of unrealized capital gains and favourable treatment of dividends paid and realized capital gains. Unlike preferred shares, common shares provide investors with voting rights and a say in how the company in which they have invested capital is managed. While more risky than many other securities, common shares offer plenty of variety and can allow such unique and profitable maneuvers as stock splits and stock consolidations.

High Yielding Common Shares: these shares produce dividends in much the same way as preferred shares, except the yield is usually lower. Common shares that pay high, regular dividends are often associated with good quality, well-managed and sizeable companies. This, however, has not always been the case. *Royal Trustco,* for example, had a reputation for being a generous dividend producer, but it eventually disappeared as a result of poor management of its international real estate portfolio. A high yielding common share is usually sought by growth-oriented investors who want the potential for above-average capital growth, but do not want too much capital risk in the form of high-share price volatility.

Aggressive Common Shares: these securities are often associated with mid-sized companies that are growth-oriented. They reinvest almost all of their profits back into their businesses and therefore do not pay dividends to their common shareholders. As growth companies, their common shares often grow well in good economic times, but head downwards quickly during periods of economic volatility or stagnation. These shares are the property of aggressive investors with a long-term investment horizon.

Speculative Common Shares: these shares pay no dividends, are quite volatile over the short term and are usually issued by junior or poorly capitalized companies. They issue stock to garner quick infusions of capital that is used to finance a yet-to-be productive venture. Only the most experienced and aggressive investor will own this kind of security. The risk of loss of capital is quite high.

Real Estate Securities

A carefully chosen real estate property can be a good investment, especially if it is well-priced, well-located and in good repair. But, regardless how good a property, the fact is you cannot eat bricks and mortar. When thinking about real estate as a component of your overall retirement accumulation portfolio, most investors think of their home first and an investment property second. Only investors who are particularly aggressive or who have lots of capital to purchase a second property will use real estate as part of their long-term retirement programme.

Other real estate based investments, such as shares of real estate firms and developers and real estate mutual funds, are better suited for a long-term retirement capital accumulation plan. This is because such securities have much higher capital liquidity than hard real estate assets. As we noted earlier in this chapter, it can sometimes take years to turn real estate into cash. In the case of a real estate mutual fund, you can usually buy and sell your interests daily, subject only to transaction fees, where applicable. In cases where investors like real estate, but either do not have enough cash to purchase a property outright or lack the necessary experience to purchase, a real estate mutual fund may be just the ticket. This fund allows investors to become owners of various real estate investments under a managed asset scenario.

A NOTE ON MUTUAL FUNDS

I have left the topic of mutual funds until now because a mutual fund represents a selection of different securities purchased and bundled under the direction of a broad investment mandate and managed by investment professionals on behalf of their many investors. In this regard, most mutual funds are like individual asset classes, except that they can hold securities found in several classes under one roof. If you understand the difference between classes of assets and individual securities comprising each asset class, you likewise have a good idea of how a mutual fund is structured and what it tries to accomplish on behalf of its respective investors.

Mutual funds have several characteristics that are often sought by both experienced and novice investors alike. First, mutual funds are capital pools, where investors pool their capital together and reap the rewards of mutual fund investment in proportion to the number of fund units or shares owned. Second, these capital pools are managed by professional investment managers and take away the responsibility of investors to make regular investment decisions. Third, where an individual investor may require a lot of capital to include securities from two or three asset classes, mutual funds can use their large capital pools to diversify for an investor. All the investor has to do to participate in this diversified capital pool is purchase comparatively few shares of the fund itself. Securities diversification is much easier to achieve through a mutual fund. Fourth, under almost all circumstances, investors can liquidate their fund holdings on any regular business day. This superior liquidity gives mutual funds definite capital management advantages over individual securities. Fifth, mutual funds provide excellent investment flexibility. Investors can move capital from one to another with relative ease; they can reinvest any dividends or take them as cash. They can opt for capital growth or pure income or any combination of the two and investors can choose their own level of risk-reward from more than 1,800 mutual funds available today. Finally, mutual funds provide the opportunity to apply a variety of unique investment strategies that can often enhance an investor's means of achieving financial independence more efficiently and over a much shorter time period than might otherwise have been possible.

RISK MANAGEMENT REVISITED

As we noted at the beginning of this chapter, the concept of risk-reward is the key to understanding how all investments work. To reiterate the point, risk-reward represents your willingness to lose a certain amount of capital value in exchange for the potential for higher rate of return on your invested capital. Portrayed in this way, it's easy to conclude that all investments, regardless of what they are, incur varying levels of risk-reward. But simply choosing what you consider to be a selection of appropriate investments doesn't mean necessarily that you have mitigated risk to what you consider to be an acceptable level. All investments are subject to forces that are both within and beyond your control. Inflation risk, default risk, financial risk, interest rate risk, callability risk and foreign exchange risk are examples of uncontrollable risks, risks that rest beyond your ability to mitigate their effects to any great degree. These risks are distinct from risks that you can control, such as business risk, liquidity risk and non-market risk.

The most often cited form of risk that you cannot control, however, is called *market risk*. This is the risk associated with fluctuating money market, bond and stock market prices. No matter how much you diversify across different asset classes and individual securities, the essential integrity of your portfolio will follow the gyrations of these markets as

well as the future fortunes of our economy. The more volatile the gyrations, the more risk of loss in value of your invested capital you have to
swallow. Most investors regularly track stock market activity, for example, and relate such activity back to the value of their investments.

Even though market risk is essentially uncontrollable, there are two
risk management concepts that have been used by investors to help offset
market volatility over the years. The first risk management method is
called *buy and hold*. The second is *market timing*.

Proponents of the *buy and hold* approach believe that uncontrollable
market volatility can be mitigated by purchasing quality securities and
holding onto them for the long term. They cite history as proof that
securities of good quality companies will always override what proponents call short-term market fluctuations. While prices of such securities
rise and fall in sympathy with market volatility, they will always recover
and grow handsomely over the long haul.

Proponents of *market timing*, on the other hand, believe there are
periods when investors should not be invested in anything but low-risk
cash and cash equivalents. They reason that you can avoid periods of
declining markets and the drop in value of your securities by timing
when you're in and out of the market concerned. By liquidating your
assets at appropriate times during your investment programme, you can
enhance the end-value of your capital dramatically.

Research has shown, however, that neither buy and hold nor market
timing proponents have had the last word on controlling market risk.
They each have flaws. Successful investors, today, however, often rely on
both buy and hold and market timing together, taking the most productive ideas from each and combining them into one solid long-term
investment strategy. My five capital accumulation strategies outlined
below make intelligent use of both the buy and hold and market timing
approaches and offer the best chance of building your retirement nest egg
quickly with a minimum of risk.

FIVE RETIREMENT CAPITAL ACCUMULATION STRATEGIES

Lump Sum Investing

If you have a lump sum of cash that you've allocated to your retirement
capital accumulation programme, you have to put it to work in the most
effective fashion possible. Depending on your penchant for risk and the
time frame you have available, it is usually prudent to invest it now. By
doing so, your capital is put to work immediately and depending on
your portfolio and its securities, it will compound and grow faster than
by any other investment format. Lump sum investing, of course, is the

preferred way to go when stock markets are in the early stages of recovery from a market correction or recession. But this should not be your biggest concern. You should look at the time horizon you have to work with and, where you have 10 years or more to invest before needing your capital at retirement, you should be prepared to invest anytime, regardless of what stock markets are doing. Buy and hold proponents have history on their side since stock markets have always grown over the long term as shown in Figure 3.7 (below). The only *caveat* I would add here is that you should be prepared to purchase only quality securities, especially if you are inclined to look at stocks and bonds. Just because bond and stock markets go up doesn't mean necessarily that the securities you have purchased automatically will do the same. Their ultimate result will depend on the quality of the underlying bond issuer or company concerned.

Diversification Can Protect Your Assets

One of the largest benefits of lump sum investing is *diversification.* If you have a cash lump sum to invest for your retirement accumulation programme, you can spread the proceeds across securities from several asset classes. This has two major benefits—*risk reduction* and *enhanced rates of return.* By purchasing several securities instead of just one or

Figure 3.7

Performance of the Dow Jones Industrial Average (DJIA) from 1897 to 1997

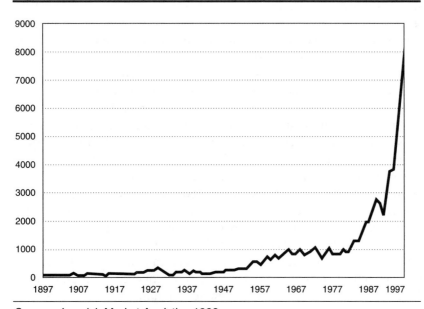

Source: Lowrisk Market Analytics 1998.

two, you have effectively reduced the amount of risk to your capital by a substantial margin. Let's look at a recent and colourful example. Remember Bre-X? Of course you do! If you had taken the advice of your brother-in-law and put your accumulated savings in Bre-X shares in August of 1996 you would have lost either a bundle or all of it, depending when and if you sold your stock. If, on the other hand, you had put 20 per cent of your capital in Bre-X, 30 per cent in Bombardier and the remaining 50 per cent in bank stock, you would have done very well, despite the failure of Bre-X. This is perhaps not the best example, but it certainly brings home the point. By simply buying a selection of securities, instead of just one or two, you can avoid risking your capital. By lowering the risk to the value of your capital, you automatically enhance your future rates of return.

But risk can also assume the form of a loss of potential investment returns. Here's an illustration. Most traditional bank-spawned GICs and trust company term deposits lock up your capital for a period of up to five years. If you managed to do so at the peak of an interest rate cycle, you would have done quite well indeed. But, if you did so just as interest rates were beginning a long climb up, then you would be kicking yourself silly. Your inability to dispose of your certificates and reinvest the capital at higher rates of interest would cost you a lot, depending on how high future interest rates would have gone. This lost opportunity could have been avoided if you had purchased a money market mutual fund with some of your capital and a bond fund that invested in short-term bonds and debentures. Since money market securities are of short duration, their interest yields rise as domestic interest rates rise, giving you a superior return. Money market mutual funds are highly liquid, too, and you can cash them to invest in any securities you wish at your convenience. A short-term bond fund can provide you with better returns as well. This is because short-term bonds are easier to sell by the fund to generate cash to purchase newer bond issues that offer higher interest yields.

Another benefit of lump sum investing is your ability to shelter earnings from excessive income tax. By keeping your capital aside in GICs, term deposits and other conservative interest-generating securities, you are exposing what earnings you have accumulated to annual income tax. As we learned in Chapter Two of this book, income tax can have a devastating effect on the ability of your capital to grow over time. If you pay income tax at a high marginal tax rate, your future investment earnings potential will be severely blunted. By investing your capital in tax-deferred and tax-preferred securities, your capital will appreciate far more effectively than if you did not. As a consequence of this, inflation's long-term corrosive effects will likewise be minimized, making for a far more valuable nest egg when you retire.

Systematic Investing

Systematic investing incurs less risk than the lump sum approach for three reasons. First, by making systematic investments you are reducing your exposure to market risk. Second, you are taking advantage of volatile bond and stock prices to increase your investment returns over the long term. Third, by making regular contributions to your retirement nest egg, you are learning how to build capital systematically as part of your overall financial plan. As you may have guessed, proponents of market timing endorse this investment strategy.

Systematic investing is the act of making regular, usually monthly, contributions to your investments. It can be used with any kind of security. Systematic investing, though, will work best with stocks and equity growth mutual funds. This is because systematic investing allows you to purchase stocks and shares of equity growth mutual funds as these securities rise and fall in value. Most seasoned investors will tell you that it is difficult to know the best time to buy equity growth securities. Sometimes a stock's price is lower in value and presents a good purchase opportunity; on other occasions, the price of the same stock will be higher than average and more expensive. In this instance, seasoned investors would avoid purchasing the stock. Since we can never know the best time to purchase securities, setting a specific day each month to make our investments will help average out the cost of acquiring our stocks and mutual fund shares. A synonym for systematic investing is *dollar cost averaging* and is most popular with equity growth stocks that offer an automatic dividend reinvestment programme (DRIP) or mutual funds that have a high level of share price volatility. Here are three illustrations of how dollar cost averaging can work.

Figure 3.8A shows the number of shares purchased when $100 is invested each month for 120 months during a steadily rising stock market. The total shares purchased amount to 1,725 at a cost of $12,000. The end value of this invested capital is $17,251 for a total capital gain or profit of $5,251. The value of the shares doubled from $5 to $10 each over the 10-year period.

Figure 3.8B shows how dollar cost averaging works during a 10-year period of volatile stock market prices. Dollar cost averaging allows investors to average out the purchase cost of their shares—some are purchased at a higher price while other shares are purchased when the prices are low. In this example, the number of shares purchased increased to 2,206 for a 10-year end value of $22,062 and a $10,062 profit.

As shown in Figure 3.8C, the worth of dollar cost averaging really shines during an elongated stock market decline and eventual recovery over the 10-year period. Here, investors averaged into declining share values up until the end of the fifth year, after which stock market prices

Figure 3.8A Steadily Rising Fund Share Price

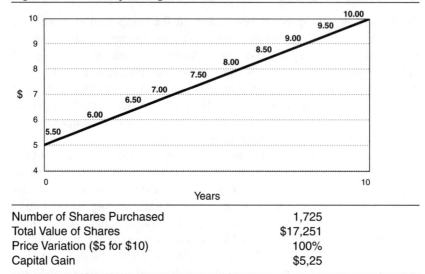

Number of Shares Purchased	1,725
Total Value of Shares	$17,251
Price Variation ($5 for $10)	100%
Capital Gain	$5,25

Source: Global Strategy Financial Inc., Toronto, Ontario.

Figure 3.8 B Fluctuating Fund Share Price

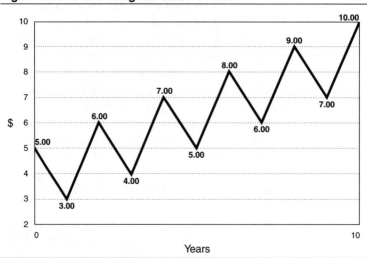

Number of Shares Purchased	2,206
Total Value of Shares	$22,062
Price Variation ($5 for $10)	100%
Capital Gain	$10,062

Source: Global Strategy Financial Inc., Toronto, Ontario.

Figure 3.8C Fund Shares Dropped and Returned to Initial Share Price

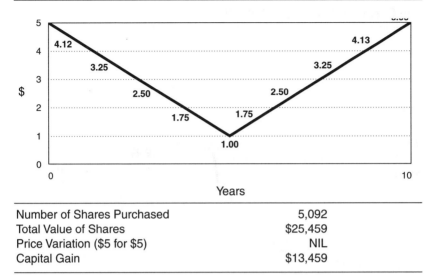

Number of Shares Purchased	5,092
Total Value of Shares	$25,459
Price Variation ($5 for $5)	NIL
Capital Gain	$13,459

Source: Global Strategy Financial Inc., Toronto, Ontario.

began to recover. In this example, investors started out at $5 per share, dropped 80 per cent to $1 and eventually returned to a $5 value at the end of the tenth year. The total number of shares purchased amounted to 5,092 and resulted in the highest profit of all—$13,459!

As mentioned earlier, market timers like the idea of dollar cost averaging. One of their biggest complaints about buy and hold strategies is the fact that, on some occasions, simply buying quality securities and holding onto them for the long term can sometimes turn into a lifetime. Take Japan and the Japanese stock market (Nikkei) for example. Market timers would argue that even an investment comprised of shares of such quality companies as Honda, Mitsubishi, Matsushita Electric and Tokyo Marine wouldn't have helped buy and hold investors in the crash of 1989. In fact, had investors held onto their stocks, they would have suffered a pretty hefty loss in the year following 1989's market decline. The Nikkei index peaked at 39,915 on December 29, 1989 only to fall to 14,194 by August, 1992. Today, the Nikkei has only managed to rally to around 15,000. As market timers will point out, 10 years is a long time to hold onto an investment that has essentially done nothing except possibly produce a moderate stream of dividends.

Market timing proponents would argue that investors should have disposed of their Japanese securities between 1988 and 1989 and then repurchased them after the market correction. Of course, many investors would have looked to other stock markets in which to invest. If you wanted to stick with the Nikkei, dollar cost averaging would have been

Figure 3.9
The Great Nikkei Bear (1989-1998)

Source: Lowrisk Market Analytics.

the way to do it, especially if you had begun your systematic investment programme at the peak of the market in December 1989. As the Japanese index and many of the stocks on it began their decline, you would have been purchasing more and more shares with the same monthly investment amount. As you can see from Figure 3.9, from 1992 onwards, the Nikkei's performance emulates illustration Figure 3.8B.

Systematic investing works best when the value of your equity growth securities is dropping in value. But, it also gives you an opportunity to take earn excellent rates of return during particularly volatile economic periods. For those of you who find it difficult, or have yet to take a disciplined approach to save and invest regularly, dollar cost averaging is the way to initiate and reinforce the task.

Lump Sum and Systematic Investing Combined

A third capital accumulation strategy is simply combining the lump sum approach with systematic investing.

If we return to Figure 3.9 above, buy and hold proponents would argue against the viability of dollar cost averaging by pointing to the fact that the latter concept would work poorly during the long bull market (where share prices are increasing) experienced by Japan from late 1977 to the end of 1989. Using dollar cost averaging during this period would cause investors to purchase shares at ever-increasing prices. As a result, dollar cost averaging would cost investors a fortune in lost earnings, rather than enhance their rates of return. Let's examine the facts.

If you had decided to invest $10,800 in the Nikkei index on December 31st, 1980, your capital would have grown to $81,654 by December 31st, 1989. If you had followed the market timing approach and invested $100 each month over that same time period, your $10,800 would have been worth just $46,604.

Obviously, based on this scenario, the buy and hold proponents win hands down. Making a lump sum investment, especially during an economic and market upswing, is far more profitable than systematic investing. But closer scrutiny of the facts reveals the interesting fact that, while a lump sum investment doubled your end result, dollar cost averaging actually was more efficient at earning its returns over the same time frame. The average annual return for the lump sum approach was 25.20 per cent and a cumulative total return of 656.05 per cent. Dollar cost averaging, to the contrary, managed an average annual return on money invested of 31.49 per cent and a cumulative total return of 1,074.71 per cent! The effectiveness of the dollar cost averaging approach was 25 per cent better than lump sum investing and generated a 63.8 per cent increase in cumulative total return over the nine-year period. As a consequence of these figures, we have proof positive that, while lump sum makes us more money, dollar cost averaging is more efficient at making investors money by taking advantage of the regular ups and downs in the value of stocks.

So, which approach is correct—proponents of buy and hold or market timers? The truth is neither. As I explained in the previous section of this chapter, both schools of thought have merit. The fact is, however, that combining a lump sum approach with dollar cost averaging gives you the best of both worlds, and will help you make money now and over the long term, while minimizing the risk of loss in value of your capital.

Leveraging

But what if you are unable to invest a cash lump sum? Are you then restricted to dollar cost averaging? No, not necessarily. You can borrow money from your bank or trust company (called *leveraging*), and invest it. By doing so, you have a lump sum of money to put to work towards the accumulation of your retirement nest egg.

Let's assume you earn a salary in a 40.3 per cent marginal tax bracket, have adequate emergency savings, little debt, a well-balanced monthly budget and a good disability insurance policy. You haven't been able to save money until recently, but now you can easily put away $650 before tax each month. You are 50 years of age and figure you have 15 years to retirement. Your goal is to invest and earn as much as you can over the

Figure 3.10
Borrowing Money to Invest

Criteria	Leveraged Results	Regular Lump Sum Results
Amount Invested Earning 11% Per Year	$60,000	$36,000***
Annual Loan Interest Rate	10%	—
Loan Period	15 Years	—
Regular Monthly Payment	$637.36	—
Loan Balance at Year 15	None	—
Income Tax Savings	$22,054.09*	—
End Value of Capital	$287,075.37**	$172,245.27

* Total interest paid equals $54,724.80 over 15 years recovered at 40% marginal tax rate each year.

** This amount excludes tax savings of $22,054.09, which, if added, will enhance the investment's end value.

*** To invest $60,000 out of your savings, you would have had to earn $100,000 before tax at a marginal rate of 40%. So, to make a fair comparison, take 40% of $60,000 which equals $36,000.

next 15 years. You would be happy with an 11 per cent average annual compound rate of return on your investments. Under this scenario, your retirement nest egg would amount to $169,583.93 at the end of 15 years. If you were to have borrow $60,000 and invest it under the same conditions, however, the value of your investment would have appreciated to $287,075.37, representing a capital increase of $117,491.44 or 69.28 per cent! This is the result of leveraging or borrowing money to invest. Figure 3.10 shows how it works.

The difference between saving $650 per month out of your monthly income and leveraging rests with the fact that your $650 savings was before income tax which means that you would really be investing about $388 per month after income tax of 40.3 per cent ($650 – (× 40.3%). Under the leveraged investment, however, the loan interest portion of your loan payment is *tax deductible at your marginal rate of 40.3 per cent*. This means that you have been able to maximize your monthly investment savings by being able to put the entire monthly amount to work in the form of a large lump sum of money. As we've seen previously, it is more profitable to put a lump sum of capital to work, than a monthly amount.

But, as good as leveraged investments can be, there are a number of *caveats* of which you should be aware. A great deal of positive publicity has been given to *leveraging*. One well-known financial speaker encourages you to pull the equity out of your home in the form of a collateral mortgage bond and invest the proceeds, arguing that real estate equity is a non-performing asset today. By borrowing against the value of your home, you have ready cash to invest in other securities such as stocks and stock mutual funds.

What this individual doesn't do, unfortunately, is tell you what you can do should stock markets fall in value. When you borrow to invest, you can dramatically increase your returns. You can likewise magnify your losses if stock markets begin to fail, too. If you borrowed $60,000 and the market dropped, resulting in a 20 per cent reduction in the value of your investments, the value of your borrowed capital would now be just $48,000. Lenders don't like to see this kind of thing and, where capital value drops below 10 per cent, for example, your lender can request $12,000 from you to bring the value of your investment back to par. Such a request is known as a *margin call.* This situation will always occur when you have borrowed money and have assigned the investments you purchased as collateral for the loan. Things can become particularly nasty if you had decided to pay only loan interest and not repay the loan principal. The result can be absolutely devastating where you have taken advantage of highly leveraged "two for one" loans offered by more aggressive lenders. If you don't have the cash to cough up to bring your loan "back on side," you've got big trouble. Figure 3.11 gives just one illustration.

Figure 3.11

The Effect of a Margin Call on An Investment

Amount Borrowed – $60,000

Loan Terms – monthly loan interest payment only @ 10 per cent per year

Number of Years Invested So Far – one

Security Purchased – back-end load equity growth mutual fund @ 6 per cent at the end of first year

Today's Security Value – $48,000

Margin Call – $12,000

Decision Made – cash out investment and repay lender

In this case, your losses would be comprised of $12,000 capital, a back-end mutual fund fee of $2,880 and loan interest cost of $6,000 ($60,000 × 10%, for a total capital loss of $20,880 or 34.80 per cent over one year). This isn't the way to build sufficient retirement capital! Think of the consequences if you had decided to invest in the Pacific Rim in August 1997! Losses in capital value exceeding 30 per cent alone over just a few months were not uncommon. What if you had invested in Canada's resource sector in April 1996? Most likely the value of your capital would have been halved at today's prices.

But, when structured properly, leveraged investments can be a great proposition. Here are some guidelines that, if implemented, will make a leveraged investment programme well worth the effort and expense.

- Never borrow more than the equivalent of 30 per cent of the value of your net assets.
- Always ensure that the gross carrying cost of your investment never exceeds 30 per cent of your net monthly income.
- Ensure you have the financial reserves to cover potential investment losses.
- Make sure your career or profession is secure.
- Remember that investment loan interest rates will float and, if they increase, will likewise increase the carrying costs of your loan.
- Take out life insurance on your investment loan and ensure you have sufficient disability insurance coverage should you become injured and unable to work.
- Note that most lenders have the right to call in your loan at their convenience, not yours, and that such action could cause you to incur administration, redemption or trustee fees, taxable capital gains, or a loss due to deflated securities markets.
- Where your loan is in the form of a secured line of credit, margin calls are reduced, but not eliminated.
- Know your penchant for risk and tolerance for swings in market value.

The Ultimate Money Accumulation Programme— *Risk Master Technology*™

Some investors have low risk tolerance levels, but they think aggressively when it comes to earning significantly higher rates of return. They are often seasoned investors and understand well the important relationship between risk and reward. They appreciate the importance of maximizing rates of return at the lowest level of risk to their capital. This situation, however, is one of the most difficult challenges to meet.

Aside from manipulating asset classes, investment diversification and dollar cost averaging, how can investors have the best of both worlds— low, low risk to invested capital and high long-term rates of return? One possible answer is the application of my patented investment concept called *Risk Master Technology*™ or *RMT*™.

RMT™ is a strategy that encourages investors to invest any time through the use of both buy and hold and market timing strategies. When implemented properly, *RMT*™ can generate generous rates of return for investors, regardless of what securities markets are doing. In fact, *RMT*™ works best when stock markets are at their worst as far as price volatility is concerned. The greater frequency in the rise and fall of market indices, the more money you make with *RMT*™. Sound impossible?

Risk Master Technology™ is based on the premise that you do not have to expose your investment capital to an inordinate amount of risk in

Figure 3.12

Real Life Results of *Risk Master Technology*™

Capital Invested ($)	Asset Class Used	Horizon In Years	Risk Tolerance	Income Amount ($)	Avg. Annual Return (%)	Investment End Value ($)
25,000	CCE/EG	10	Low	17,183	28.43	76,218
50,000	FI/EG	10	Low-Med	37,062	28.43	165,475
100,000	FI/EG	10	Low-Med	84,455	28.43	397,146
250,000	EI/EG	10	Medium	193,377	28.43	913,266

order to earn above-average rates of return. This is a radical premise because we've seen previously in this chapter that the greater the investment return you want, the more risk of loss in capital value you must assume to do so. As long as your investment horizon is at least six years, *RMT*™ will work for you. Where you have 10 years or more, as would be the case for most retirement capital accumulation programmes, your results would be outstanding. I have outlined a few real life results of my investment strategy in Figure 3.12.

As you can see from Figure 3.12, your average annual rate of return has been a whopping 28.43 per cent per year over 10 years, commencing July 31st, 1988! But, particularly interesting is the fact that these rates of return have been accomplished with investment portfolios designed to reflect low- to medium-risk investor tolerance levels.

RMT™ has been designed specifically to keep your original investment capital intact while making it work to its maximum capacity. It is superior to the concept of market timing because it encourages investors to take advantage of volatile equity markets, rather than run from them. It is also superior to the concept of buy and hold because it encourages all types of investors to invest on a lump sum basis, anytime. The true benefit of *RMT*™, however, is that, aside from providing capital stability and excellent investment returns, it offers a range of traditional investment qualities in one package that no other investment strategy has or can provide. First, *Risk Master Technology*™ can use both managed assets as well as single securities. Second, it makes use of investment diversification to help protect the value of your capital and future long-term growth. Third, investors can adjust their portfolio anytime they wish, providing excellent investment flexibility and liquidity over the short-, medium- and long-term.

If you return to Figure 3.12 above, securities from the first asset class or cash and cash equivalents can be used to hold your original capital. Your interest earnings can then be used to invest systematically in aggressive equity growth securities such as common shares or common stock growth mutual funds. Your host security would be virtually risk-free, a good example being a five-year income GIC or a mortgage mutual fund that invests almost exclusively in first mortgages. Securities from the second asset class or fixed income can be used as source investments while transferring earnings from these securities to an equity-growth portfolio. Since fixed income securities often generate higher levels of investment income, the amount of reinvested earnings is higher and purchases more equity-growth securities. Bonds and bond mutual funds represent the second form of fixed income class, and, while more risk-prone than mortgaged-based securities, often offer capital growth in addition to generating high investment income. Equity-income securities are the fourth and final form of *RMT*™ host security. Dividend mutual funds and high-yielding preferred shares represent this asset class and dividends generated by these host securities are reinvested in more aggressive and potentially higher rewarding common shares or stocks and stock-based growth mutual funds.

Finally, for those investors who do not have a lump sum to invest but would like to get into the market, *RMT*™ is the perfect solution for leveraged investments. Not only will it eliminate many risks incurred by borrowing money to invest, but it also can provide excellent returns without having to expose your capital to excessive income tax or the prospect of sudden margin calls.

CHAPTER FOUR

HOW TO PLAN YOUR RETIREMENT FINANCES

P lanning your retirement finances is not much different than the process you had to implement to set a good long-term money accumulation plan in place in Chapter Two. But, because retirement involves such a major shift in lifestyle, the financial plan that you had in place previously must now be completely revised. After all, you spent the last 30 to 40 years generating income from your employment. Now, you have to prepare to generate sufficient income from your retirement assets. Here's how to do it.

MANAGING YOUR CASH

Increasing cash flow to replace lost employment income is the most important aspect of retirement planning. It doesn't matter how much or how little retirement income you have. Managing your cash effectively should be your first priority. To be effective, though, you should be able to construct appropriate solutions to the following issues:

- an analysis of your first year retirement income requirement
- an estimate of your annual retirement income needs in today's dollars
- the analysis of the amount of *pre-tax* income your resources will generate in your first year of retirement
- a study of the *after-tax* income you will have to fund your retirement lifestyle
- a vision as to which capital assets will have to be converted to income-generating investment, as opposed to emphasizing long-term capital growth.

CALCULATING YOUR RETIREMENT INCOME NEEDS

The easiest way to calculate your retirement income needs is to take your present combined after-tax income and multiply it by a percentage reflecting your lower cost of living in retirement. For example, let's say you live well on an *after-tax* employment income of $50,000 per year. Since you expect your monthly expenses to drop by at least 15 per cent on retirement, your first year after-tax retirement income requirement is just $42,500 ($50,000 × 85%).

Where things become complicated, however, is figuring just how much of a drop in income and expenses you will actually experience in your first year of retirement. Most financial planners will tell you to revisit your monthly budget or "cash receipts" section of your net worth statement. Depending on your financial circumstances, you will have likely paid off the mortgage and enjoy lower transportation costs since you no longer have to head to the office. UI and CPP payments and contributions to your company's pension plan will have disappeared and union dues and professional expenses will also have ceased. Costs associated with disability, life and medical insurance will have been reduced or eliminated, depending on your employer's benefit package. Hopefully, much of the debt you carried during your lifetime will have been reduced or eliminated, allowing your increased disposable cash flow to be directed to other more enjoyable pursuits. Expenses associated with education, domestic help and other miscellaneous items will have disappeared, too. But don't forget that many of the living costs you suffered while employed will often reappear in the form of various retirement activities, such as hobbies, clubs, social programmes and travel.

A general guideline is to apply an "80 factor" when making an initial retirement income needs analysis. You should be prepared, however, to rationalize this factor to ensure its accuracy. To do this, complete another "cash receipts" statement, including regular savings where applicable, and then multiply the after-tax result by 80 per cent. Most financial planners advise repeating this process annually to ensure your income needs remain current.

Adjusting Your Income Requirement for Inflation

Calculating how much income you will need in your first year of retirement has to be accomplished with care. This is because your answer is the foundation on which all of your other retirement analysis is based.

However, you should also have a good idea of the income you will require later in your retirement. As we saw in Chapter Two of this book, one of the biggest problems that we face when calculating our future net worth is inflation. Inflation increases the cost of living but adds no value to it. As such, how we live today and what it costs to do so will be affected by the amount of inflation found in the economy. For those of us who enjoy earning an income, inflation is still a nuisance but it can be offset somewhat by our future earnings potential. When it comes to retirement, though, most of us do not have the luxury of being able to simply increase our income. Yes, you could get a part-time job, but working isn't my idea of a happy retirement. To offset the long-term corrosive effects of inflation, you have to factor its effects into your future income requirements. Figure 4.1 demonstrates a handy formula that I have used in the past for many of my clients. For those of you who are computer literate, rather than use this formula, there are many financial software programmes that can do this calculation and many other handy calculations, at the touch of a key.

Figure 4.1
How to Factor Inflation into Your Future Income Needs

Gross up for
Estimated Income Tax
(divide total after-tax income
required by 1.00 less
expected average tax rate)   Divided by

Total Pre-tax
Income Needs $

Future Value Factor
For Number of Years
(Until Retirement _____At
Projected Inflation Rate
Of _____Per Cent)   X

Total Retirement Income
Needs In Future
Dollars $_____

Here is the way to factor inflation into your future income needs. First, let's assume you are five years from retirement and you've decided that you will need 80 per cent of your current *net* income to maintain a comfortable lifestyle. Based on a net annual income of $50,000, you would need $40,000 at retirement five years down the road. You discover, however, that, as a contract professional, your employer does not index your income to inflation, which has averaged three per cent annually for the last ten years. This means that your current $50,000 income will probably have depreciated in terms of its current value by three per cent per year by the time you retire. Second, as a result, you now have to calculate the real value of your $50,000 income for each of the five years. In this case, you can use a *declining balance method.* Based on this method, simply multiply your $50,000 sum by three per cent and deduct the result. Then take the balance and once again multiply it by three per cent and deduct the result, and so on for the remaining three years. The value of your $50,000 income, which is subject to three per cent per year inflation, is now worth just $43,130.44 measured in terms of today's dollars. To offset this corrosive effect of inflation, you would have to increase the percentage rate of your current income of $50,000 to approximately

93 per cent from 80 per cent to ensure that you have achieved your $40,000 minimum inflation adjusted income target at the end of your fifth year.

Now that you have a good idea as to what you will need as a retirement income for your first year, you also know that, should long-term inflation continue at three per cent, each year you will have to increase your income requirement by an equivalent amount. This sounds easy to calculate and it is. Simply raise the level of income you wish by three per cent each year.

Gross versus Net Retirement Income

When we think about how much we earn per year, we often think about our gross income, that is, what we earn before income tax. When it comes to figuring how much income you'll need at retirement, it's a good idea to continue using gross income in your initial calculations. First, it is easier to work with gross amounts, and second, you can then figure what income tax you'll pay on your gross income. What you take away after income tax at retirement, though, will depend on what kind of income it is—employment, pension or investment—and how much of each you will report for tax purposes. Starting from a known commodity and working down from that figure to a net figure is a more accurate and logical way of calculating what the bottom line will be. So, if you need an inflation adjusted pre-tax retirement income of $46,500 ($50,000 × 93%), for example, you could figure on a combined federal and provincial tax rate of 41.34 per cent. Of course, this doesn't mean that you will pay 41.34 per cent tax on this entire income amount. You have various tax credits to apply to your income before Revenue Canada takes its share. But, for every unprotected dollar you bring into income, yes, the tax could cut as much as 41.34 cents right off the top.

EVALUATING RETIREMENT ASSETS

I mentioned at the beginning of this chapter that retirement signals a complete change in lifestyle. From a financial perspective, it also means a change in how you view your accumulated retirement assets. You are no longer earning income from employment. You are now looking to generate that lost income from the resources you have at hand. While you may have a pension from your employer, you will also have RRSPs and various investments outside of such registered plans. In these instances, you will now have to interpret these and other investment assets as income sources. RRSP conversion options will have to be reviewed, deferred annuities will have to be considered, and all of those bonds, common stocks and equity growth mutual funds will have to be examined as potential sources of additional retirement income. RRSPs can be converted into registered retirement income funds (RRIF), life income retirement accounts (LIRA) can be converted to life income funds (LIF), deferred annuities can be activated into regular monthly income streams, and bonds, stocks and stock-based mutual funds can provide valuable dividend income. How you restructure these and other accumulated assets will depend on your own particular financial situation.

CONVERTING ACCUMULATED ASSETS TO RETIREMENT INCOME ASSETS

There are three major income sources you can draw from to finance your retirement. They are *employer-sponsored pensions, government pensions* and *accumulated investment capital. Employer-sponsored pensions* are fixed income sources and the amount you receive will depend on the kind of registered pension plan you participated in and for how long. From a retirement planning perspective, there isn't a lot of flexibility when it comes to these kinds of income resources, except if you are receiving lump sum benefits when you leave your job. You receive what it is you are entitled to for a designated period of time.

The situation is the same for *government-sponsored pension resources* as CPP and OAS. You can split some of this income with your spouse as well as defer receiving payment on CPP benefits, but these two items are the only two options that provide any real planning flexibility.

Where you do have a great deal of flexibility to control and generate retirement income is through your *accumulated assets*. These can be in the form of RRSPs, registered or non-registered deferred annuities, proceeds from non-registered insurance policies, and an entire array of investments such as GICs, bonds and mortgages, preferred and common stocks and mutual funds. By mixing, matching and altering these and other similar assets, you can change the kind and origin of your retirement income to meet your annual adjustments in capital liquidity, income level, income tax and inflation. A truly planned retirement portfolio will provide you with optimum flexibility. You should be able to access your retirement assets anytime you should need a cash lump sum. You should also be able to increase or decrease the level of income whenever you deem it necessary. As income tax rules change, you should be able to alter the kind of income you enjoy to match such changes and allow you to keep your income tax under tight control. Finally, you should be able to change your income requirements and the investments that you utilize to generate retirement income anytime. This way you can control your financial future, rather than it controlling you.

As a point of reference for our discussion of retirement income strategies outlined in later in Chapter Six of this book, you should take note that most sources of pension income are not liquid and the level of income you receive is fixed. All pension income is also taxed fully at your combined federal and provincial tax rate, called your marginal rate. Regardless of the kind of pension income you receive, you pay a standard federal rate of tax, while your provincial rate, which is a percentage of the standard federal rate, will depend on where you live in the country. Where you receive pension income, you will receive a small pension tax credit on your T-1 General tax return. Your pension income may be indexed to help offset the long-term effects of inflation; however, it will depend on the kind of pension plan you have and its benefits. The rate of inflation indexing you enjoy will also vary, depending on how the long-term inflation rate is calculated by your plan.

Neither Canada Pension Plan nor Old Age Security offers any capital liquidity, so, unless CPP owes you some back pension as a result of late application processing, you can depend only on a monthly income from these resources. You receive your benefits as a monthly stipend that has inflation indexing based on the rise or fall of the *Consumer Price Index* (CPI). CPI is the cost of purchasing a typical basket of consumer goods and is factored into your pension payment on a semi-annual basis. There are no tax advantages to receiving either of these pension benefits.

Income from such registered assets as RRIFs, annuities and registered life insurance policies all qualify for the pension tax credit mentioned above. But only RRIFs offer the combination of capital liquidity, the choice of income level and inflation indexing. A RRIF is simply RRSP capital that has been converted into an income mode. You can take a minimum amount of income from your RRIF, thereby avoiding having to pay withholding tax on the income, or you can withdraw a lump sum, providing tax is paid before your receive your capital. If you decide to simply take a certain income from your RRIF, you can index your monthly income according to the presiding inflation rate. RRSPs are great vehicles because they, too, can be accessed at your convenience, providing you are willing to pay the accrued withholding tax. As long as you leave your capital untouched inside your RRSPs, it will continue to grow untouched by taxes. While RRSPs will not act as a source of regular income like a RRIF or registered annuity, RRSPs can provide you with a lot of protection against inflation as a result of the fact that earnings are allowed to compound on a tax-deferred basis until redeemed.

Keep the Liquidity of Your Assets in Mind

All of the securities you have from the first five asset classes offer varying degrees of capital liquidity. *Cash and cash equivalents* provide low returns, but they provide excellent capital liquidity. You can easily access capital kept in chequing and savings accounts, money market and T-bill mutual funds, T-bills, BDNs, commercial and finance paper. CDs and

GICs are not as liquid due to their capital lock-up feature of up to five years. Still, most CD and GIC issuers offer some liquidity although there may often be an interest rate penalty attached. There are no income tax benefits accruing to securities found in this asset class, and no inflation protection. You can generate an income by use of income, as opposed to compound, term deposits.

Fixed income securities offer good capital liquidity. Depending on the quality of each security, you are usually able to either cash them immediately as in the case of CSBs, or within three to five days in the case of bonds, debentures, mortgage-backed securities and strip bonds. Where a bond earns a capital gain, you have preferential tax treatment of your profit. Because these securities often offer higher long-term returns than cash and cash equivalents, inflation is less of a problem for investors. Depending on the kind of fixed income security you own, you can generate varying levels of investment income.

Equity income securities provide superior capital liquidity, too. But, preferred shares involve a greater amount of investment timing than securities found in the previous two asset classes. This is because preferred shares trade on the stock market, rather than a bond or money market. The gyrations that often accompany daily stock market activity will carry over to preferred shares, making them harder to liquidate during volatile or declining market activity. The amount of liquidity you enjoy will also depend on the kind of preferred shares you own. Preferred shares provide varying levels of investment income, which again depend on the kind of shares you own. These equity income securities also provide good tax savings if their dividend income stream is from distinctly Canadian corporations. Some preferred shares will not only provide a high level of tax-preferred investment income, but they offer the opportunity to grow in capital value as well. This growth is usually in the form of capital gains, which also enjoy preferred tax treatment and provide some protection from the corrosive effect of long-term inflation.

Equity growth securities provide the least amount of capital liquidity. This is because common shares and stocks are associated with high short-term price volatility. This market risk goes with the territory and always has to be considered before accessing your capital. Common shares and stocks do not generate income and they, therefore, are not good sources of retirement income. We will see in Chapter Six of this book, however, that equity growth securities can be good sources of retirement income, providing certain criteria are addressed beforehand. Owning securities of the equity growth asset class bring some of the best tax savings available. This is due primarily to tax-deferred growth. As far as inflation is concerned, equity growth securities provide above-average inflation protection over the long haul.

The fifth asset class, *real estate,* offers comparatively poor capital liquidity, but securities found in this class can often generate good pre-tax cash flow in the form of rental income. Depending on the security, such as residential, commercial and industrial property, real estate investors can enjoy favourable tax treatment of rental income as a result of capital cost allowance (CCA) or depreciation, and preferred tax treatment of unrealized capital growth in the value of their property. Real estate has traditionally been considered a bulwark against inflation.

HOW TO CONTROL INCOME TAX IN YOUR RETIREMENT YEARS

Even after you have retired, income tax will continue to be the single largest barrier to a financially secure future. Unfortunately, there is no reason to believe there will be any relief from this problem soon. There are, however, many things that you can do to soften the tax bite when preparing for your retirement years. Some of these items you have already used during your drive to accumulate a retirement nest egg; others are new. Either way, making a concerted effort to take advantage of every tax reducing strategy available will go a long way to keeping your tax liability under tight control.

Income Splitting

Income splitting between you and your spouse can be a great way of lowering your combined tax burden. This is because your spouse can assume some of the income that is taxed in your hands and use his or her own non-refundable tax credits to both reduce and/or eliminate taxes that would otherwise accrue to income received in your hands. The CPP allows you and your spouse to split CPP benefits under certain conditions. Where your spouse does not earn much income, it is often an excellent idea to split investment income. Special rules apply here, though.

If you still have interests in your business, and you have children who were shareholders in your company prior to your retirement, they will likely remain so through your retirement years. Income that is generated by your business is paid to shareholders, usually in proportion to the percentage of the company owned by each. This means that income that would otherwise be taxed to you, is split among family members, often at lower rates of tax.

Of course, where you still can contribute to an RRSP and you can afford to do so, consider making a contribution in the name of your spouse. By doing so, taxes will accrue to your spouse's income, not yours. This maneuver is called a spousal RRSP.

Investment Income

Investment income is of four principal types—capital gain dividends, dividend dividends, interest and rental income. Preference should be given to dividend dividends and capital gain dividends, followed by rental income and then interest. This is because Revenue Canada treats interest just like employment and pension income for tax purposes. If you earn interest from your investments, you pay tax at your marginal tax rate. Rental income fares slightly better. This is because rental income is often offset by a tax credit generated by write-offs in the form of property depreciation. Providing the property is not liquidated or sold, the depreciation a person claims is not recovered later by Revenue Canada. Capital gain dividends pertain to fixed income, equity income and equity growth mutual funds. Depending on a mutual fund's securities portfolio, whenever the fund's management team sells off a security at a profit, such profits are distributed to the fund's shareholders in the form of a capital gain dividend. Only 75 per cent of capital gain dividends are subject to tax, regardless as to whether these dividends are reinvested in the fund or distributed directly as cash. Dividend dividends, to the contrary, can result in as much as a 35 per cent tax saving when compared to an equivalent amount of interest. On occasions where an investor has no other income, he or she can earn substantial levels of dividend income and pay no tax whatsoever.

Tax Deferral

You can save valuable tax dollars by choosing to draw as much tax-preferred income as you can, rather than access retirement resources that offer little or no tax relief. Only use RRSPs and registered annuities as a last resort to fund your retirement. Once you reach age 69, of course, you have no choice but to do so. However, the longer you put off accessing these and other registered assets, the longer capital inside these plans has to compound on a tax-deferred basis. Where you are forced to convert your RRSPs to a RRIF, for example, you have the option to take only a specified minimum amount of income each year. No withholding tax is paid if you elect to take this minimum amount each year. If you have capital invested in a regular, non-registered deferred annuity, make sure you elect to prescribe the annuity payments when you decide to access it. Prescribing annuity income allows you to spread accumulated interest over the entire term of the annuity, rather than getting hit with it over a comparatively short period of time. Where you have built a sizeable chunk of capital in a universal or whole life insurance policy, don't access it until absolutely necessary. This is because, in most instances, policy earnings are tax-deferred indefinitely or until the conditions of the policy are realized, for example, death or liquidation. You can delay receiving CPP benefits until you reach your seventieth birthday, too. So, where you have sufficient sources of tax-preferred income, deferring receipt of CPP payments can earn you handsome tax savings over the years.

Tax Deductibility

If you were fortunate enough to have invested in a good quality tax shelter or used leverage to help build your investment nest egg, carrying such investment strategies over to your retirement years can provide additional sheltering of otherwise taxable retirement income. Depending on what kind of tax shelter you purchased, you could still use whatever tax deductible expenses remain—for example, foreign net business losses, foreign net rental losses, capital cost allowance (CCA) and limited partnership loss carry-forward amounts. You could also have unused capital losses, business investment losses, carrying charges, foreign and domestic tax paid, charitable donations, gifts to Canada or a province, Canadian exploration expenses (CEE) and unclaimed investment tax credits.

If you borrowed money and invested it in quality investments that have continued to perform well, then you may wish to consider continuing the strategy into your retirement years. The interest charged by your lender for your borrowed capital is tax deductible at your marginal tax rate. Providing your investment rate of return continues to be higher than the after-tax cost of your loan interest, it is probably worth hanging onto the investment. Sometimes, where your capital has grown substantially, you can elect to take tax-preferred income from it in amounts that do not inhibit future potential growth of the underlying investment.

Special Rollovers

While we will discuss this topic in greater detail in the next chapter, it is worth noting here that you can roll over certain kinds of income upon retiring from your employer. Proceeds in the form of a lump sum payment from a company-sponsored pension plan can be rolled over tax-free into your RRSP. The amount allowed depends on the number of years of service you provided to your company and the number of years your company did not contribute to your registered pension plan. Severance payments can be transferred on a tax-free basis, too, and special payments in the form of sick leave and gratuities also qualify for registered retirement savings plans. Where you receive the company's contributions to your pension plan, you can roll over the proceeds to a LIRA.

Other Tax Reducing Ideas

Other books on retirement planning give long lists of how to reduce your income tax. The problem with the majority of these other tax reducing ideas is that they often assume that you have *too much* retirement income. This is the reasoning behind such strategies as charitable donation credits, registered education savings plan contributions for grandchildren, inheritance planning for people other than a spousal beneficiary, and lending or giving money to your spouse or your children. If you find yourself in the position of having too much retirement income, then some of these maneuvers will be of benefit.

Better alternatives that will help save you income tax through your retirement years, however, involve taking advantage of all available tax credits and deductions such as:

- child and attendant care expenses
- allowable business investment losses (ABILs)
- moving expenses
- alimony, support and child care payments
- various carrying charges like safety deposit box fees, accounting fees, investment counsel fees and investment loan interest
- stock option and shares deductions
- capital loss deductions
- Northern residents deductions
- age and spousal tax credit
- equivalent-to-spouse credit
- pension income credit
- disability credit
- tuition and education credit
- credits transferred from your spouse
- medical tax credit
- labour-sponsored funds tax credit
- provincial tax credits.

These additional deductions and tax credits will help keep your combined income below $53,215 (1997 rate), which is the threshold beyond which a claw-back of OAS benefits begins. For every dollar above this income threshold, about 15 cents of pension income must be repaid. At a combined annual income of approximately $85,000, all of your OAS benefits must be repaid.

Details of each of these deductions and credits are available from Revenue Canada in *Information Circular 91-1, Guidelines for Preparation of T1 Returns.*

Don't forget that if your income is low enough, you will be eligible for either a full or partial rebate of goods and services tax (GST) you paid up to a maximum annual amount of $199. If you still have dependent children you will be eligible for an additional annual maximum of $105 per child.

MANAGING LIFE RISK

Studies conducted by the *Life Underwriters Association of Canada* (LUAC) have shown repeatedly that the majority of retired Canadians are either underinsured or have inappropriate insurance products for themselves and their families. Various reasons are cited for this situation, however, the most important one is the failure on the part of consumers to review and modify their insurance strategies as they move through their respective life cycle. Yet providing adequate insurance against disability or premature death is very important today, especially now that our federal and provincial governments are busy looking at how they can generate greater and greater revenues.

Protecting Your Income

Disability insurance protected your income while employed in the event you were disabled and couldn't perform your normal job. This kind of insurance was often part of your employer's group benefits package and normally covered up to two-thirds of your pre-tax income or salary up to age 65. If your employer paid your disability insurance premiums, your benefit was taxable to you. If you paid the premiums, the benefit was essentially tax-free. Disability income insurance pays out only two-thirds of a person's pre-tax income in order to emulate approximately what you would receive after tax when working. Most policies paid benefits to you if disabled through accident or sickness and after a "waiting period" of up to 120 days. The exact benefits would depend on your company's group benefits package as some packages now provide short-term disability benefits which kick in sooner.

It is important to note that disability income coverage normally ceases when you retire from your place of work or when you reach age 65. Sometimes, enriched or executive benefits programmes offer disability coverage that will continue as if you were employed right up to age 70. Most private policies that you can purchase on your own, though, will be issued only until your reach age 45. If you retire earlier than age 65, you may be in the fortunate position to have disability coverage in force even though you are no longer employed.

Protecting Your Family

Life insurance is far more important than disability insurance when contemplating your retirement. This is because life insurance coverage will protect your spouse and children with an estate asset that is paid tax-free in a lump sum, often within 14 days of the death of the insured. This cash lump sum can mean the difference in allowing your surviving spouse to carry on the lifestyle you intended. In the case of the death of both you and your spouse, for example, life insurance proceeds can often be used to preserve the value of your estate from the attacks of creditors, estate settlement costs and Revenue Canada Taxation. We will discuss this briefly in Chapter Eight of this book.

Making good insurance choices can mean low costs and maximum insurance benefits. If you had life insurance as part of your employer's group benefits package, you are often covered up to age 70 under the original package. Other programmes cover your life until age 65. Still other benefits packages allow you to convert your group life coverage to an individual policy upon retirement without further medical evidence of insurability and will continue in force as long as you continue to pay the insurance policy premiums.

Prior to retiring, it is often good planning to purchase enough of the right kind of insurance to protect your estate and the income of your surviving beneficiaries. To protect your estate from settlement costs and income tax, you have to estimate such costs in advance with the help of a lawyer or your local library. Estate settlement costs will include legal fees, administration fees, trustee fees, burial or internment costs and investment management costs. These are in addition to executor fees paid for the time your designated *executor* took to settle your estate and provincial administration fees (called *probate* fees). Federal income tax must also be calculated, often with the help of a chartered accountant (CA). Once these costs have been tallied, you can then go shopping for an appropriate amount of insurance. Sometimes, a comparatively low cost *Term to 100* policy is the best kind of insurance policy. This is because it is usually cheaper than the alternative *universal life policy* (U-life policy). On the other hand, a U-life policy can grow beyond its original face value (insured amount) because of compounding interest and dividends contained in the policy. Your choice will depend on your particular circumstances. Where there are two spouses, a jointly owned, last-to-die insurance policy is often the best route to go when planning for estate preservation.

When looking to protect the financial welfare of your spouse or other dependant beneficiaries, you have to calculate what loss of income would occur on your death and how such losses would affect your survivors. In many cases of premature death of the principal income earner, pensions from employers will either cease or be reduced by up to 50 per cent. An Ontario secondary teacher, for example, will lose up to 40 per cent of his or her teacher's pension should he or she pass on, leaving only 60 per cent for a surviving spouse or dependent child. Investments that were held in the deceased's name only will be frozen and form part of the deceased's estate and could adversely affect the current income of a surviving spouse or other dependent beneficiaries. The same goes for OAS benefits, which cease on the death of the annuitant. CPP benefits pose an interesting problem inasmuch as these benefits cease yet reappear as survivor's benefits, often at a decreased level. In many instances, uninsured debts of the deceased will have to be paid outright and any other assets that are jointly owned or otherwise may have to be liquidated to pay such indebtedness. Once these potential problems are factored into the insurance equation, you have a pretty good idea regarding the amount of life insurance you really need.

PLANNING FOR YOUR ESTATE

While we will visit this topic in detail in Chapter Eight, it is important to mention some of the most important items here as a point of introduction.

Depending on which province you reside in, your estate could end up paying as much as 50 per cent of its total value in taxes. Whatever unrealized profits we show in the year of our passing both the federal and provincial government will tax at the highest possible marginal rate. Many estates will have unrealized profits that, when combined, will equal income levels that are equivalent to the highest income bracket possible. In Ontario, for example, you've reached this magic income level if you have taxable income of at least $66,105 in the year of your death. Imagine paying income tax of more than 52 per cent! This is why planning for the preservation of your estate is so important for the majority of Canadians.

Tactics that you can use to help obviate this and other kinds of costs, such as administration fees, processing or probate fees, trustee fees, legal, tax preparation and accounting fees and executor fees, include:

- an appropriate amount of life insurance
- capital gains exemption for qualifying businesses
- charitable gifts
- capital loss carry-backs (as opposed to forwards)
- an estate freeze
- farm rollover
- gifts and loans
- joint ownership of property
- an irrevocable *inter vivos* trust
- net capital losses
- family testamentary trusts
- preferred beneficiary election
- spousal testamentary trust
- wills
- spousal trust rollover
- shareholder's agreements
- spousal rollover
- revocable trust
- principal residence exemption
- income splitting
- sale of property and capital reserve transfers
- use of segregated investment funds.

CHAPTER FIVE

TODAY'S RETIREMENT RESOURCES

Now that you have a good idea as to how best plan your retirement finances, the next step is to note the many different financial resources you can draw upon. This chapter surveys the major sources of retirement income and outlines the principal features of each. These resources include CPP, OAS, Guaranteed Income Supplement (GIS), Spouse's Allowance (SPA), private pension plans and individual resources such as RRSPs, LIRRSPs, LIRAs, RRIFs, LIFs, LRIFs, annuities and investments. This survey of today's retirement resources will set the stage to learn how to actually generate sufficient retirement income in Chapter Six.

PUBLIC PENSION PLANS

Public pension plans are those designed, funded and operated by our federal government. The CPP is the principal source of pension income and is funded by contributions from working Canadians. OAS is an age-based pension that is funded out of general revenues of the federal government. The GIS, on the other hand, is a pension income supplement and is available to Canadians who have low levels of retirement income.

Principal CPP Benefits

The CPP began on January 1st, 1966 and everyone age 18 years and older who received employment income was a member and made contributions to the plan. As a member of the plan, you can receive any of six benefits:

- a retirement pension commencing at age 60
- survivor's benefit to your spouse should you decease while collecting your retirement benefit
- lump sum benefit to your estate upon death
- a disability pension should you be unable to continue working
- income to your dependent children while you are disabled
- survivor's benefit to your spouse and any dependent children if you decease before retirement.

The amount of your retirement benefit is based on how much money you contributed to your portion of the plan and for how long. You can begin collecting a retirement pension as early as age 60 or defer receiving CPP benefits until the end of the year in which you turn 70. If you are between age 60 and 65, you must have ceased working and, should you begin collecting a CPP entitlement before you reach your sixty-fifth birthday, your CPP income will be reduced by six per cent for each year you take your benefit in advance of age 65. At age 60, for example, your CPP pension would be reduced by a total of 30 per cent (six per cent × five years). After age 65, you can collect benefits as well as continue to work. The amount of CPP benefit you receive increases by six per cent for every year you defer taking income, for up to five years. Your retirement benefit is indexed to inflation and is adjusted every six months. Your CPP retirement income benefit is fully taxable at your marginal tax rate. Your CPP benefits are summarized in Figure 5.1.

Figure 5.1

CPP Benefits

Type of Pension	Amount	
1998 Maximum CPP Pension At Age 65	$744.79 Monthly	
Early Retirement Pension (Age 60-65)	Maximum Penalty Amount 30%	Penalty Per Calendar Year 6.0%
Late Retirement Pension (Age 65-70)	Maximum Credit Amount 30%	Credit Per Calendar Year 6.0%
Maximum Disability Pension	$895.36 Monthly	
Maximum Survivor's Pension	Over Age 65— $446.87/Month	Under Age 65— $410.70/Month
Dependent Children	$169.80 Monthly	
Lump Sum Death Benefit	$2,500 Once Only	
Maximum Combined Survivor/ Retirement Pension	At Age 65— $744.79	
Maximum Combined Survivor/Disability Pension	At Age 65— $895.36	
1998 CPI Indexing Rate	1.5% Adjusted Every 6 Months	

Special note should be made of the fact that provisions are made under the plan to allow spouses to split CPP income so that both spouses can receive the same benefit amount where one spouse has a higher marginal tax rate than the other. Both you and your spouse must have contributed to the CPP and applied for benefits under the plan. Also, it is important to note that your CPP credits may be divided equally with your estranged spouse in the event of divorce.

Collecting Your OAS Entitlement

All Canadians who reach age 65 are entitled to benefits under the Old Age Security programme, providing you are a Canadian citizen or a legal resident. Your maximum benefit under OAS is $407.17 per month at 1998 rates and is indexed to inflation in the same way as your CPP entitlement. Indexing, however, is adjusted quarterly in January, April, July and October.

To qualify for OAS benefits, you must have fulfilled *one* of the following requirements:

- resided in Canada for at least 40 years after age reaching age 18
- must have been age 25 or older on July 1st, 1977 and resided in, or had a visa to enter Canada
- resided legally in Canada prior to July 1st, 1977 and, after reaching age 18, must have lived in Canada for a minimum of 10 years prior to applying for OAS benefits
- if you were absent during the 10 year period mentioned above, your residency in Canada must have been at least triple the number of years you were absent and you must have been a resident for at least one year prior to applying for OAS benefits.

You are eligible for partial OAS benefits and any adjustments made are based on a complicated formula based on residency rules similar to the above.

OAS benefits are outlined in Figure 5.2.

Figure 5.2

OAS Benefits

Maximum 1998 OAS Pension	$407.15 At Age 65	
OAS Claw-back Level	Commences At $53,215 Income	No OAS Benefits Paid At $84,977 Income

To prevent abuse of the plan, OAS benefits are recovered through a claw-back mechanism, which reduces your benefits once you earn an income of $53,215. Your benefit gradually reduces the more total income you earn so that, by the time you reach $84,977, no OAS benefits are payable. There are no survivor's benefits for either spouses or dependent children under the OAS benefit plan and your OAS payments are taxed at your marginal tax rate.

The Guaranteed Income Supplement—Do You Need It?

The guaranteed income supplement (GIS) is just as it says—a pension income supplement for pensioners with little or no other sources of income other than OAS benefits. If you earn under a specified income for the preceding calendar year and are receiving OAS benefits, you are entitled to additional GIS pension income. GIS benefits are not taxable and are included with your regular OAS benefit cheque. Your total income ceiling excludes OAS payments. The benefits and conditions pertaining to the GIS are outlined in Figure 5.3.

Figure 5.3
GIS Benefits

Benefit	Amount	Cutoff Level
Maximum GIS Payment For Single Individuals	$483.86 Monthly	Annual Income $11,448 Excluding OAS
Maximum GIS Benefit Paid To Individual Married To Non-Pensioner	$483.86 Monthly	Combined Annual Income $27,744 Excluding OAS
Maximum GIS Benefit Paid To Individual Married To A Pensioner	$315.17 Monthly	Combined Annual Income $14,928 Excluding OAS
Maximum GIS Paid If Spouse Receives Spousal Allowance	$315.17 Monthly	Combined Annual Income $27,744

The Spouse's Allowance (SPA)

The spouse's allowance is a benefit paid under OAS, in the same way as the GIS. The SPA is paid to a pensioner's spouse and widowed individuals who are between the ages of 60 and 64. This supplementary benefit ceases to be paid if the recipient dies, reaches 65 years of age, is no longer is classified a spouse or becomes separated. The SPA is given on the basis of a certain combined income threshold. The maximum benefit received for 1998 if you are married to a pensioner is $722.32 and is reduced $3 per month for every $4 of income earned beyond $21,360. If widowed, the SPA benefit is increased to $797.45 with your combined annual income cutoff being $15,672. SPA benefits are not taxable.

PRIVATE OR REGISTERED PENSION PLANS

Compared to private pension or registered pension plans (RPP), government-sponsored pensions are pretty simple to understand, as there are essentially only three pension plans to consider. Private pension plans that are offered through your employer vary widely in complexity and suitability. Fortunately, however, all of these plans are derived from two principal types of private pension plans: *defined benefit* and *defined contribution* pension plans. By understanding the features of each of these principal types you will also have a good grasp of the many other available plans.

The Security-Flexibility Trade-off—The Defined Benefit Pension Plan

If you worked for a company that had a *defined benefit pension plan* (DBPP) and you participated in it, you will receive pension benefits in addition to available CPP and OAS payments. The actual amount you receive, however, is based on a certain predetermined percentage of your employment earnings, the level of earnings you enjoyed and the number of years you were employed by your company.

Let's look at an example. Assume that your company agreed to set your DBPP's percentage of earnings rate at two per cent and you earned an average annual salary of $45,000 over 25 years. Based on these numbers, you could figure on a pension of $22,500 in your first year ($40,000 × 2.0% × 25).

Your actual level of pension income, however, will depend on what kind of DBPP you have: a *final average pension plan, career average earnings pension plan* or *flat benefit pension plan*. If you have a *final average pension plan* (FAPP), your pension amount is determined in exactly the same way as above. Your earnings component, though, is based on either your last five years prior to retirement if they represent your highest income years, or your five highest income years during the last 10 years prior to your retirement. If you were a public servant, teacher, railway employee or worked for a chartered bank, insurance company or some other well-established Canadian company, the chances are you have a final average pension plan. It is the most generous plan of the three and will usually pay at a two per cent of earnings rate.

A *career average pension plan* (CAPP) bases your pension on an average of your earnings throughout your entire career. As a result, this kind of DBPP pays a lower pension amount than a FAPP.

Here's an illustration. If you worked for a company for 30 years where your income varied from $30,000 to $60,000 and your average earnings amounted to $45,000, based on 1.5 per cent of earnings, you could expect a maximum initial pension of just $20,250 ($45,000 × 1.5% × 30). While it is a lower paying kind of pension plan, figuring out your CAPP is easy. This is because your years of service and earnings to date are known. Once you know what your plan's percentage of earnings factor is, you can make the calculations yourself.

A *flat benefit pension plan* (FBPP) gives you a pension that is based on a set dollar amount for every year of service you give to your company. The amount of income you earn (earnings) is not a factor in calculating your benefit entitlement under the FBPP. For example, if you are credited with $750 for each year of employment and you've worked for 30 years, your FBPP entitlement will amount to $22,500 ($750 × 30). This kind of DBPP is often used by unions, which negotiate future contribution rates through collective bargaining. Different contribution rates are used where different employees receive widely divergent employment earnings.

All defined benefit pension plans share several important characteristics. The most important characteristic is that all DBPPs will define *in advance* what your anticipated pension benefits will be once you join the plan. This is a big benefit. Depending on the type of DBPP you participate in, you will have a good idea of the pension income amount you can expect upon retirement. This means that your employer promises to pay you a specific pension amount. This virtual guarantee is why such plans are referred to as *defined benefit* plans. Your company is on the hook to ensure that its pension fund managers invest the plan's capital so as to be able to fund your promised pension. Where there is a shortfall, the company itself must make up the shortfall with cash from other resources. As a consequence, there is no risk to you. Your pension contributions are invested in a DBPP after two years of continuous employment with your firm and membership in the plan is compulsory for as long as you are with your company. The DBPP can be contributory or non-contributory as well. In the first case, both you and your employer contribute to the plan. In the other instance, your company funds your DBPP entirely.

DBPPs provide other benefits as well. Assets in the plan are held apart from your company and this will protect your accumulated interest in the plan from corporate bankruptcy. Rigorous federal legislation provides strict rules for the management and investment of pension contributions and the plan is reviewed annually by the plan's actuarial department to ensure the plan is on track. Of particular importance is the fact that many DBPPs offer inflation indexing to its members, making this part of retirement planning a much easier task. Your maximum pension is the lesser of two per cent of your average highest earnings times the number of years service or $1,722.22 times your years of service to a maximum of 35 years.

DBPPs do have some drawbacks. While you are secure in the knowledge of what your pension will be in advance, you cannot opt out of the plan before retirement. Your income, too, is inflexible. This is due to the fact that you receive benefits in the form of regular, usually monthly, payments. You cannot take a cash lump sum from your plan. Another drawback is that payments from a DBPP have ceilings and these ceilings have varied in the past. If you are security conscious and willing to forgo some flexibility, however, then a DBPP is the right plan for you.

The Flexibility-Security Trade-off—The Defined Contribution Pension Plan

The *defined contribution pension plan* (DCPP) is the other major type of RPP. It is also known as a money purchase pension plan (MPPP). The major difference between this plan and a DBPP is that under a DCPP you *do not* know what your pension will be in advance of your retirement. There are important reasons for this feature.

While both you and your employer both contribute to the plan based on a fixed percentage of earnings, you are ultimately responsible for the end-value of your DCPP at retirement. This is because you make the decision as to how you want to invest your capital. A number of investment options are made available through the DCPP, but you have to decide where both your contributions and those of your employer are to be invested. So, regardless of your salary, the end-value of your contributions will be related directly to how well you've invested your capital. This means, of course, that, while you enjoy increased flexibility in the form of investment management, your employer is under no obligation to direct your investment strategy or to guarantee in any way what your actual pension will be. It is a double-edged sword—make good investment decisions and you will have a superior pension, make poor ones and your pension payment will decrease accordingly.

Some other potential drawbacks exist for DCPP participants. First, when it comes time to access your plan, you can only elect to use an annuity. An annuity is an insurance-based product that pays you a portion of your capital as well as ongoing interest earnings on a periodic, usually monthly, basis for a specified period of time. But, because an annuity is a contractual agreement, your RPP capital is locked up and you are no longer able to access it other than in the form you elected at the time you purchased the annuity. What could be particularly hazardous is the timing of your annuity contract. If consumer interest rates are at 10 per cent and above, the prospect of locking up your capital is offset by a good investment yield. If interest rates are low, say five or six per cent, then you do not have a very good yield and your total monthly annuity payment will be low as well. Second, there are numerous types of annuities, guarantees, and other options you can add to your annuity. For every enhancement or benefit you add to your basic annuity your annuity payment is reduced by a certain amount.

One positive feature that can be quite valuable is the DCPP plan's portability. Should you leave your employer, you can take the full accumulated value of your plan, which includes all contributions and the earnings accrued to termination from your job.

Your contributions and your employer's contributions to your DCPP are a percentage of your annual earnings. Five to eight per cent is a typical contribution amount. You are allowed to contribute up to 18 per cent of your *pensionable earnings* per year or $13,500 (for the years 1998-2004), whichever is less.

The Profit Sharing Pension Plan (PSPP)

A *profit sharing pension plan* (PSPP) is really a DCPP, except that your employer's contributions to the plan are based on your company's annual profits, rather than on a predetermined fixed percentage of your salary.

A PSPP can be particularly attractive during sustained periods of corporate profitability. If your agreement states that you are entitled to 12 per cent of the company's profits, for example, during periods of positive economic growth, contributions could be substantial. But, the reverse is true, even though most PSPP agreements guarantee a certain minimum annual contribution of one per cent or more. A variety of investment alternatives are used, including company shares. The major risk to you is an under-funded pension at retirement.

As with all DCPPs, contributions are deductible for tax purposes; pension income is received on retirement or termination; payments must be received as an annuity or LIF; proceeds can be transferred to a locked-in RRSP or LIRA; and pension proceeds are taxable at your marginal tax rate.

The Multi-Employer Pension Plan (MEPP)

The *multi-employer pension plan* (MEPP) is available for employees of two or more employers. This kind of plan is ideal for companies that operate several closely tied subsidiary companies under one roof. Instead of having multiple pension plans which add to administrative and management costs, a MEPP can have obvious advantages for the corporation by eliminating superfluous costs at bay. MEPPs can take the form of either a DBPP or DCPP, but they are most often flat benefit pension plans. Contributions to a MEPP are based on the employee's combined years of service for two or more participating companies. Contribution rates are the same as those for DBPPs and DCPPs.

The major drawback of MEPPs is that, more often than not, your retirement benefit is not guaranteed in the case of DBPPs. If the funds contributed by your employers are not sufficient to provide the intended pension, the actual pension you receive at retirement may in fact be lower than anticipated.

The Hybrid Combination Pension Plan (HCPP)

The *hybrid combination pension plan* (HCPP) is a mix of both the DBPP and the DCPP. In many cases, your employer will contribute to, and fund, the DBP portion, while your contributions fund the DCP portion of your plan. Your retirement pension will be based on the total value of the two plans. Your pension payment, though, is based on the greater of the two types of pensions. The advantage of a hybrid combination pension plan is that you can often spread the funding risk or pension result between the two plans and choose the best pension payment. The drawback of the HCPP is that you have to choose between the two at retirement, which, in many cases, could be a tough decision where your pension amount is the same.

The Individual Pension Plan (IPP)

The *individual pension plan* (IPP) is an important development for business owner-managers who earn in excess of $80,000 per year. It is a registered pension plan or RPP, but it has all of the features of a DBPP. It is designed solely for one person instead of a group of individuals. Its job is to provide valuable pension benefits in situations where there is only one highly compensated person involved. If you are self-employed, an IPP is worth investigating. On retirement, the annuitant or owner of the IPP receives all of the contributions and earnings.

The major benefit of owning an IPP is that you can contribute more to an IPP than RRSPs in some circumstances. At the very least, by becoming a member of an IPP you can maximize your RPP contributions yet still make a minimum additional contribution to an RRSP. In many cases, the proceeds of an IPP are protected against creditors.

The drawback of owning an IPP is that it is an RPP and therefore requires actuarial analysis and yearly reporting. This means extra costs to you. Also, an IPP is less flexible than a regular RRSP and doesn't allow you to income split in the form of a spousal RRSP contribution.

Deferred Profit Sharing Plans (DPSP)

You may not know it, but you could be a member of a *deferred profit sharing plan* (DPSP). Under this programme, your employer is sharing its profits with you and other employees of the firm. The maximum amount your employer can contribute is one-half the rate allowed for DCPPs. Your employer's contributions are tax deductible to you. As an employee, you cannot contribute to this plan.

You should note that employer contributions to a DPSP appreciate on a tax-deferred basis until you retire. Once retired, you can elect to purchase an annuity for pension income purposes. But, be aware that, like a PSPP, the value of your DPSP will depend ultimately on the profitability of your company since your employer's contributions are related directly to the profits earned each year. DPSPs are close cousins to RRSPs. They must invest in "qualified investments" and adhere to the same foreign content rules.

The Retirement Compensation Arrangement (RCA)

Some companies offer a *retirement compensation arrangement* (RCA) to help supplement employee pensions. All RPPs have pension income ceilings. If you've been an exemplary employee or high-ranking executive, your company may decide to provide additional benefits to you over and above your regular retirement pension through the use of an RCA. An RCA works in the following way. Your employer appoints a trust or insurance company as its custodian to hold whatever contributions the company deems appropriate on your behalf. Your company's contributions are tax deductible to the company. The custodian, however, must pay a 50 per cent tax on all corporate contributions. Once you retire, however, taxes paid by the custodian are credited back to your plan. You then pay tax on your RCA income at your marginal tax rate.

What makes RCAs particularly attractive is that they allow companies to contribute as much as they want to assist their employees in their future retirement without being limited by contribution caps as exist with all RPPs. In the case of RCAs, your company allows you to build up retirement assets on a tax-deferred basis in much the same way as you do with an RRSP. It is based on a tax flow-through arrangement where everyone benefits, including our federal and provincial governments.

Group Registered Retirement Savings Plans (GRRSP)

Most employers, today, have implemented *group registered retirement savings plans* or GRRSPs. These plans are simply an RRSP with multiple members and are administered and managed by a financial institution such as a bank, trust or insurance company.

Companies like GRRSPs because such plans are low cost and low maintenance when compared to any other kind of private plan. The most a company has to do is ensure monthly contributions on behalf of the plan's employee-participants are made on an accurate and timely basis. Contributions to the plan are made through payroll deduction. The amounts involved are usually determined by the employee and are based on a minimum-maximum contribution formula agreed to by both the company and the employee.

But, the low cost of operating a GRRSP may not be as important as the pros and cons of membership in the plan. First, while most companies will match an employee's contributions to the GRRSP, an employee is not obligated to either join the company GRRSP or continue with it if already a member. In the majority of cases, participation in a company-sponsored GRRSP is voluntary. Second, dealing with just one financial institution may limit the number of investment alternatives. Third, you have to make all of the investment decisions, which, if not done well, can lead to a costly retirement nest egg shortfall down the line. Fourth, most GRSSPs allow you to access your cash any time, providing you pay the federal withholding tax on the withdrawn amount.

OTHER NON-REGISTERED RETIREMENT SAVINGS PLANS—EPSPs AND DCAs

There are two other retirement savings plans available in today's marketplace: the employee profit sharing plan (EPSPs) and deferred compensation arrangement (DCA). These two plans are not registered pension plans, but they have valuable features and benefits, so I have included a brief discussion of them here.

Employee Profit Sharing Plan (EPSPs)

An *employee profit sharing plan* or EPSP is a trust arrangement that allows employees to purchase shares of their employer's company. In good economic times, participation in an EPSP can be a good move, especially if your company is enjoying above-average net earnings. Since employees usually have a better inkling as to how well the company is doing, participation in an EPSP can often be a better option than putting all your money in some other security.

The EPSP is not constrained to pension regulation and is therefore much more flexible than RPP-based savings vehicles. If you are a member of an EPSP, note that earnings are taxable and contributions are not tax deductible. You can liquidate your holdings at any time, however, and employer contributions to your portion of the EPSP are tax deductible.

There are no investment ceilings to the EPSP and membership in the plan is usually up to your employer, in other words, membership is discretionary.

Deferred Compensation Arrangement (DCA)

Membership in a deferred compensation arrangement or DCA is one of privilege. This is because the DCA is often a reward to high-ranking or well-regarded executives of a company. The DCA allows a company to further reward key employees by making tax-deductible contributions to the plan and allowing earnings on such contributions to grow on a tax-deferred basis. At retirement, the executive includes the entire plan in income and the taxes that were deferred and deducted by the company are recaptured in the hands of the executive.

DCAs are attractive vehicles for the highly paid executive. Cash bonuses and other similar forms of executive compensation are taxed at the highest marginal tax rate, leaving less than one half of the original compensation. Tax-deferred earnings in a DCA work in exactly the same way as those inside an RRSP. Over the long term, tax-deferred earnings can amount to substantial sums. There are usually no ceilings as to the amount that can be contributed by your employer to a DCA. To be tax deductible to the company, however, contributions made on your behalf have to be reasonable. At retirement, you are allowed to receive the proceeds of the DCA and, depending on how you elect to receive your capital and your level of income, proceeds could be taxed at a lower rate. Companies will sometimes use a life insurance policy on your life that builds up cash dividends as a DCA while the company is named as policy beneficiary. This is because earnings inside of a participating life insurance policy grow on a tax-deferred basis. The life policy performs double duty since, should you decease, the proceeds of the policy will help compensate the company for losing you and your services. In this instance, insurance policy funding costs are not a taxable benefit to you. Your company pays these costs.

INDIVIDUAL RETIREMENT RESOURCES— REGISTERED

For many Canadians, proceeds from public and private pension plans will form a good portion of their retirement income. While this provides a certain amount of security, such dependence on government-sponsored pension funding, as we saw earlier in Chapter One, may not be in your long-term interests.

Neither should you depend on your company to look after you. This is because there has been an increasing trend among corporations to opt out of DBPPs and DCPPs and focus on group RRSPs, which, as we know, offer far fewer benefits than RPPs. Looking toward your retirement, it is always better to have your own assets that you can draw upon. As you will see in the remainder of this chapter, having your own retirement assets will give you a great deal more flexibility to meet the challenges and changes that your retirement years will no doubt bring. How successful you are at creating sufficient retirement income will depend on how much you have been able to save for your retirement and how you disburse your accumulated capital during retirement.

To help you in this task, I have outlined the pros and cons of the principal retirement income vehicles currently available to Canadians.

The Case for Annuities

Annuities are insurance-based contracts where you give a certain amount of capital to an insurance company, which then provides you with a set amount of income. The income you receive is a blend of original capital plus accrued interest earnings. The amount you receive is paid out in regular amounts at regular intervals. The frequency of payments can be annually, semi-annually, quarterly or monthly.

The amount of money you receive is determined by several factors, such as the amount of money involved, annuity type purchased, age, health and sex. The most important factors, though, are your life expectancy and interest rates. Insurance companies use life expectancy tables to determine how long people live. Based on statistical information gleaned from various sources, your annuity payment will be determined in part by how long the insurance company expects you to live. Insurance companies do not know who will live for what period of time, but they know just how many people in the same age group will expire over a specified period of time. The value of annuity payments is based also on where interest rates are at the time the annuity is purchased. Once you have purchased your annuity, the interest rate locked in by your purchase remains the same for the life of the annuity contract.

There are two groups of annuities: registered and non-registered. *Registered annuities* are derived from proceeds from DBPPs, DCPPs, PSPPs, IPPs, RRSPs, LIRAs and other similar sources of registered capital. The income you receive from registered annuities is fully taxable at your marginal tax rate. This is because capital you invested in such registered plans provided you with a tax benefit and is treated as pre-tax capital by Revenue Canada once you begin to draw from these sources. *Non-registered annuity* income is treated more favourably because you used after-tax capital to purchase the annuity. By electing to *prescribe* your non-registered annuity income you reduce tax. This is because the interest earned on your capital is spread across and paid out over the life of your annuity contract. Only the interest earned is taxable.

There are several different types of annuities, which will offer you a variety of features and benefits. The most common is a *single life annuity with guarantee*. This is one of the highest paying annuities because the insurance company only has to pay for as long as the annuitant lives or the payment-guarantee period is in force. A *joint life annuity* is an annuity that includes a spouse. This kind of annuity pays less as a result of it being a contract between two annuitants. Both annuitants have to decease before the insurance company is off the hook. Of course, the chances of this happening soon is much less than with the case of the single annuitant. Payment levels decrease again should you include a guarantee period in your joint annuity contract. An *indexed annuity* can use any kind of regular annuity contract and its job is to increase your income every year to protect your long-term purchasing power. This feature is also known as inflation indexing. You should take note that inflation indexing is a costly annuity feature and will cut into the level of annuity income you receive.

Another type of annuity is the *variable annuity*. This vehicle invests your capital in segregated (mutual) funds, such as mortgage, bond and equity funds. The assumption here is that such alternative fund investments will earn you more and your capital would last longer than with fixed interest rate annuities.

An *installment refund annuity* is a vehicle that guarantees it will pay at least the equivalent of what you had originally invested to purchase the annuity upon your death. It can be paid as a lump sum or in the form of regular annuity payments. Another type of annuity is called an *insured annuity*. This vehicle is a combination of annuity income and life insurance. It provides you with regular income and a lump sum to your estate that is both tax-free and creditor proof. It is most widely applied to individuals who want the added security of regular, fixed income as well as provide a cash lump sum to help preserve the value of their estates and provide for their beneficiaries.

One other popular annuity is called *a term certain to age 90*. This annuity is a repayment of principal and interest in equal installments until your ninetieth birthday. It has special features and benefits. First, on your death, the remaining installments are paid to your spouse, or if other than your spouse, are commuted to a lump sum and then paid to the named beneficiary. In the latter case, all earnings are taxed to you. Second, a term certain annuity can be locked or cashable. Higher rates are paid to annuitants willing to lock up their investment capital. Third, these annuities can be either registered or non-registered. Fourth, a cashed term certain annuity can be reinvested in another annuity or committed to a RRIF on a tax-free basis.

You may have heard about *deferred annuities*. They are sold as annuities that you can purchase today and realize income on your retirement. In reality, all you are doing is providing an insurance company with cash flow until you retire, after which time the insurance company pays you back your principal plus accrued interest. Rather than pay the insurance company a lump sum, you are actually paying them in installments over a long period of time. As you know, there are better investments than this in today's marketplace.

Should you purchase an annuity? As a Certified Financial Planner, I use annuities sparingly. The reasons for this are as follows:

- Annuities lock up your capital and provide no future flexibility should you need money.
- Your annuity rate of return is fixed for the life of your annuity and, should interest rates rise, you will not be able to lock into these escalating rates of return.
- Should you require additional features attached to your annuity, such as indexing, joint ownership, or some other item, your annuity payment is decreased accordingly.
- Annuity pay-out rates can be punitively low during periods of prolonged deflation.

On the other hand, you should consider the benefits of owning an annuity, such as creditor proofing, locking into high interest rates for exceptionally long periods of time and capital safety. Up to $2,000 per month of annuity income is guaranteed by the *Canadian Life and Health Compensation Corporation (Comp Corp)* should your annuity issuer default through bankruptcy or some other hazard.

Registered Retirement Savings Plans (RRSPs)

I have left any real discussion of RRSPs until now because this strategy is one of the best money accumulation and income-generating vehicles in Canada. If you think back to Chapter Two of this book, you will recall that two of the biggest problems facing Canadians today are efficient investment compounding and taxation. Between these two items, the potential to build long-term retirement capital is greatly diminished. Any strategy that can effectively eliminate or reduce the effects of poor investment growth and taxation is a welcome strategy. RRSPs are one of the best ways of doing so.

First, registered retirement savings plans were introduced in 1957 to assist federal government employees to save for their retirement. Later, as this vehicle was introduced to the general public, people with highly taxed incomes began to use them as simple tax shelters. The rules for saving tax haven't changed. Essentially, for every dollar of income you earn and deposit to your RRSP, you will save income tax at your marginal rate. So, where you have a total income of $60,000, for example, you pay income tax at a marginal rate of 49.43 per cent. For every dollar you deposit in your RRSP, you will save tax of 49.43 cents. Deposit your RRSP maximum of, say, $10,000 and your tax savings amount to $4,943.

Second, RRSPs provide the most efficient means of building capital than any other vehicle. This is because annual earnings on your RRSP capital compound on a tax-deferred basis for as long as your money is left in your RRSP. As you can see from Figures 5.4A-B, the difference

Figure 5.4A
Investing Within an RRSP: A Comparison

Year	Investment $	Total Investment $	Total Value $
1	10,000	10,000	11,100.00
2	0	10,000	12,321.00
3	0	10,000	13,676.31
4	0	10,000	15,180.70
5	0	10,000	16,850.58
6	0	10,000	18,704.15
7	0	10,000	20,761.60
8	0	10,000	23,045.38
9	0	10,000	25,580.37
10	0	10,000	28,394.21
11	0	10,000	31,517.57
12	0	10,000	34,984.51
13	0	10,000	38,832.80
14	0	10,000	43,104.41
15	0	10,000	47,845.89
16	0	10,000	53,108.94
17	0	10,000	58,950.93
18	0	10,000	65,435.53
19	0	10,000	72,633.44
20	0	10,000	80,623.12

Based on a one time investment of $10,000. Saved at an Effective Interest Rate of 11%. Over 20 years.

Figure 5.4B
Investing Outside of an RRSP: A Comparison

Year	Investment $	Total Investment $	Total Value $
1	10,000	10,000	10,557.00
2	0	10,000	11,145.02
3	0	10,000	11,765.80
4	0	10,000	12,421.16
5	0	10,000	13,113.02
6	0	10,000	13,843.41
7	0	10,000	14,614.49
8	0	10,000	15,428.52
9	0	10,000	16,287.88
10	0	10,000	17,195.12
11	0	10,000	18,152.89
12	0	10,000	19,164.00
13	0	10,000	20,231.44
14	0	10,000	21,358.33
15	0	10,000	22,547.99
16	0	10,000	23,803.91
17	0	10,000	25,129.79
18	0	10,000	26,529.52
19	0	10,000	28,007.21
20	0	10,000	29,567.22

Based on a one time investment of $10,000. Saved at an Effective Interest Rate of 5.57% (11%—Tax at 49.43%). Over 20 years.

Figure 5.5A

Making Regular Contributions within an RRSP: A Comparison

Year	Investment $	Total Investment $	Total Value $
1	10,000	10,000	10,000.00
2	10,000	20,000	21,100.00
3	10,000	30,000	33,421.00
4	10,000	40,000	47,097.31
5	10,000	50,000	62,278.01
6	10,000	60,000	79,128.60
7	10,000	70,000	97,832.74
8	10,000	80,000	118,594.34
9	10,000	90,000	141,639.72
10	10,000	100,000	167,220.09
11	10,000	110,000	195,614.30
12	10,000	120,000	227,131.87
13	10,000	130,000	262,116.38
14	10,000	140,000	300,949.18
15	10,000	150,000	344,053.59
16	10,000	160,000	391,899.48
17	10,000	170,000	445,008.43
18	10,000	180,000	503,959.36
19	10,000	190,000	569,394.88
20	10,000	200,000	642,028,32

Based on an annual investment of $10,000. Saved at an Interest Rate of 11%. Over 20 years. Annual deposit made at the beginning of each year.

between tax-deferred and tax-prone compounding can be dramatic, especially over the long term. If you purchased an interest-generating security earning 11% outside of an RRSP and you paid tax at 49.43 per cent, each year your compounded earnings would be reduced by the tax you would pay on those earnings leaving an effective interest rate of 5.57% (See Figure 5.5A). Inside an RRSP, however, your annual earnings are left to compound on a tax-deferred basis. Under an RRSP as in Figure 5.4A, you would have accumulated $80,623.12. Outside of an RRSP, your investment would have grown to just $29,567.22 because of the impact of taxes on the effective interest rate.

Tax-deferred <u>versus</u> Taxable Compounding

Most RRSP participants make more than one deposit to their RRSPs. If we examine the consequences of putting aside $10,000 into both registered and non-registered investments each year as demonstrated in Figure 5.5A-B, the results are even more dramatic. Which would you rather have at retirement—$642,028.32 as shown in Figure 5.5A or $351,296.51 as shown in Figure 5.5B?

Figure 5.5B
Making Regular Contributions Outside an RRSP: A Comparison

Year	Investment $	Total Investment $	Total Value $
1	10,000	10,000	10,000.00
2	10,000	20,000	20,557.00
3	10,000	30,000	31,702.02
4	10,000	40,000	43,467.83
5	10,000	50,000	55,888.99
6	10,000	60,000	69,002.00
7	10,000	70,000	82,845.41
8	10,000	80,000	97,459.90
9	10,000	90,000	112,888.42
10	10,000	100,000	129,176.30
11	10,000	110,000	146,371.43
12	10,000	120,000	164,524.31
13	10,000	130,000	183,688.32
14	10,000	140,000	203,919.76
15	10,000	150,000	225,278.09
16	10,000	160,000	247,826.08
17	10,000	170,000	271,629.99
18	10,000	180,000	296,759.78
19	10,000	190,000	323,289.30
20	10,000	200,000	351,296.51

Based on an annual investment of $10,000. Saved at an Effective Interest Rate of 5.57% (11%—Tax at 49.43%) Over 20 years. Annual deposit made at the beginning of each year.

Obviously, it makes more sense to use an RRSP as your preferred long-term investment strategy when faced with the problems of efficient investment compounding and taxation. This is why good financial planners recommend you start investing in your RRSP as early as you can.

Invest Your Tax Refund Too!

But, don't forget about investing your income tax refund for more long-term tax savings. If you paid enough income tax during the course of the year, you would receive a cash refund of $4,943 for every year you made an RRSP contribution. If you in turn invested this capital in a regular investment (as shown in Figure 5.6) that earned an annual after-tax return of just 5.57 per cent (adjusted for tax), you would have acquired an additional $179,399 to use during your retirement years.

THE FUTURE VALUE OF REINVESTED TAX SAVINGS

As good as RRSPs are, our federal government isn't about to give away the store. You are allowed maximum annual RRSP contribution limits

Figure 5.6
Invest Your Tax Refund Too!

Year	Investment $	Total Investment $	Total Value $
1	4,936	4,936	4,936.00
2	4,936	9,872	10,146.94
3	4,936	14,808	15,648.12
4	4,936	19,744	21,455.72
5	4,936	24,680	27,586.80
6	4,936	29,616	34,059.39
7	4,936	34,552	40,892.50
8	4,936	39,488	48,106.21
9	4,936	44,424	55,721.72
10	4,936	49,360	63,761.42
11	4,936	54,296	72,248.94
12	4,936	59,232	81,209.20
13	4,936	64,168	90,668.55
14	4,936	69,104	100,654.79
15	4,936	74,040	111,197.26
16	4,936	78,976	122,326.95
17	4,936	83,912	134,076.56
18	4,936	88,848	146,480.63
19	4,936	93,784	159,575.60
20	4,936	98,720	173,399.96

Based on an annual investment of $4,936. Saved at an Effective Interest Rate of 5.57% (11%—Tax at 49.43%). Over 20 years. Annual deposit made at the beginning of each year.

and any contributions made beyond your allocated maximum is not deductible for tax purposes and will incur a monthly penalty of 1 per cent of the ineligible contribution amount. As a general rule, you are allowed to contribute 18 per cent of your qualified *earned income* to a maximum of $13,500, whichever is less. These maximum contribution limits are listed below in Figure 5.7.

Don't forget that your total RRSP contribution limits include contributions made to your registered pension plans less UI and CPP contributions, where applicable. Your pension plan contributions normally show up on your T4 annual income slip under pension adjustment (PA) in Box 52. A one-time non-deductible over-contribution of $2,000 can be made to your RRSP without penalty. Making your maximum over-contribution makes sense for tax-deferred compounding purposes if you invest it for 10 years or longer. As an added bonus, if you failed to make RRSP contributions in past tax years, you are allowed to carry-forward your outstanding RRSP contribution amounts indefinitely to a time when you can afford to make them. As far as income options are concerned, when you decide to access your RRSP assets you have several options available. You can take out capital in the form of a lump sum, you can convert all or a portion of your RRSP capital to a registered life or term certain annuity or you can convert all or part of your RRSPs to a registered retirement income fund (RRIF).

Figure 5.7

Maximum RRSP Contribution Limits (1995-2006)

Taxation Year	Maximum RRSP Contribution
1995	$14,500
1996-2002	$13,500
2003	$13,500
2004	$14,500
2005	$15,500
2006	Indexed to the average industrial wage

The Locked-In Registered Retirement Savings Plan (LIRRSP)

The *locked-in registered retirement savings plan* (LIRRSP) is an RRSP derivative which was designed to hold the proceeds of your registered pension plan or deferred profit sharing plan when you terminated your employment or were given early retirement. The proceeds from your RPP or DPSP are those monies that had been vested on your behalf plus accrued earnings, while you were a member of the plan. These monies are "locked-in" and cannot be withdrawn until you reach age 55. Even then, the manner of withdrawal is restricted, so care must be exercised when looking to access your account. You cannot make further contributions to your LIRRSP, and you cannot co-mingle these monies with other regular or spousal RRSPs. You can only transfer locked-in money to an LIRRSP and you must begin withdrawing from your LIRRSP no later than the end of the year in which you turn age 69.

Of particular importance, however, is the fact that LIRRSPs lose their locked-in status on your death and can be transferred tax-free to your surviving spouse's RRSP or RRIF. You should note that monies paid to you as a result of termination do not have to be transferred to a LIRRSP. You can leave your money with your previous employer's pension plan to grow there and eventually pay you a reduced retirement pension or you can transfer the commuted value of your RPP to a deferred registered life annuity.

The Locked-In Retirement Account (LIRA)

A *locked-in retirement account* or LIRA is an accumulation plan that allows proceeds from an RPP commutation to compound on a tax-deferred basis until you draw from it. It is quite similar to a LIRRSP. As of 1998, Alberta, Manitoba, New Brunswick, Nova Scotia, Ontario and Saskatchewan all have the LIRA in place. British Columbia, Newfoundland and Prince Edward Island use the LIRRSP.

RETIREMENT INCOME OPTIONS

Prior to 1981, Canadian retirees had only two retirement income options: life and term certain annuities. Only insurance companies, and the occasional trust company, could offer these products. After a year or two of intense negotiations between consumer groups and government, the latter finally recanted and revoked the insurance industry's stranglehold on retirement planning by introducing several novel income alternatives. Over the years we've seen the implementation of such income alternatives as the registered retirement income fund (RRIF), the locked-in retirement income fund (LRIF) and the life income fund (LIF). These three income options comprise almost 85 per cent of the income vehicles used by retired Canadians, today.

The Registered Retirement Income Fund

The *registered retirement income fund* or RRIF is the most popular retirement income vehicle available. An RRIF is like an RRSP insofar as all growth, regardless as to kind, compounds on a tax-deferred basis until you begin to withdraw capital from your plan. But, where you put money into an RRSP to build a retirement nest egg, the RRIF's job is to supply you with retirement income. You can take as much as you wish from an RRIF, providing you are willing to pay federal withholding taxes listed below:

Figure 5.8

Withholding Taxes on an RRIF

Amount Withdrawn	Quebec Withholding Tax	Remainder of Canada
$1—$5,000	21%	10%
$5,001—$15,000	30%	20%
$15,001 +	35%	30%

You must take a minimum amount when you convert your RRSPs to an RRIF, regardless of your age. If you are younger than age 69, you can convert only a portion of your total RRSPs. If age 69, you must convert all of your RRSPs to an RRIF. Figure 5.9 below provides the minimum RRIF withdrawal requirements in percentages. If you take the minimum amount from your RRIF, no withholding tax is levied at the time you make your withdrawal. You pay tax on it later when you file your annual T1 General tax return.

Figure 5.9

Minimum RRIF Withdrawal Requirements

Age at Start of Year	RRIFs Set Up Before 1993 %	RRIFs Set Up After 1993 %
65	4.00	4.00
66	4.17	4.17
67	4.35	4.35
68	4.55	4.55
69	4.76	4.76
70	5.00	5.00
71	5.26	7.38
72	5.56	7.48
73	5.88	7.59
74	6.25	7.71
75	6.67	7.85
76	7.14	7.99
77	7.69	8.15
78	8.33	8.33
79	8.53	8.53
80	8.75	8.75
81	8.99	8.99
82	9.27	9.27
83	9.58	9.58
84	9.93	9.93
85	10.33	10.33
86	10.79	10.79
87	11.33	11.33
88	11.96	11.96
89	12.71	12.71
90	13.62	13.62
91	14.73	14.73
92	16.12	16.12
93	17.92	17.92
94 & Over	20.00	20.00

One of the signal characteristics of an RRIF is its flexibility. You can convert all or a part of your RRSP holdings to an RRIF anytime you wish prior to age 69. You can take whatever amount you wish subject only to the annual minimum withdrawal amount. Like an annuity, you can elect to receive RRIF payments on a monthly, quarterly, semi-annual or annual basis. You can have more than one RRIF and with more than one financial institution, just like RRSPs. You can also use any kind of asset class or security you wish as investments, subject to just a few government restrictions.

Some of the most common RRIF payment options are as follows:

- minimum withdrawal option
- interest-only withdrawal option
- the smoothing withdrawal option
- level withdrawal option
- term withdrawal option.

We will examine these later in Chapter Six.

The Life Income Fund (LIF)

The *life income fund* or LIF is the locked-in RRSP income equivalent to an RRIF. Prior to the introduction of the LIF, locked-in RRSPs could only be converted to income through the use of an annuity. The LIF gives you greater flexibility. Now, you can elect between a minimum and maximum LIF income each year prior to age 80. At that age you must convert the remaining LIF assets to purchase a registered life annuity, although this conversion can take place anytime before. Your spouse is normally the beneficiary of your LIF and on your death the LIF becomes liquid and can be converted to a regular RRSP or RRIF.

Determining the minimum amount you can withdraw from a LIF uses the same formula as the one used to calculate minimum RRIF payments. To determine the maximum amount, you must use a complicated formula based on the current yield rate of Government of Canada Long-Term Bonds (CANSIM Series B14013). Figure 5.10 outlines a LIF minimum and maximum withdrawal or payment schedule. Note that you cannot take lump sums from a LIF and once the plan is started, it cannot be turned back into a LIRA in the same way an RRIF can be turned back into an RRSP prior to age 69.

The Locked-In Retirement Income Fund (LRIF)

The *locked-in retirement income fund* or LRIF was introduced after the LIF and life annuities. The LRIF allows you greater flexibility when it comes to determining how much income you need to live for your retirement years. The LRIF uses the same withdrawal formula as the RRIF and LIF, but its maximum payment formula is calculated differently and is based on the LRIF's investment earnings.

Figure 5.10

Minimum and Maximum LIF Withdrawal (Payment) Schedule

At Age	LIF Minimum %	Maximum (based on CANSIM Dec. 1997) %
55	2.86	7.31
56	2.94	7.38
57	3.03	7.45
58	3.13	7.52
59	3.23	7.59
60	3.33	7.68
61	3.45	7.77
62	3.57	7.86
63	3.70	7.97
64	3.85	8.09
65	4.00	8.21
66	4.17	8.35
67	4.35	8.50
68	4.55	8.67
69	4.76	8.85
70	5.00	9.06
71	7.38	9.28
72	7.48	9.54
73	7.59	9.82
74	7.71	10.14
75	7.85	10.51
76	7.99	10.93
77	8.15	11.42
78	8.33	11.99
79	8.53	12.69
80	Purchase a life annuity	

The maximum LRIF withdrawal is calculated using the LRIF's investment earnings for the previous year or the sum of all investment earnings not withdrawn in prior years, or whichever is greater. The LRIF also does not have to be converted to a life annuity at age 80. Most other characteristics remain the same as LIFs and RRIFs.

INDIVIDUAL RETIREMENT RESOURCES— NON-REGISTERED

In addition to all of the above registered income options, you have countless non-registered sources of retirement income. For the sake of expediency, I have divided investments that generate income into three types: *capital preservation-high income; capital preservation-growth and income; and capital preservation-high growth and tax-preferred income.* Although a somewhat novel set of categories, I believe you will find them useful when attempting to determine what kind of investments you have, which ones can generate retirement income and which ones have to be altered to do the same. It is obviously not possible to mention in a book this size even a reasonable portion of the many investments available to you, today. These three categories, you'll discover, will act as comparative foils against which to judge investments that could not be included here.

Capital Preservation-High Income Investments

Unless you are well off or you live frugally, investments that you have managed to build up outside of your RPP, RRSPs and other registered plans will likely have to be converted to produce additional retirement income. The amount of retirement income you do generate from your investments will depend on where your capital has been invested, the kind of investment earnings you generate and what level of tax you pay on those earnings.

Traditionally, those investments that pay the highest level of pre-tax investment income fall under the cash and cash equivalent asset class. Figure 5.11 shows that Canada Savings Bonds, Guaranteed Investment Certificates and 91-day treasury bills have produced comparably high pre-tax income over the last 15 years. This investment income is in the form of interest.

According to Figure 5.11, Canada Savings Bonds have been able to generate a 15 year average annual interest yield of approximately 7.3 per cent, while five-year GICs and 91-day treasury bills generated 8.7 per cent and 8.3 per cent, respectively. This means that you would have received an average of 8.1 per cent on investment capital that had been allocated in equal amounts to each of these three securities. This means that a $100,000 investment made at the beginning of your retirement 15 years ago would have provided you with a pre-tax income of $8,100 per year. Within the context of the cash and cash equivalent asset class, the risk of loss of capital to you is low. The earmark of these kinds of securities is that they generate a high level of pre-tax income without encroaching on the original value of your invested capital. In this case, at the end of 15 years, your original $100,000 worth of capital would still be intact and you would have received a total of $121,500 in retirement income.

On the surface, this situation looks inviting. When you factor inflation and taxation into the formula, however, you may find that your net retirement income may not be as attractive as you first surmised. In our

Figure 5.11

Rates of Return for Canada Savings Bonds, Five Year GICs and 91 Day T-Bills

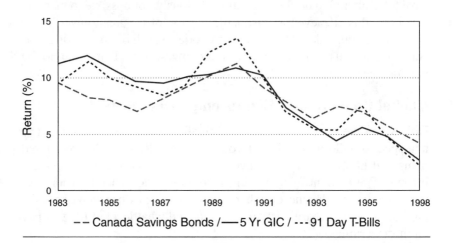

example above, our gross income yield was 8.1 per cent. Inflation over this same period was 3.1 per cent per year. So, while your nominal yield of 8.1 per cent appeared to be a fair reward for no risk to your capital, your real yield (after inflation yield) is much lower. In terms of today's dollar value, your combined 15-year income of $121,500 generated by an original $100,000 investment has been reduced to a real capital value of just $63,258.66 as a result of an average annual 3.1 per cent inflation rate. Your real current income of $8,100 would be reduced in purchasing power to a mere $5,123.95 by the end of your fifteenth year.

Add back income tax on your investment income and things become meager, indeed. For example, if you have retirement income in excess of $10,000 in interest, you will be paying income tax at a federal rate of 17 per cent and a provincial rate of 48 per cent (Ontario). This means that, even at this income level, you'd still see your 8.1 per cent gross income reduced to 6.07 per cent after tax (17% + (× 48%) × (17% − 8.1%)) and just 2.97 per cent (6.07 − 3.1%) after long-term inflation. Could you live on an annual net income of $2,970 from a $100,000 capital investment?

Using such conservative securities from such a risk-averse asset class does have big risks—the cumulative erosive risk associated with inflation and taxation. Your average marginal tax for the years 1992 to 1997, which apply to securities found in the capital preservation-high income investments category, are outlined in Figure 5.12.

Figure 5.12

A Comparison of Marginal Tax Rates on Interest Income

Interest Income Amount $	Amount of Tax Payable Per $100 Income
15,000	27%
32,000	42%
65,000	50%

Capital Preservation-Growth and Income Investments

This category is equivalent to the fixed income asset class and the securities contained in it. The most common fixed income securities are bonds. The average annual rate of return for these kinds of securities was 10.1 per cent over a 15-year period, ending December 31st, 1997. The average income yield was about 7.2 per cent, with the remaining 2.9 per cent representing appreciation in the value of original invested capital. This means that a $100,000 bond investment would have generated $7,200 each year for a total of $108,000 worth of retirement income. After income tax at the same marginal tax rate of 25.16 per cent, you would have netted 5.39 per cent or $5,390 per year. The big difference comes when we realize that the effects of inflation has almost been eliminated because of the additional 2.9 per cent growth attributed to your original invested capital. In this example, your $100,000 is now worth $97,047.46 when inflation of 3.1 per cent is entered into our calculations. The use of these kinds of securities has provided $680 less income per year, but the inflation-adjusted value of your nest egg has grown from a mere $63,258.66 to $97,047.96 in current value as a result of the extra capital growth bonds can produce. The effect of marginal tax rates on bond income is the same as for securities from the cash and cash equivalent asset class. But unrealized capital gains in the form of appreciated bond prices are not taxed at all and where capital gains are in the form of income dividends the tax liability is still better than that which applies to interest earnings as shown in Figure 5.13.

Capital Preservation-High Growth and Tax-Preferred Income Investments

Securities found in the equity income asset class represent this investment type. The principal security that comprises the equity income asset class is preferred shares or stocks. The average 15-year annual rate of return for preferred shares is 11.1 per cent, ending December 31st, 1997. The average income yield over that period amounted to about 6.8 per cent, with the remaining 4.3 per cent representing an appreciation in

Figure 5.13

A Comparison of Various Taxes Paid on Interest Earnings, Capital Gain Dividends and Unrealized Capital Gains (Uncashed Profits)

Interest Income Amount $	Tax Paid Per $100 Income %	Capital Gain Dividend Amount $	Tax Paid Per $100 Income %	Unrealized Capital Gains $	Tax Paid Per $100 Income %
15,000	27	15,000	20	15,000	0
32,000	42	32,000	31	32,000	0
65,000	50	65,000	37	65,000	0

capital value. If we used the same $100,000 and invested it in a selection of preferred securities, you would have earned $6,800 per year for a total of $102,000 over the 15-year period. The value of your original $100,000 capital investment would be worth $119,593.53 after long-term inflation of 3.1 per cent. And as good as these results are, preferred shares issued by distinctly Canadian corporations generate dividends that qualify for the Canadian dividend tax credit. The amount of tax you pay on Canadian dividends is as follows:

Figure 5.14

Tax Payable on Dividend Income

Dividend Income Amount ($)	Amount of Tax Payable Per $100 Income (%)
15,000	8
32,000	27
65,000	34

In this instance, by generating dividend income from Canadian corporations, your income tax savings can be substantial when compared to interest earnings generated by cash and cash equivalents and various kinds of bond-based securities. As a general rule, your tax savings on dividends will average about 32 per cent, depending on your marginal tax rate. So, where you have earned 7.2 per cent in interest income, your equivalent pre-tax dividend yield would amount to about 9.5 per cent (7.2 × 1.32). Based on our example above, a dividend of 6.8 per cent is equivalent to 8.98 per cent in pre-tax interest income.

As these computations indicate, your overall increase in net worth with capital preservation—high growth and tax-preferred income investments, after inflation and income tax, is far superior to the previous two investment types. But, after all is said and done, your penchant for risk or price volatility will be a principal determinant of which major investment type you utilize in your drive for adequate retirement income.

CHAPTER SIX

TWELVE SUPER INCOME STRATEGIES

This chapter represents the core of this book. In it you will find 12 strategies to help you generate the highest retirement income possible. These strategies have been drawn from my 16 years as a practicing Certified Financial Planner and, in many ways, have formed the core of many of the financial plans I have developed and implemented on behalf of my clients over those years. So, in one context, these 12 income strategies do work well, having been field-tested time and time again. On the other hand, these strategies should not be construed as ready-made systems that you can pick and choose from and apply on your own. They should be part of your financial plan and form the constructs that provide strength and direction to your total financial programme. In this regard, your general financial plan is your road map to financial prosperity. My 12 retirement income strategies are the vehicles that you can use to travel across that financial road map to achieve your life's short-, medium- and long-term financial goals, whatever they may be.

THE PROBLEM WITH PENSION INCOME

Short of being able to provide you with a small break in the form of a pension tax credit at age 65, pension income, while a welcome addition to anyone's retirement cash flow, can become a problem for many retired Canadians.

Government-sponsored pensions such as the CPP, OAS, the GIS and SPA do not qualify for the pension tax credit, located on line 314 of your T1 General tax return. These pension sources also do not provide you with any flexibility or liquidity. Short of inflation indexing, the pension you receive and the circumstances involved remain the same, unless our federal government decides to change them. What this means is that this pension income is fully taxable, GIS and SPA benefits excepted. In addition to being fully taxable at your marginal tax rate, these pension resources are illiquid, too. If you need a lump sum, don't look to CPP or OAS for relief. Two advantages that the CPP does offer you though, are the ability to split your CPP income equally with your spouse and to defer receiving CPP benefits until the end of the year in which you turn age 70. Where your spouse has either no taxable income or enjoys a lower marginal tax rate than you, an income split of this kind can save you precious tax dollars on the CPP amount that you have shifted to your spouse. Deferred income means deferred taxes and savings now. But, this is no real retirement income strategy, since the whole idea behind building a financial nest egg is to generate adequate income for your retirement years.

Private pensions, such as DBPPs and DCPPs, also offer very little, if any, capital liquidity unless your plan allows you to transfer a portion to a RRSP which is not locked-in at retirement or termination. For the most part, if you are looking for a lump sum handout from regular pension income, forget it. Benefits are usually paid out on a regular, often monthly, basis. Private pension plans do offer more flexibility than government plans. This is because of special rollover provisions that allow you to transfer all or a portion of your RPP entitlement to your own RRSPs at retirement. However, unless you receive a severance amount and additional sick leave credits, you either receive an annuity-like income from your past employer's RPP or a moderately variable income in the form of a LIF or LRIF, depending on where you live in Canada. The benefit of private pension plan income is that it does qualify for the federal pension income amount of up to $1,000 and subsequent tax credit.

When it comes to actually leaving your employer, there are four items with which you will usually have to deal. They are the benefits package, employer pension, severance (where applicable) and termination pay. When you are fired or quit your employer, your group benefits usually cease. If you are laid off or you retire, your benefits will sometimes be convertible to individual coverage or be extended to a certain age, often age 65. These group employee benefits include life and disability insurance, dental coverage, vision care and extended medical coverage. If you are laid off or fired, you have the option to transfer any contributions made to your company's registered pension plan to another RPP or have your plan amount commuted to a lump sum which is then transferable to your own "locked-in" RRSP. If you retire and are a member of a DBPP, you normally receive a regular company pension. In the case of DCPPs and DPSPs, you can often elect to transfer those proceeds to your own RRSP or LIRA. If you are severed from your company, you can transfer all or part of any severance payment (i.e., one week of pay for every year's service) that your company gives to you directly to an RRSP up to a maximum of a 26 week equivalent. You can also receive a retiring allowance and transfer up to $2,000 for every year of service you have provided to your company prior to 1996 as well as an additional $1,500 for every year your company did not contribute cash to your pension plan or DPSP prior to 1989. This severance package includes retiring allowances and sick leave credits. Depending on the province in which you live and work, you may be entitled to a payment in lieu of notice of up to 16 weeks salary in the event you are fired or laid off without advanced notice. The number of weeks you are entitled to will depend on the number of employees who work at your company and/or the number of years you worked for the company.

TWELVE SUPER INCOME STRATEGIES

Now that you've acquired your retirement nest egg, it's time to conduct an inventory of the retirement assets you have and how they can best provide you with the ideal retirement income. When considering retirement income options, you should be prepared to analyze them according to several important criteria. By doing so, you will have all the information you need to build the best possible retirement income strategy available. These criteria are as follows:

- income generating capacity
- capital liquidity
- capital flexibility
- inflation control
- tax savings
- investment selection
- rate of investment return.

REGISTERED RETIREMENT SAVINGS PLANS AND OTHER REGISTERED INVESTMENT VEHICLES

Properly speaking RRSPs are not income generating vehicles. They are used by taxpayers to save tax at their marginal rate and to allow invested capital to grow efficiently on a tax-deferred basis until retirement. They are, as the plan name attests, savings vehicles.

But, RRSPs offer excellent liquidity and are restricted only by the underlying investments comprising the plan. Providing you are willing to pay the federal withholding tax on amounts you draw from your RRSP, such a tactic can provide you with cash lump sums whenever you need them.

RRSPs offer excellent capital flexibility, too. Not only can you get at your cash whenever you need it, but you can convert all or part of your RRSP to more systematic income delivery vehicles such as registered annuities, RRIFs and LIFs. With the exception of registered annuities, such income conversions can occur without disturbing the investment portfolio that comprises your RRSP.

RRSPs offer the best inflation fighting capacity of any other investment strategy in Canada. This is due to the ability of RRSPs to protect compounded earnings year after year. We saw the advantages of such tax-deferred earnings previously in Chapter Five.

Of course, tax savings are the best with RRSPs. In addition to the huge benefits of tax-deferred compounding, a deposit made to an RRSP is tax deductible on your total annual income and can save you thousands of precious tax dollars every year, depending on your marginal tax rate.

You can choose from one of the widest selections of investments when looking for an investment vehicle for your RRSP capital. Your rate of investment return, of course, is proportionate to the earnings potential of the investments you choose for your RRSP.

RETIREMENT INCOME STRATEGY # 1

If you are forced to redeem capital from your RRSP, do so in amounts of $5,000 or less. Federal withholding tax will be limited to just 10% of the amount withdrawn. If you need more than $5,000 in one calendar year, make several withdrawals, none of which exceeds the $5,000 threshold. The majority of financial institutions will allow you to do this. Make sure you date each withdrawal at least one business day apart and be prepared to pay additional income tax at the end of the year.

Registered Life Annuities

Registered life annuities are often the only income option for members of registered pension plans. But, individual RRSPs can also be converted to provide income using a registered annuity.

Registered annuities will provide a level of retirement income that is both level and systematic. It will give you a fixed income amount that can be paid on an annual, semi-annual, quarterly or monthly basis. Your actual payment from a registered annuity is comprised of a blend of original capital and interest earnings.

If you are security conscious and prefer the idea of a systematic monthly income, then a registered annuity may be the ticket for you. But, once purchased, an annuity cannot provide you with any additional cash lump sums. Your capital is locked away for good or until you decease, whereupon any remaining annuity value will be commuted to a lump sum, if elected, and paid to your designated beneficiary.

There is no capital flexibility with a registered annuity. There are no investment decisions to be made. It is strictly an insurance contract with a fixed rate of interest attached. Regular registered annuities will not usually provide any real long-term inflation protection, unless you purchased your annuity during peaks in the interest rate cycle or if you purchase an inflation-indexing option and attach it to your annuity. As with all registered sources of retirement income, there are no tax savings available for registered annuity income, except for the pension tax credit that was mentioned previously.

Investment selection is restricted to long-term Government of Canada bonds and is the purview of the annuity provider. Your investment rate of return is fixed for the life of the annuity and the only shot you get to determine your investment return is at the time you purchase your registered annuity.

RETIREMENT INCOME STRATEGY # 2

Always consider converting a portion of your RRSP capital to a registered annuity. Before doing so, however, ensure that your investment rate of return will match a minimum semi-annual compound rate of nine per cent. While today's market interest rates are low by comparison, you should always be prepared to lock-in higher interest rates for part of your retirement income portfolio.

Registered Retirement Income Funds

A registered retirement income fund is simply an RRSP in reverse. Instead of depositing capital into your RRSP and enjoying a tax deduction as well as long-term, tax-deferred compounding, you are now making capital withdrawals. The difference is that making withdrawals incurs income tax.

As an income-generating option in retirement, there is no better financial instrument. Nowadays, RRIFs provide excellent income opportunities. You can take a minimum payment as per a defined RRIF formula and pay no federal withholding tax or you can take out a lump sum at your convenience. You can elect to receive any income amount you wish on whatever periodic basis you wish, or, you can raise and lower your income requirements at any time. It's even possible to set a fixed income level and the RRIF automatically will index your income to a preset inflation rate that can be adjusted at any time. Also, you don't have to reach a particular age before you can commence receiving RRIF payments. You can start anytime, but you cannot defer receiving RRIF income beyond the end of the year in which you turn age 69.

The *minimum withdrawal option* is based on the standard minimum formula outlined previously in Chapter Five. If you use this option, you won't begin to eat into the value of your original captial until around age 80. Base it on the age of the younger spouse, and you receive even less RRIF income. By taking the minimum prescribed amount according to Revenue Canada's present formula, you pay no federal withholding tax, allow more of your capital to compound and grow on a tax-deferred basis.

You can also elect to take all of the RRIF capital's earnings each year until the minimum payment requirement exceeds your annual RRIF earnings. This strategy pays you a higher income than the minimum payment option, but it leaves your capital intact until you reach 80 years of age, approximately. This is referred to as the *interest only withdrawal option.*

The *smoothing withdrawal option* is simply an income that is based on a fixed percentage of the value of your RRIF. Providing it meets or exceeds the minimum payment option, it is an effective means of providing a relatively fixed income level that is also indexed for inflation, for example.

The *level withdrawal option* allows you to receive a level or fixed income amount in exactly the same way as a term certain annuity to age 90 (or 100). Your payment is a blend of earnings plus capital and is designed to pay itself out over your lifetime to age 90. So, you have security in the form of a fixed income stream like an annuity but you enjoy being able to transfer the remaining funds to your spouse in the event you decease prematurely.

The last RRIF payment alternative is called the *term withdrawal option.* You can elect to have a systematic payment for a specified period of years. This would be used in cases where other financial resources would be available sometime in the future or where your health is in decline.

As far as access to your capital is concerned, RRIFs are as liquid as cash, depending on the investments you have used inside of the RRIF. It does take up to 10 business days to get your capital, sometimes longer, but, providing you are prepared to have withholding tax taken off your withdrawal, RRIF liquidity is as good as it can get.

When it comes to capital flexibility, you can convert all or a portion of your RRIF to a registered annuity of your choice should interest rates justify the conversion.

RRIFs are based on a minimum payment formula (see Chapter Five) which automatically indexes your income to help offset long-term inflation. While an assumed inflation rate of three per cent is the norm, you can increase your initial payment amount to whatever level you wish and, at the end of every year, increase your payment by whatever the inflation rate has been over the preceding year. You, of course, have to be cautious in determining the amount of capital you should or can take out of your RRIF, since too much of a withdrawal will encroach on the capital value of your retirement nest egg.

RRIFs offer three great tax savings opportunities. First, like RRSPs, investment earnings are allowed to continue to grow on a tax-deferred basis for as long as capital remains in your RRIF plan. Second, where you are experiencing a higher-than-required level of retirement income, you can base your minimum RRIF payment on the age of the younger spouse.

This maneuver allows you to reduce the minimum payment even further. This is particularly effective when you are forced to convert your RRSP to income at the end of the year in which you turn age 69. Third, should you be receiving RRIF income and you suddenly receive a lot of income from an inheritance, for example, you can convert your RRIF back to an RRSP, providing you receive the minimum RRIF payment as cash for that year and you are under age 69. This can save you thousands of precious tax dollars.

The investments you can use are exactly the same as those that are eligible for RRSPs. The *Income Tax Act* is quite specific about which investment types qualify, but it is quite a comprehensive list.

Having such a wide selection of investments to choose from, your potential investment rates of return can range far and wide. It is usually prudent to choose a larger proportion of securities from the fixed and equity income asset class than equity growth securities. This will provide you with more consistent investment earnings and lower risk.

RETIREMENT INCOME STRATEGY # 3

Where you turn age 69, consider taking minimum RRIF payments first and base these payments on the younger spouse's age. You can always adjust your payments upwards should you require increased income. By doing so, you will keep income tax at a minimum and allow your investment earnings to compound more efficiently over time. Where you are still suffering too much of a tax liability and the younger spouse has yet to reach the end of the year in which he or she turns age 69, consider making a contribution to an RRSP in your spouse's name. This is called a spousal RRSP. You get a tax break and your spouse gets your money!

Annuities or RRIFs—Which to Choose?

For my dollar, I gravitate towards the RRIF. However, financial markets can provide unique opportunities where purchasing an annuity in fact may be an opportune course of action. Annuities can be attractive alternatives to RRIFs where annuity interest rates have risen to nine per cent and beyond. But, there are several other considerations as well.

First, when it comes to management of your retirement nest egg, the RRIF is far more flexible than an annuity. You have full control of your retirement finances with the RRIF. An annuity is a long-term illiquid contract where the management of your retirement assets is in someone else's hands. On the other hand, if you don't want the responsibility of managing your retirement assets and prefer a guaranteed life income, then the annuity is the best route to go.

Second, when it comes to retire income, you have a variety of annuities from which to choose, and you can custom fit an annuity to meet your current financial circumstances. But, for every additional feature you attach to the basic annuity, the costlier the product. You do not pay for this up front like some mutual fund fees. The annuity issuer simply pays you a smaller amount. Not only can costs be higher, but once in place, your annuity and its features cannot be altered. The only restriction you'll face with a RRIF is the required minimum payment schedule.

Third, a non-registered annuity can have tax benefits not shared by RRIFs. This tax benefit we have already described under prescribed income above.

Fourth, if your annuity does not have a guarantee period and you die, any remaining annuity capital is lost to the issuer. Joint annuities just forestall the inevitable. With the death of the second joint annuitant, any remaining cash goes to the insurance company. This does not apply to term certain annuities. Sometimes the commuted value of an annuity on the death of the annuitant can incur substantial charges, depending on the issuing insurance company involved. RRIF proceeds ultimately will go to the estate of the deceased in the event of a single person and to the surviving spouse of a married annuitant.

These main distinctions aside, making a decision as to which vehicle to use will really depend on your own unique financial situation. For example, if you already have a company pension through an RPP, you may not need another comparatively inflexible resource like an annuity. If, on the other hand, your family has a history of longevity and you find yourself in excellent health, an annuity may be a good vehicle, especially where annuity interest rates are high. Can you imagine the benefit of locking into a double digit interest rate for 20 years? This is exactly what some smart consumers did in 1981 when rates catapulted to 17.5 per cent.

RETIREMENT INCOME STRATEGY # 4

If you have non-registered investments that generate a fixed income, owning a RRIF will give you superior flexibility, tax savings and more growth than an annuity. If you have pension income from an RPP in addition to the above, the value of owning an annuity is substantially diminished because of its inflexible, illiquid nature.

LIFs and LRIFs

A *Life Income Fund* (LIF) operates in much the same way as a RRIF. You use a LIF to generate income from your locked-in retirement account (LIRA). There are important differences, though.

First, the amount of income you receive is limited to a formula for minimum and maximum payments. The minimum RRIF payment schedule is used to calculate the minimum amount you can receive from your LIF. To figure out your maximum payment, you have to use a more complicated formula that is based on yields produced by long-term Government of Canada bonds. At age 65, your minimum LIF payment, for example, amounts to four per cent of the value of your LIF, while your maximum pay out is 8.21 per cent.

Where you can redeem as much of your RRIF capital as you wish, you are not allowed to liquidate lump sums from your LIF. Your capital liquidity is restricted to the variance between your minimum and maximum payment options. This situation becomes even worse at age 80, at which time your remaining LIF capital must be converted to a life annuity. Things are not much better when considered from the perspective of capital flexibility. In a nutshell, you have little if any opportunity to do anything with your LIF, other than alter the minimum-maximum amount of income you receive each year. You can have as many LIFs as you want, however.

A LIF can provide some inflation protection through the minimum-maximum payment schedule. It is certainly lost, though, when it is converted to a life annuity.

As far as tax savings are concerned, once you begin a LIF, you cannot convert it back to a LIRA. It will continue until you decease, after which it becomes unlocked and transformed into an RRSP or RRIF for your surviving spouse. You cannot base your minimum payment amount on the younger spouse's age, like the RRIF. LIFs offer no real tax advantages other than on tax-deferred earnings to age 80. Until you reach age 80 and convert to a life annuity, LIFs can incorporate the same wide selection of "qualifying investments" as the RRIF and, where you choose superior securities as repositories for your LIF capital, you can continue to build the value of your LIF well beyond the income stream that you are withdrawing from it.

The *Locked-In Retirement Income Fund* or LRIF is a special alternative to LIFs and life annuities. The advantages of owning a LRIF are twofold. First, you do not have to convert your plan assets to a life annuity at age 80. Second, the maximum withdrawal you can make from a LRIF will equal the LRIF's investment earnings for the calendar year or the sum of all investment earnings not withdrawn in earlier years, whichever is greater. The LRIF is the preferred vehicle but it is only available in Alberta and Saskatchewan as of 1997 and beyond. The rollover and retirement options for commuted locked-in pension monies are listed in Figure 6.1.

Figure 6.1
Rollover and Retirement Options By Province

Province	Rollover Option	Retirement Income Option
British Columbia	LIRA	Life Annuity, LIF
Alberta	LIRA	Life Annuity, LIF, LRIF
Saskatchewan	LIRA	Life Annuity, LIF, LRIF
Manitoba	LIRA	Life Annuity, LIF
Ontario	LIRA	Life Annuity, LIF
New Brunswick	LIRA	Life Annuity, LIF
Nova Scotia	LIRA	Life Annuity, LIF
Newfoundland	Locked-In RRSP	Life Annuity
Prince Edward Island	Locked-In RRSP	Life Annuity

RETIREMENT INCOME STRATEGY # 5

If you have other assets, such as RRSPs and non-registered investments, defer converting your locked-in capital to a LIF for as long as you possibly can (end of the year in which you turn age 69).This will allow you to fatten up your locked-in capital, so that when you are forced to convert, your LIF income payment will be much larger than if you took your income earlier in your retirement. It's important to remember that you will need the greatest amount of flexibility in your financial plan in your early years. RRIFs and other non-registered investments can provide all the flexibility you could possibly need. LIFs and, to a lesser extent LRIFs, provide very little financial flexibility.

NON-REGISTERED INVESTMENT INCOME

Generating retirement income from non-registered investments, such as non-registered annuities, GICs, bonds and common stocks, is easier than from pension and other similar registered income. The level of income you can generate from non-registered capital can be substantially more than what could be produced by an equivalent amount of registered capital. Depending on the securities you use, you often have excellent capital liquidity and flexibility. Inflation protection is a snap, if you set up your income plan properly, and tax savings can be formidable. You have hundreds of securities to choose from and you can very easily choose the investment rate of return that is most suitable to your needs and wants. Here are several of the most popular securities that should find their way into your retirement income portfolio.

Non-Registered Annuities

Non-registered annuities are exactly the same as the registered variety, except that non-registered annuities offer some added benefits that registered annuities do not. Non-registered annuities usually offer no capital flexibility or investment selection. They do offer the potential for enhanced income, tax savings, a higher net investment return and capital liquidity. Non-registered annuity income can be taxed preferred. This is because you are using after-tax capital to invest in such an annuity, compared to pre-tax capital that you have used to purchase a registered annuity (remember, you received a tax deduction for your pension or RRSP contribution). In the case of the former, only the interest earnings that form part of your annuity income is taxed at your marginal tax rate. The capital portion of your annuity payment is tax-free. This means that you have more money to spend and a higher net investment return when expressed as a percentage of invested capital.

In many cases, though, non-registered annuities offer an annuitant the option to prescribe their annuity income. Under normal circumstances, annuity income is comprised primarily of accrued interest earnings during the first several years of the annuity term. Only after this period do interest earnings decrease in favour of an increasing capital payment. In this situation, you will pay a good chunk of your interest earnings to taxes in the early years. A prescribed annuity spreads the interest earnings of your annuity over the life of the contract, so that the tax you pay is also spread over the same term. You end up paying less tax at the beginning and therefore keep more of your annuity income for yourself. The tax you will save by prescribing your annuity can add as much as 50 basis points or one-half percentage point to your investment yield.

Many of today's non-registered annuities are cashable contracts. This can be a real boon should you suddenly need capital for some unforeseen emergency or expenditure. In these cases, though, your investment yield will be less than a regular annuity contract and, should you cash out of your annuity, there will be a hefty penalty in the form of a negative interest yield adjustment. Cashable annuities are usually term certain annuities and do not qualify for prescribed treatment of earnings.

RETIREMENT INCOME STRATEGY # 6

If you are comfortable with the interest rate offered, a non-registered annuity can be a good addition to your retirement income portfolio. If you do choose a locked-in annuity, as opposed to a cashable one, always prescribe your annuity earnings.

Canada Savings Bonds

CSBs have been around for years and most Canadians at least recognize the name. As income generators, CSBs are about as perfect a vehicle as you can find. This is because they are issued in two formats: compound and income. The income variety is designed to pay out its interest earnings, while compound CSBs reinvest earnings at a predetermined rate. CSB income is regular. But, our federal government does reserve the right to adjust your interest earnings, any time it wants to. This is a good thing during protracted periods of rising interest rates, but not good during periods of declining rates. Since CSBs are a means of borrowing heavily from the public purse, the federal government must maintain competitive rates in the marketplace or you and I will find some better paying security. Of course, during periods of decreasing interest rates, there is even more pressure on government to maintain a decent rate of return. CSBs also offer excellent capital liquidity. You can cash them any time and without penalty if you redeem them at month's end.

Aside from their liquidity, CSBs offer some flexibility, too. Government guaranteed CSBs are considered to be an indisputable asset that can be used as collateral for a loan. During retirement or any time, a loan may be needed to cover a major purchase such as a car or an unforeseen emergency or bridge financing for a new home purchase. Since you do not have to cash them in, you can retain their benefits without disruption. Of course, should you need to cash them to pay the loan, you can do so within minutes at your local bank or trust company.

There is a cost for these features, though. First, where you elect to purchase the income variety or R-class or regular income CSB, your underlying capital has no inflation protection. This type of CSB pays out all of its interest earnings, leaving nothing in reserve. As we saw earlier in Chapter Two of this book, long-term inflation can devastate the future value of your capital. Second, should you find yourself in a high marginal tax bracket, your interest earnings will be whittled down by as much as 50 per cent. It doesn't matter if your CSB earnings are paid to you as cash or reinvested in the form of a C-class or compound interest bond.

CSBs offer little in the way of investment selection. They represent one security with an adjustable yield. This yield, as we've seen, floats as a result of mid-term interest rate trends coupled with the willingness of the federal government to attract capital from the public domain. CSBs have earned an annual average compound rate of return of 7.3 per cent over 15 years, ending December, 1997. Compared to bank and trust company savings accounts, which offer similar capital liquidity, CSBs are a much better alternative.

RETIREMENT INCOME STRATEGY # 7

As good as CSBs can be, Canada Savings Bonds should never be used as income generators to help fund your retirement income. This is because the capital value of R-class bonds will depreciate in purchasing power due to inflation. What makes CSBs an attractive retirement asset is their high level of liquidity, adjustable interest

yield and collateral value. Use CSBs only as vehicles for an emergency capital reserve. Buy only compound or C-class bonds and purchase only enough to fund the equivalent of between three and six times your monthly expenditures.

Guaranteed Investment Certificates

Today, there are three kinds of fixed deposits available to consumers: compound GICs, income GICs and cashable GICs. Compound GICs are just like C-class CSBs, except your capital is locked-in for a specified term of anywhere from one to five years, sometimes longer, depending on the issuer. As retirement income vehicles, income GICs pay a higher rate than CSBs, because you have given the issuer your capital to work with over a specified period of time with no cash-out option. Cashable GICs can be either compound or income products. The rates paid on these certificates of deposit are always lower than the locked-in version because you are given various options to break your GIC contract.

Depending on the GIC you choose, the level of capital liquidity and flexibility you enjoy will vary. Compound GICs offer no liquidity, except at death. Income GICs, though, can be sold by trading them through a stockbroker. You will usually get whatever interest has accrued to your GIC up to but excluding your next payment, but you get more or less of the original capital value, depending on what interest yield you are earning compared to the yields offered by current income GICs. If your certificate is earning a higher rate of interest than exactly the same certificates issued today, you could earn an additional profit in the form of a capital gain. If, however, your certificate is earning less, you could end up with less capital than what you had originally invested.

Unless you use a compound GIC, there is no inflation protection available. Like CSBs, income-generating GICs pay out all of their earnings in the form of an income stream to you. As a result, the value of your original capital will depreciate in direct proportion to the amount of inflation you experience over the term.

Since GICs only generate interest, net earnings after income tax will lower your disposable investment income. Coupled with the effects of long term inflation, income tax on your GIC earnings can reduce your net income by up to 80 per cent, sometimes more during periods of exceptionally high inflation. In July 1981, inflation was running at approximately 12 per cent. Five-year GICs could be had for 17.5 per cent. If you paid income tax at 41.34 per cent, your real net return after your first year would have been an astonishing –2.1 per cent!

GICs are like CSBs. They offer no investment variety. In the case of GICs, they are really investment derivatives that are based on first mortgages owned by the bank or trust company. As a result, your GIC is tied solely to what the mortgage market produces in terms of mortgage interest rates. Your GIC rate of return, however, is not the equivalent of the presiding mortgage rate. It is configured on what your GIC issuer can earn by investing your capital in quality first mortgages less its profit on those mortgages. So, if you are earning 6 per cent on your $100,000, for example, there's an equally good chance that your bank or trust company is earning at least 0.5 to 1.5 percentage points over and above your return.

GICs offer better rates of return than CSBs. GICs have earned an annual average rate of return of 8.7 per cent over last 15 years, ending December, 1997. The difference in earnings is the premium your GIC issuer is willing to pay you to lock up your capital for a specified time period. GIC rates rise and fall according to current market interest rates.

RETIREMENT INCOME STRATEGY # 8

If you wish to use GICs as a source of retirement income, purchase income GICs only to maximize your rate of return and provide a measure of capital liquidity. If trading GICs through a stockbroker is too awkward for you, simply purchase several GICs and stagger their maturities so that you have at least one GIC maturing as often as you deem necessary, usually once each year. Be careful to compare the total yield of a staggered GIC portfolio with that offered by a five-year cashable income GIC. In certain cases, you would be better off with the cashable version, even though cashable GICs offer the lowest yields of all three GIC types.

Government of Canada Bonds

Government of Canada bonds will sometimes offer great income potential, depending on when you purchase them and the term of the bonds involved. Government of Canada bonds can be for periods of up to 20 years and beyond. Bonds with a maturity of three years or less are called short-term bonds. Bonds with a maturity of between three and 10 years are medium-term. Bonds with a maturity of ten years or longer are long-term bonds. So, if you are lucky enough to purchase a long-term Government of Canada bond that offers a high interest yield, you have a guaranteed high income for the duration of your bond term. Traditional long-term bonds have paid much higher yields than GICs.

Government of Canada bonds are less liquid than either CSBs or cashable GICs. However, they do offer more liquidity than compound and non-cashable income GICs. If you purchase a 20-year Government of Canada bond, for example, and you decide to liquidate the bond to raise cash or to redirect your capital to a different security before your bond matures, the only way to do so is to offer it for sale through a stockbroker. A stockbroker will evaluate the worth of your bond to other investors and then post it for sale on an informal trading exchange called the *over-the-counter market* (OTC). Where an investor likes your bond, a purchase is made, your broker takes his or her commission, and you receive the remaining cash.

What you actually receive will depend on a number of important factors. In the case of Government of Canada bonds, they are perceived to be very low risk, so you will enjoy above-average capital liquidity at a very reasonable price. You are guaranteed to receive any outstanding interest that has yet to be paid to you, but the amount of original capital you get back could vary as a result of how competitive the interest rate of your bond is compared to yields offered on newer bond issues. The amount of money you receive will also depend on the time remaining before your bond matures. If you have a substantial number of years left before your bond expires and the interest rate on your bond is higher than current yields on the same kind of bond, then you can expect to receive your original invested capital plus a handsome capital gain. This capital gain is a kind of bonus in the form of a premium paid by another investor who wants to have a higher yielding security than what is currently available. This is a good example of how Government of Canada bonds and other similar securities can provide not only higher long-term yields, but bonuses and a return of original capital value. This relatively high level of capital liquidity and flexibility is a welcome feature of these kinds of securities.

The danger of owning these securities, though, is due to the prospect of rising interest rates. Should bond interest rates move upwards, the market value assigned to your lower yielding bond can result in an irrecoverable capital loss. You will still receive the interest that you have earned up until your bond is sold, but you will normally have to reduce the capital value of your bond to make it attractive enough to sell to other investors. For example, if the *face value* of your bond was $50,000 and you were earning 8 per cent per year, you might have to reduce the face value of your bond by $6,000 where exactly the same but newer bond issue was paying 9 per cent instead. So, while you would receive interest owed to you to the point of sale, you would only receive $44,000 of your original $50,000 invested capital. Where this occurs, you are subject to *bond discounting*.

Government of Canada bonds do not normally have any kind of inflation indexing potential. This is because interest earnings are paid to you, the investor. So, original invested capital is exposed fully to the corrosive effects of inflation, just like R-class CSBs and income GICs. However, they do have some potential for tax savings. Wherever you sell off a bond and earn an additional capital gain, only 75 per cent of your capital gain is taxable, while accrued interest is fully taxable at your marginal tax rate.

There is a constant flow of new issues of federal bonds from which to choose. As a result of this process, you can often build a portfolio of Government of Canada bonds that offer different yields and varying investment terms. The 15-year average annual compound rate of return for Government of Canada bonds has been a very attractive 10.1 per cent, ending December 31st, 1997. While there is no inflation protection offer by Government of Canada bonds, a yield of 10.1 per cent is much better than either CSBs or GICs.

RETIREMENT INCOME STRATEGY # 9

If you invest in Government of Canada bonds, be aware that making a long-term commitment of 10 years or more will incur much more capital risk than might first appear. For example, should bond interest yields rise substantially, you will be unable or unwilling to cash out to repurchase these higher yielding bonds because of the potential capital loss you could sustain by doing so. While income from Government of Canada bonds can be superior when compared to other securities such as CSBs and GICs, care must be exercised to ensure that you are purchasing your bonds at an appropriate time in the interest rate cycle. Buy these securities for the long term and, should you be in a position to realize a substantial capital gain, be prepared to liquidate your bonds with a clear eye to purchase more effective securities later.

Preferred Shares and High-Yielding Common Stock

Depending on the kind of *preferred shares* you choose, they can provide a continuous source of high income coupled with the potential for additional capital gains. Preferred shares are low to moderate risk securities that are built primarily to generate income to investors. A typical average annual dividend yield for Canadian preferred shares has been around 6.8 per cent, with additional capital appreciation in the 4.3 per cent range per year. If you factor the tax benefits attached to dividends paid by Canadian corporations into the equation, a 6.8 per cent yield competes well against high-yielding GICs. A 6.8 per cent dividend is equivalent to a nine per cent interest yield before tax.

Preferred shares offer an average level of capital liquidity. You can buy and sell preferred shares only on the stock market. They are, however, far less volatile in price than other securities such as common stocks. So, when stock markets drive downwards, preferred shares will often decrease marginally in value, sometimes not all, depending on the kind of preferred shares you own and the quality of the issuing corporation. While you have to trade preferred shares on the market, they are usually the easiest of all equity securities to sell.

Preferred shares also offer unique capital flexibility. Unlike CSBs, GICs and Government of Canada bonds, preferred shares allow you to undertake a number of different maneuvers. First, you can purchase straight preferred shares, which simply pay out a high dividend to you, while allowing any future appreciation in the share value to remain as an unrealized capital gain. Second, you can take advantage of increasing stock prices by electing to convert your preferred shares to common shares of the same issuing company. You could earn substantial capital gains if done at the outset of a positive rise in the market. Third, you could also have preferred shares that allow you the option to force the issuer to buy back your shares should the price of your preferred shares be worth more than what you paid for them. Fourth, you could purchase preferred shares that offer a floating dividend rate, which could rise substantially should you enter a period of sustained positive economic growth.

High yielding preferred shares are the first security that can provide an effective bulwark against the corrosive effects of inflation. This is because of their propensity for capital growth over and above regular dividend income. When you invest in preferred shares you participate directly in a company's profits in the form of an earnings stream. But, because you are also a shareholder, your preferred shares will often react like common shares and move up in value as investors begin to invest in the common shares of the company. Preferred shares normally do not show great promise as a capital gain security, but they will rise in value as the underlying company gains financial strength. If you earned a 6.8 per cent dividend, you would have additional capital growth of 4.3 per cent based on our 15-year average annual return of 11.1 per cent. Since the average inflation rate was 3.1 per cent per year ending December, 1997, your capital in fact would have grown in value by one percentage point per year after income and inflation. If you had invested $50,000 in preferred stock 15 years ago, took all of the regular income dividends of $51,000 and adjusted the value of your capital for inflation, the value of your original $50,000 investment would be $58,048.45.

In addition to having excellent inflation protection, preferred shares provide excellent tax protection because of the federal government's preferred treatment of Canadian dividends. As we saw in the previous chapter of this book, your average after-tax yield on dividends is 32 per cent higher than taxes paid on interest. So, based on the information above, nine per cent interest will net 4.5 per cent after tax while a tax-preferred dividend will net you approximately 5.9 per cent at a 50 per cent marginal tax rate.

There is a wide array of preferred shares from which to choose. You have straight preferred shares, convertible preferred shares, retractable preferred shares, variable or floating rate preferred shares, foreign-pay preferred shares and class "A" preferred shares.

While your future rates of return will vary, tax-preferred treatment of dividends coupled with additional long term capital appreciation goes a long way to make preferred shares a very attractive alternative to cash equivalents, GICs and bonds.

While I am not a proponent of using high yielding common stocks as a source of retirement income, some individuals will no doubt want to incorporate them into their retirement income strategy. Common stocks have the greatest potential for good dividends as well as superior long capital growth. But, as we know, the greater the potential for growth, the greater the volatility the security incurs. As we know from August and September of 1998, stock market downturns can be savage and, depending on the kind of common stocks you invested in, your equity could have been reduced by more than 30 per cent over just a few days. If you had invested in Toronto Stock Exchange (TSE) listed stocks in January, 1997, today, whatever gains you earned to the end of June, 1998 would have been erased completely. I find it difficult to believe that investors who need income from their investments at retirement would be so venturesome as to invest in common stocks. It is true that stocks of proven, stable, quality corporations such as banks, for example, do pay good dividends that can add to your retirement income stream. These dividends, however, are often much lower than preferred share dividends. As we saw in August 1998, even bank common shares can drop by more than 40 per cent when the circumstances are right!

If you are still determined to incorporate a selection of high yielding common shares into your income portfolio, you should be aware of the following characteristics. One, when markets are rising, you often have excellent liquidity if you want to sell off all or a portion of your common shares. Two, high yielding common shares will often outpace inflation by a wide margin. The S & P 500 Index, which is comprised of common stocks, has averaged 18.5 per cent per year over the last 15 years, ending May 31st, 1998. Three, tax savings are generated by tax-preferred dividends and by unrealized capital gains of stocks held in your portfolio. Four, you have a huge variety of different securities to choose from, and, five, your investment rate of return can be remarkable during long periods of positive economic growth.

RETIREMENT INCOME STRATEGY # 10

Preferred shares are one of the best retirement income securities available today. Make sure you choose these securities from established,

quality companies that show high, long-term, stable earnings. Ensure that preferred dividends are paid to you as cash and retain any growth in the value of your preferred shares as a bulwark against future inflationary trends. If you need to maximize your retirement income, choose to invest in straight preferred shares. Use quality floating rate preferred shares during periods of volatile interest rates. Retractable preferred shares are great vehicles for investors who intend to generate income but will gladly collect a capital gain should these preferred shares rise in value. Invest in quality convertible preferred shares if you want both good dividend yields and the opportunity to invest more aggressively in common shares at some opportune time down the line.

RETIREMENT INCOME STRATEGIES USING MUTUAL FUNDS

Until the crash of August, 1998, mutual funds have been the darlings of novice and professional investors alike. As managed pools of capital, mutual funds allow you to invest in a wide selection of different securities without having to worry about the mechanics and maintenance of your portfolio. All you have to do is ensure that your choice of mutual funds is in accordance with your personal financial goals, risk tolerance level, level of investment expertise and personal financial circumstances.

These items aside, what many Canadians fail to recognize is that mutual funds offer some of the best retirement income strategies available. The following seven income strategies are the best of the pack and you should study them in detail.

We have already discussed a few of the pros and cons you'll experience by using income generated from certain types of individual securities. One of the problems we ran up against with many of these securities was the lack of growth of our original capital. Some preferred shares and high yielding common stocks excepted, after taking the income stream in the form of retirement income, our original capital was not capable of growing beyond what a person had invested originally. The result was a loss in capital value due to long-term inflation. Many mutual funds offer protection from this kind of situation.

Lump Sum and Partial Capital Withdrawals

Depending on the kind of mutual fund you own, you can simply withdraw all or a portion of your mutual fund assets any time you wish. This is because mutual funds are structured to be able to constantly issue and redeem shares. This feature is particularly important because you in fact redeem capital by way of a redemption of shares (or units). Publicly traded companies are allowed to manufacture and issue only a finite number of shares for sale in the form of an initial offering. Investors purchase these shares and trade them on the stock market on which the company is listed. Because the number of shares is limited, investors can experience liquidity problems as a result of tight share availability. Mutual funds normally do not run into this problem because they are allowed to constantly issue and redeem shares as required. This means that mutual fund investors enjoy some of the highest capital liquidity levels of all, making lump sum withdrawals a breeze.

The only restrictions mutual fund investors have to face are share-price variability and transaction fees. The amount of variability in capital value you will incur depends on the kind of mutual fund you own. Fees will depend on whether you purchased a load or no load fund.

Dividends and Distributions

Mutual fund investors can receive dividends as cash, just like individuals who own bonds and stocks. They leave their capital alone and take only dividends that their mutual fund produces. Mutual funds such as mortgage and bond funds produce the highest amount of pre-tax dividends. Occasionally, a mutual fund will pay a special distribution called a capital gain dividend. This dividend is the result of a mutual fund selling off some of the securities it owns in its portfolio at a profit. This profit is then divided among the shareholders of the fund in proportion to the number of shares or units held by each investor and paid towards the end of each calendar year. While you can elect to receive this dividend in cash, it is usually more prudent to allow the dividend to be reinvested to purchase more shares and subsequently fatten the value of your fund over term. Figure 6.2 outlines the various types of mutual funds available and the dividends and distributions you can expect from each.

The Systematic Withdrawal Plan (SWP)

Taking cash dividends from your mutual fund portfolio is an excellent way of generating retirement income from non-registered investments. But the one drawback to using just dividend distributions is that you limit your income stream to the amount of dividend income your mutual funds produce. By now you know that you have to try and choose between high income and pure capital growth inasmuch as these two aspects of investment are mutually exclusive. You can enjoy high pre-tax income but your long-term growth potential will be curtailed. Where inflation is a concern, an investment that is growth-oriented will obviate inflation, but reduce the amount of income you can receive. A much better means of generating retirement income from your funds is to enact a *systematic withdrawal plan*. By doing so, you can control and set the level of income you need and modify the long-term growth potential of your invested capital. There are four systematic withdrawal plans you can use.

Figure 6.2

Types of Mutual Funds and Their Dividends and Distributions

Mutual Fund Type	Interest Dividend	Dividend Dividend	Capital Gain Dividend	Pure Capital Growth
Money Market	Low	—	—	—
Mortgage	High	—	—	—
Bond	High	—	Low-Moderate	Low
Dividend	—	High	Moderate	Low
Real Estate	Rental Income	—	Low	—
Balanced	—	Moderate	Moderate	Moderate
High Yield Growth—Domestic	—	Moderate	Moderate-High	Moderate-High
High Yield Growth—Foreign	—	Low-Moderate	Moderate-High	Moderate-High
Pure Domestic Growth	—	—	Low	High
Pure Foreign Growth	—	—	Low	High
Speculative Common	—	—	—	Very High

Ratio Withdrawal Plans

The first is called the *ratio withdrawal plan*. According to this plan, you reinvest all dividends and capital gain distributions to purchase additional shares or units of your mutual fund, but redeem shares or units of your fund to generate income. You decide what percentage of the value of your mutual fund investment will suit your income needs. The actual percentage you use will vary depending on the kind of fund you own and whether you want to preserve, enhance or deplete the value of your original invested capital. If you choose this plan, however, you probably want to either maintain your capital value or, where inflation is a concern, increase the value of your investment over the long term. If you use fixed-income funds, such as mortgage and bond, I recommend anywhere from six to eight per cent as a good income ratio. If you use equity income funds a similar percentage ratio of between six and eight per cent will suffice. This is because your after tax return will be higher than with fixed income funds. If you use equity growth mutual funds, you can use anywhere from eight to ten per cent, providing you are aware that the

Figure 6.3
An Example of a Ratio Withdrawal Plan

Period End	Invest $	With-draw $	Charges	Income $	Capital Gains	Rein-vest $	Market Value $	Shares	NAV
7/31/1988	50,000	0	0	0	0	0	50,000	10,905	4.59
12/31/1988	0	1,681	0	2,011	0	2,011	49,958	10,977	4.55
12/31/1989	0	4,133	0	4,784	0	4,784	51,711	11,118	4.65
12/31/1990	0	3,941	0	4,666	0	4,666	50,352	11,285	4.46
12/31/1991	0	4,213	0	4,561	0	4,561	55,966	11,361	4.93
12/31/1992	9	4,525	0	4,442	0	4,442	56,872	11,345	5.01
12/31/1993	0	4,814	0	4,318	0	4,318	62,785	11,252	5.58
12/31/1994	0	4,476	0	3,919	0	3,919	53,035	11,142	4.76
12/31/1995	0	4,529	0	4,509	0	4,509	59,029	11,138	5.30
12/31/1996	0	4,704	0	4,302	0	4,302	60,504	11,061	5.47
12/31/1997	0	4,853	0	3,716	0	3,716	60,679	10,855	5.99
7/31/1998	0	2,849	0	1,958	0	1,958	59,795	10,697	5.59
Total	**50,000**	**44,718**	**0**	**43,188**	**0**	**43,188**			

Ending Amount Attributable to	Market Value	Shares	Return on the Investment	Percent
Principal:	59,795	10,697	Average Annual:	10.40%
Income:	0	0	Cumulative:	169.07%
Capital Gains:	0	0		
Total Ending Amount:	**59,795**	**10,697**		

more money you withdraw, the greater the risk of loss in value of your invested capital. Anything beyond these maximum percentages will likely encroach on the long-term value of your invested capital. Here is a real life illustration of how a ratio withdrawal plan works.

In the case of Figure 6.3 above, you invested $50,000 on July 31st, 1988 and began withdrawing eight per cent of the value of a bond mutual fund on a monthly basis until July 31st, 1998. The total amount of pre-tax income you generated from this ratio withdrawal plan was $44,718. The monthly income amount you received varied from a low of $315 to a high of $431 (although because the chart only shows year-end figures, these monthly figures are not available here). Note the end value of your mutual fund, which has appreciated by $9,795 as well, representing an average annual return of 10.4 per cent.

Fixed Dollar Withdrawal Plans

The second type of plan is the *fixed dollar withdrawal plan*. According to this plan, you simply choose the fixed dollar amount you need, determine the payment frequency and set the plan in motion. What this format

Figure 6.4A
A Fixed Dollar Withdrawal Plan in an Ascending Market

Period End	Invest $	With-draw $	Charges	Income $	Capital Gains	Rein-vest $	Market Value $	Shares	NAV
10/31/1987	50,000	0	0	0	0	0	50,000	3,023	16.54
12/31/1987	0	832	0	0	0	0	48,846	2,971	16.44
12/31/1988	0	4,992	0	603	948	1,552	49,655	2,776	17.89
12/31/1989	0	4,992	0	376	780	1,156	54,825	10,344	5.30
12/31/1990	0	4,992	0	301	1,102	1,402	42,734	9,582	4.46
12/31/1991	0	4,992	0	185	1,757	1,942	50,161	8,989	5.58
12/31/1992	0	4,992	0	0	3,831	3,831	52,539	8,786	5.98
12/31/1993	0	4,992	0	0	2,386	2,386	65,740	8,417	7.81
12/31/1994	0	4,992	0	0	2,217	2,217	63,294	8,073	7.84
12/31/1995	0	4,992	0	0	2,595	2,595	66,967	7,787	8.60
12/31/1996	0	4,992	0	0	3,098	3,098	73,807	7,585	9.73
10/31/1997	0	2,912	0	0	3,469	3,469	81,328	7,629	10.66
Total	50,000	48,672	0	1,465	22,184	23,650			

Ending Amount Attributable to	Market Value	Shares	Return on the Investment	Percent
Principal:	78,679	7,381	Average Annual:	13.75%
Income:	0	0	Cumulative:	262.57%
Capital Gains:	2,649	249		
Total Ending Amount:	81,328	7,629		

does is redeem enough shares on a periodic, usually monthly, basis to generate the required income amount. Mutual fund investors who use the fixed withdrawal plan must be aware that excessive share price volatility can variously affect the long-term value of their capital. If you use an equity growth fund, for example, and the stock market on which the bulk of your fund's portfolio trades declines in value over an extended period of time, then you can seriously erode the value of your fund. Where a stock market index is rising in value, you can see a significant increase in the value of your investment capital. If you use fixed and equity income mutual funds, there is less of a chance that your capital will decrease in value as a result of market volatility.

In the example shown in Figure 6.4A, an investor invested $50,000 in a well-managed equity growth mutual fund on October 31st, 1987 and began withdrawing $416 each month (shown in the chart year-end increments). This yearly withdrawal represented almost 10 per cent of the initial invested capital. After reinvesting all dividends, the value of the fund had climbed to a remarkable $81,328. So, in this instance, the investor received $48,672 income and increased the value of the original invested capital by an additional $31,328 by using a fixed dollar withdrawal plan for an average annual return of 13.75 per cent!

Where the stock market was falling in value, the results for our investor have not been as pleasant, as shown in Figure 6.4B. The same $50,000 investment made on August 31st, 1987 would have resulted in the same $48,672 income, but would have an end value of just $34,709 after a similar 10-year period. This is due to the fact that subsequent withdrawals required more and more shares to be redeemed as the value of the fund's shares decreased in value as a result of declining stock market values.

Fixed Period Withdrawal Plans

The third type of withdrawal plan is called the *fixed period withdrawal plan*. Under this plan format, you can withdraw a portion or all of your capital over a specified period of time. The goal of this plan is to provide you with a maximum income flow. Some people allocate a lump sum to a mutual fund for the purposes of funding a child's university or college

Figure 6.4B
A Fixed Dollar Withdrawal Plan in a Descending Market

Period End	Invest $	With-draw $	Charges	Income $	Capital Gains	Rein-vest $	Market Value $	Shares	NAV
8/31/1987	50,000	0	0	0	0	0	50,000	2,318	21.57
12/31/1987	0	1,664	0	0	0	0	36,523	2,222	16.44
12/31/1988	0	4,992	0	446	701	1,147	35,819	2,002	17.89
12/31/1989	0	4,992	0	268	556	824	38,070	7,183	5.30
12/31/1990	0	4,992	0	206	754	960	28,255	6,335	4.46
12/31/1991	0	4,992	0	120	1,141	1,261	31,289	5,607	5.58
12/31/1992	0	4,992	0	0	2,343	2,343	30,794	5,149	5.98
12/31/1993	0	4,992	0	0	1,367	1,367	36,100	4,622	7.81
12/31/1994	0	4,992	0	0	1,193	1,193	32,527	4,149	7.84
12/31/1995	0	4,992	0	0	1,300	1,300	31,847	3,703	8.60
12/31/1996	0	4,992	0	0	1,424	1,424	32,223	3,312	9.73
7/31/1997	0	2,912	0	0	1,460	1,460	34,709	3,167	10.96
Total	**50,000**	**49,504**	**0**	**1,040**	**12,239**	**13,279**			

Ending Amount Attributable to	Market Value	Shares	Return on the Investment	Percent
Principal:	34,052	3,107	Average Annual:	8.24%
Income:	0	0	Cumulative:	119.36%
Capital Gains:	657	60		
Total Ending Amount:	**34,709**	**3,167**		

studies. For a retired investor, a fixed period withdrawal plan might be used to fund the time between early retirement at age 55, for example, and the commencing of benefits from a DBPP at age 65. When using the fixed period withdrawal plan, care must be taken to ensure that the right amount of initial capital is invested in the most appropriate fund to provide the expected income flow over the required time period. Here is another real life illustration of the fixed period withdrawal plan.

As shown in Figure 6.5, an investor has invested $50,000 in a quality, balanced mutual fund with the intention of withdrawing as much as he could over a fixed 10-year period. Calculations proved that he could safely withdraw $640 monthly (shown in the chart in year-end increments) and his programme would last the period required. His net average annual return over that 10-year period was a very handsome 9.65 per cent.

Life Expectancy Adjusted Withdrawal Plans

The fourth and final withdrawal plan is called the *life expectancy adjusted withdrawal plan.* Using this withdrawal plan format allows you to maximize your retirement income by setting up a payment schedule that will eventually deplete the entire value of your investment.

Figure 6.5
An Example of a Fixed Period Withdrawal Plan

Period End	Invest $	With-draw $	Charges	Income $	Capital Gains	Rein-vest $	Market Value $	Shares	NAV
7/31/1988	50,000	0	0	0	0	0	50,000	4,310	11.60
12/31/1988	0	3,200	0	1,268	696	1,964	48,131	4,207	11.44
12/31/1989	0	7,680	0	2,376	630	3,006	46,263	3,827	12.09
12/31/1990	0	7,680	0	2,437	0	2,437	38,049	3,367	11.30
12/31/1991	0	7,680	0	1,918	245	2,163	36,159	2,914	12.41
12/31/1992	0	7,680	0	1,439	309	1,748	29,984	2,440	12.29
12/31/1993	0	7,680	0	1,101	1,193	2,294	28,538	2,031	14.05
12/31/1994	0	7,680	0	623	488	1,110	19,819	1,552	12.77
12/31/1995	0	7,680	0	451	449	900	15,359	1,056	14.55
12/31/1996	0	7,680	0	243	732	975	10,815	643	16.82
12/31/1997	0	7,680	0	129	309	438	4,337	246	17.61
7/31/1998	0	4,480	0	17	0	17	4	0	17.42
Total	50,000	76,800	0	12,003	5,050	17,053			

Ending Amount Attributable to	Market Value	Shares	Return on the Investment	Percent
Principal:	4	0	Average Annual:	9.65%
Income:	0	0	Cumulative:	151.16%
Capital Gains:	0	0		
Total Ending Amount:	4	0		

Obviously, this plan is designed to maximize your income as long as you are alive. Its job is to essentially exhaust the value of your invested capital by the time you decease. The difficulty of knowing when you will pass away is a characteristic problem facing this withdrawal plan. One way financial advisors get around it is to use life expectancy or mortality tables. For example, if you are a 72-year-old male, your life expectancy would be 10 years.

In Figure 6.6, a $50,000 investment that earned you about 10 per cent per year would generate $5,591 income in your first year, eventually rising to $13,874 in your last full calendar year. Obviously, your periodic income would vary. But you would maximize your income level because it is comprised of a blend of original capital plus earnings paid over a specific period of time.

The Pros and Cons of Systematic Withdrawal Plans

It's obvious from the above discussion that systematic withdrawal plans (SWP) all offer tremendous retirement income potential. All four plan types offer significantly higher income options than just receiving investment income earnings and distributions. However, particular care must

Figure 6.6

An Example of a Life Expectancy Adjusted Withdrawal Plan

Period End	Invest $	With-draw $	Charges	Income $	Capital Gains	Rein-vest $	Market Value $	Shares	NAV
7/31/1988	50,000	0	0	0	0	0	50,000	4,310	11.60
12/31/1988	0	2,110	0	1,292	708	2,000	49,239	4,304	11.44
12/31/1989	0	5,591	0	2,513	674	3,187	49,683	4,109	12.09
12/31/1990	0	5,573	0	2,733	0	2,733	43,627	3,861	11.30
12/31/1991	0	6,306	0	2,290	298	2,589	44,127	3,556	12.41
12/31/1992	0	6,843	0	1,835	401	2,236	39,189	3,189	12.29
12/31/1993	0	7,790	0	1,505	1,659	3,164	39,853	2,837	14.05
12/31/1994	0	8,511	0	909	728	1,637	29,850	2,337	12.77
12/31/1995	0	9,093	0	729	750	1,479	25,905	1,780	14.55
12/31/1996	0	11,422	0	436	1,345	1,781	20,007	1,189	16.82
12/31/1997	0	13,873	0	247	598	844	8,409	478	17.61
7/31/1998	0	8,700	0	33	0	33	0	0	17.42
Total	**50,000**	**85,812**	**0**	**14,521**	**7,161**	**21,682**			

Ending Amount Attributable to	Market Value	Shares	Return on the Investment	Percent
Principal:	0	0	Average Annual:	10.11%
Income:	0	0	Cumulative:	162.05%
Capital Gains:	0	0		
Total Ending Amount:	**0**	**0**		

be taken where you wish to preserve the value of your capital. Taking too much money from your investment can cause a rapid deterioration in its original capital value. An equal amount of care must be exercised to ensure that inflation does not continue to undo the current value of your investment nest egg. This is true if you wish to maximize your retirement income as well as increase the current value of your retirement nest egg.

Using mutual funds as repositories for your non-registered capital can pay substantial benefits inasmuch as you can liquidate your capital anytime without fear of locking up your capital. As a result of this superior liquidity, you can modify your systematic withdrawal plan any time, too. The only restrictions you may face will be the type of mutual fund you use and the amount of volatility associated with the fund.

Systematic withdrawal plans are very flexible. As we've seen, you can adjust the circumstances of the withdrawal plan you choose at any time. You can even change to a different type of withdrawal plan, and do so without disrupting the underlying mutual funds you are using currently. Protecting your non-registered retirement nest egg is a snap when using systematic withdrawal plans. This is because most mutual funds offer superior long-term rates of return and allow you to raise and lower the amount of income you receive at any time.

Of course, with more than 1,800 mutual funds on the books today, you can choose from one of the widest selection of investments available. Depending on your selection of funds, your rates of return can be substantial during both good economic times and bad.

RETIREMENT INCOME STRATEGY # 11

When choosing a mutual fund portfolio for your SWP always keep in mind your goals, your level of investment experience, your risk tolerance level and your expectation of risk-reward. Use the ratio withdrawal plan first and watch how the programme works. You can always change to a more aggressive SWP strategy that more closely matches your financial circumstances and retirement income requirements.

Taxation of Systematic Withdrawal Plans

Any dividends earned on, or distributions made from, your mutual fund investments are taxed at your marginal tax rate in the year you receive them, regardless as to whether you take them as cash in hand or reinvest them. The amount of tax you pay will depend on the kind of dividends and distributions you receive: interest, dividend dividends or capital gain dividends. These are normally reported on a Revenue Canada T3 or T5 reporting slip.

In addition, you have to report all capital gains and capital losses generated by your systematic withdrawals. This is because a SWP redeems shares or units of your mutual fund as opposed to a withdrawal scheme that allows you to simply take your fund's dividend income stream. Where your mutual fund shares are gaining in value, that is, they are valued at a price that is higher than what you paid for them, any redemption of those shares will result in a capital gain. Where your shares are worth less than the price you purchased them and you redeem them, you have realized a capital loss. If you are redeeming them at the same share price you purchased them for, then there is no tax applied. This situation would be considered a return of capital since, in the case of non-registered money, it is considered to be capital on which you already paid tax.

For tax purposes, only 75 per cent of your total capital gains (profit) are subject to income tax at your marginal tax rate. Where you have a capital loss, no tax is payable. In fact, you can deduct your capital losses against your capital gains. Should one cancel out the other, no income tax is payable. Where your capital gain is only reduced by your capital losses, then 75 per cent of your remaining capital gain is reported as "income" and taxed accordingly.

While many mutual fund companies will provide you with the numbers you need to calculate your year-end tax liability, it is important to keep a close eye on your accumulated capital gains and losses. You want to always make sure that your reporting is accurate, otherwise you could be in for a nasty surprise in the form of extra taxes to pay.

RETIREMENT INCOME STRATEGY # 12

When looking to generate retirement income through the use of a SWP, make sure that you purchase good quality mutual funds with past performance records of not less than five, preferably 10 years. This will ensure that you have a good idea as to what you can expect through good and bad stock markets. The SWP can be an excellent way of enjoying a high, tax-preferred retirement income during long periods of positive economic growth. During protracted periods of declining stock market indices, however, a SWP can reduce the value of your retirement capital quickly, depending on how much you withdraw and when the original investment was made.

If you have a low marginal tax rate, use quality mortgage and bond funds. If you have a moderate marginal tax rate, look to high-yielding dividend funds. If you suffer from a high marginal tax rate and still want to generate income using a SWP, choose a balanced fund or moderate risk, high-yielding common stock equity fund. Under no circumstances should you withdraw more than *eight per cent* of the value of your fund portfolio annually. By exceeding this withdrawal rate, you risk depleting your original capital during periods of declining markets and poor economic activity.

CHAPTER SEVEN

REAL LIFE INVESTING: FOUR CASE STUDIES

This chapter is designed to provide you with illustrations of what you can expect when planning for your retirement income. I have drawn from my files as a practicing Certified Financial Planner to provide you with four real life case studies. The first case involves the financial situation of a single, 35-year-old engineer who has specific retirement goals. My second case involves the retirement needs of a 54-year-old Ontario teacher who is thinking about taking the commuted value of his accumulated pension and re-entering the work force as a self-employed consultant. The third case concerns the income needs of a married couple who is within one year of retirement. My fourth case study examines the financial implications for a retired spouse whose husband has recently passed away.

These four case studies are intended to be summaries of the actual circumstances involved and leave much material out of the picture. In this regard, I purposely have presented each case study in a way that allows you to raise questions and work towards postulating solutions of your own. There is no one correct answer. In this way, I hope to have shown how different retirement situations require thoughtful reflection and the application of common as well as different financial planning emphases.

The names and financial circumstances of these four case studies have been altered to ensure client-advisor confidentiality.

THE CASE OF THE PRUDENT ENGINEER

John is a stress concrete engineer, single, age 35, and works for ABLE2 Engineers Ltd. His annual salary is currently $60,000 and includes a guaranteed minimum indexing of three per cent per year. He has been a member of a company sponsored GRRSP for the past five years and, today, it is worth a total of $36,706.49. His monthly RRSP contributions amount to $500, which represents a savings ratio of 10 per cent of his annual gross salary.

Retirement Goals

John figures that he will need at least $60,000 gross in today's dollars to live the lifestyle he wants by the time he retires at age 60. He enjoys entertaining, skiing and travelling.

The Query

After speaking at length with a financial planner, John wants to know what he has to do to ensure that he has enough capital to generate a current gross annual income of $60,000 by the time he turns age 60.

John is particularly concerned about his retirement nest egg because he has only a GRRSP as a company benefit and his company does not make contributions on his behalf. He is solely responsible for saving enough capital to fund his eventual retirement.

The Answer

His financial planner calculated that John would need to generate an annual income of $125,628 at retirement 25 years down the road, if inflation averaged three per cent per year, to equal a gross retirement income of $60,000 in today's dollars.

The Solution

To generate an annual income of $125,628 at retirement, John would have to accumulate a minimum of $1,448,335 by the time he retires. This sum would generate $125,628 per year for 25 years after retirement, which is the projected longevity for males who are in good mental and physical health. This lump sum figure, however, does not factor the corrosive effects of long-term inflation into the financial equation. If John wants to maintain the spending power of his retirement income over an assumed 25-year period, where inflation averages three per cent annually, then his financial nest egg requirement jumps to $1,884,000. Figure 7.1 illustrates how his nest egg of $1,884,000 would provide the desired cash flow over a 25-year period.

John is aware of the fact that should he live beyond his eighty-fifth birthday, he would need to save even more of a retirement nest egg.

But John may not have to save so much capital if he factors potential pension income into his figures. CPP benefits may be available at age 60 and OAS payments at age 65. His financial planner believes that there is a strong likelihood that such government-sponsored benefits will not exist by the time John retires. At the very least, CPP and OAS benefits will have probably changed dramatically from what they are today. John prefers to factor CPP and OAS into his retirement income calculations. So, assuming benefits are inflation indexed at three per cent per year for the next 25 years, John could expect monthly CPP benefits of $1,091.59 at age 60 ($1,559.42 − (6% × 5)) and OAS benefits of $988.26 per month commencing age 65. Now, John's retirement nest egg can be reduced to account for an additional indexed CPP income of $13,099.13 per year for the first five years of his retirement and another $11,859.12

in annual indexed OAS benefits commencing on his sixty-fifth birthday. Based on CPP pension income, John's retirement nest egg requirement is reduced to $1,687,511 instead of $1,884,000. Factor his OAS benefit of $988.26 into the equation at age 65 and the nest egg John needs to fund his retirement drops to $1,509,669.

Figure 7.1

Annual Cash Flow of John's Inflation-Indexed Retirement Income of $60,000

Amount of Initial Investment:	$1,884,000
Annual Return	8.00%
Number of Years	25
Amount of Each Withdrawal	$125,628

Withdrawal Frequency: Annually
Increase Withdrawals Annually By 3.00%

Period	Opening Balance ($)	Withdrawal Per Period ($)	Total Withdrawals ($)	Closing Balance ($)
1	1,884,000.00	125,628.00	125,628.00	1,899,041.76
2	1,899,041.76	129,396.84	255,024.84	1,911,216.51
3	1,911,216.51	133,278.75	388,303.59	1,920,172.79
4	1,920,172.79	137,277.11	525,580.69	1,925,527.34
5	1,925,527.34	141,395.42	666,976.11	1,926,862.47
6	1,926,862.47	145,637.28	812,613.40	1,923,723.20
7	1,923,723.20	150,006.40	962,619.80	1,915,614.14
8	1,915,614.14	154,506.59	1,117,126.39	1,901,996.15
9	1,901,996.15	159,141.79	1,276,268.18	1,882,282.71
10	1,882,282.71	163,916.05	1,440,184.23	1,855,836.00
11	1,855,836.00	168,833.53	1,609,017.76	1,821,962.67
12	1,821,962.67	173,898.53	1,782,916.29	1,779,909.27
13	1,779,909.27	179,115.49	1,962,031.78	1,728,857.28
14	1,728,857.28	184,488.95	2,146,520.73	1,667,917.79
15	1,667,917.79	190,023.62	2,336,544.35	1,596,125.70
16	1,596,125.70	195,724.33	2,532,268.68	1,512,433.48
17	1,512,433.48	201,596.06	2,733,864.74	1,415,704.42
18	1,415,704.42	207,643.94	2,941,508.69	1,304,705.31
19	1,304,705.31	213,873.26	3,155,381.95	1,178,098.62
20	1,178,098.62	220,289.46	3,375,671.41	1,034,433.89
21	1,034,433.89	226,898.14	3,602,569.55	872,138.61
22	872,138.61	233,705.09	3,836,274.63	689,508.20
23	689,508.20	240,716.24	4,076,990.87	484,695.32
24	484,695.32	247,937.73	4,324,928.60	255,698.20
25	255,698.20	255,375.86	4,580,304.46	348.13
Total			**$4,580,304.46**	**$348.13**

The Plan

On the advice of his financial planner, John decided to construct a retirement capital accumulation plan based on a 25-year target of $1,884,000. As John is an Ontario resident, he pays income tax at a marginal rate of 49.36 per cent. In view of this, it makes sense to deposit more than the $500 per month he is currently contributing to RRSPs. For every dollar of pre-tax income John contributes to his RRSP he saves $0.49 in tax. Based on these figures his financial planner proposed the following plan:

1. Increase monthly RRSP deposits from $500 to $900 until he reaches retirement age, earning an annual average compound return of eight per cent.

By doing so, John's RRSP nest egg will amount to $1,322,378.94. His minimum annual tax savings amount to $5,330.88 and, where sufficient income tax has been deducted from his income, John's refund will be in the form of cash each year. This leaves John with a retirement nest egg shortfall of $561,621.06.

John's financial planner pointed out that it was not wise to have all of his retirement capital in RRSPs, regardless as to how efficient they are in allowing capital to grow and the tax savings they incur. By having all of his retirement assets under a registered format, he had less flexibility regarding income tax on his retirement income. Since John's current taxable income was $49,200 ($60,000 less his annual $10,800 RRSP deposit), his marginal tax rate was still quite high at 40.3 per cent. To help build capital outside of RRSPs on an efficient basis, his financial planner proposed a long-term investment loan.

2. Borrow $50,000.00 from John's local trust company and pay it back over 25 years, with interest expense averaging 10 per cent per year, compounded semi-annually.

Here is how John's leveraged investment program was structured. By borrowing $50,000 and investing the cash in a well-balanced portfolio of quality equity-growth mutual funds, John could expect to maximize his returns by investing in high growth investments that earned tax-deferred capital gains. Over a 25-year period, John will have paid off the $50,000 loan principal and would have paid total accumulated loan interest of $84,172, as shown in Figure 7.2. Based on an average annual rate of return of 10 per cent, his $50,000 investment would have grown to $541,735.30 after 25 years.

The Results

When you add the value of his RRSPs to the value of his regular investment, John's total nest egg amounts to $1,864,114.24, which is just

$19,885.76 short of John's total capital requirement. It is important to note, however, that John's 25-year RRSP tax savings amounted to $133,272 ($10,800 × 25 × 49.36%).

John's total out of pocket costs to carry his $50,000 investment loan amounted to $134,172 over the same 25-year period. As a result, John's RRSP tax savings effectively covered the cost of his investment loan. But, John also received income tax refunds of $33,921.32 ($84,172.00 × 40.3%) as a result of tax deductible loan interest of $84,172. Add back John's additional tax savings and his retirement nest egg is now worth $1,898,035.56 ($1,864,114.24 + $33,921.32), which is more than enough to fund John's retirement income needs.

THE CASE OF THE RELUCTANT TEACHER

Barry is a Toronto, Ontario teacher, age 54, and currently earns a $65,000 salary per year. After 31 years in the "front lines," Barry is considering leaving his teaching career to join the ranks of the self-employed as an education consultant. As a teaching professional in Ontario, Barry has the option to retire with a full pension beginning the month following his fifty-fifth birthday. For the past few years, the province has offered teachers the opportunity to leave the teaching profession earlier than they might otherwise have been able. In Barry's case, the province's "85 Factor" allows him to quit teaching with no penalty, providing he resigns

Figure 7.2

Particulars of John's $50,000 Investment Loan

Loan Amount:	$50,000	**Int. Rate:**	10.000%	**Compounded:** Semi-Annually
Amortized for:	25 Year(s)	**Term:**	25 Year(s)	**Day basis:** 365
Pay Frequency:	Montly	**Pay Type:**	Blended	

First Payment Date: Oct 05, 1998   **Interest Adjustment Date:** Sep 05, 1998
Advance Date: Sept 05, 1998   **Payment Amount:** $447.24

Prepayments:
Annual Prepayment: $0.00

	Payment ($)	Principal ($)	Interest ($)	Balance ($)
Term Totals:	134,172	50,000	84,172	.00
Amortization Period Totals:	134,172	50,000	84,172	.00
Years to pay off:	25.00		**Interest adjustment:**	.00

prior to age 55. The "85 Factor" equals Barry's age plus his years of service. Where the number equals 85, Barry, and other teachers like him, can retire with a full teacher's pension.

Retirement Goals

Barry has tired of teaching, but he enjoys the education field. His dream is to retire early, take a pension and return to the provincial Ministry of Education as a self-employed education consultant. While he believes his prospects for consulting are good, he is not sure if taking a teacher's pension is the right way to go. Under a provincially mandated retirement option, Barry can elect to commute the value of his accumulated pension amount and receive it as a lump sum. By doing so, he can manage his own retirement nest egg and provide superior income options for his spouse should he decease prematurely. More important, though, is the fact that Barry estimates his first year consultant income will amount to about $60,000 before expenses. With an anticipated teacher's pension of approximately $45,000, Barry would earn a minimum of $105,000 in his first year as a consultant. Barry doesn't need this much income at retirement and he doesn't want to suffer a potential annual tax liability of $50,000 either. For Barry, it's not a question of having too little income, but having too much income in his retirement years!

The Query

Barry wants to know how to retire early, defer his teacher's pension and protect his spouse from financial destitution should he pass on prematurely. Barry knows that if he takes his teacher's pension, rather than commute his accrued pension amount, on his death his spouse would receive only 60 per cent of his retirement pension of $45,000 or $27,000. Although he has the option to increase the amount to his widowed spouse by 10 per cent or $31,500 ($45,000 x 10% + $27,000), his own initial pension income would be reduced to purchase that extra income protection. He is also aware that should he and his wife both pass on, the Teacher's Pension Board keeps the remainder of his pension nest egg. "No deal" says Barry. But what are the alternatives?

The Answer

If Barry quits teaching prior to his fifty-fifth birthday, he can elect to commute his accumulated pension benefits to a cash lump sum and roll over the proceeds to his own registered retirement plan. Barry figures on an accumulated pre-tax sum of $600,000. By doing so, Barry essentially defers receiving a pension and can continue to do so until the end of the year in which he turns age 69. This meets Barry's first challenge, which is to avoid receiving pension income while he pursues his consultant career.

Second, by transferring his accumulated pension amount out of the pension system, he now manages his own retirement nest egg. This allows Barry more flexibility when it comes to his spouse. On Barry's death, his surviving spouse would now receive all of his retirement nest egg tax-free under the spousal rollover provision for individual retirement plans. His spouse could then generate whatever pension income she wishes, rather than live on a reduced pension of just $31,500. After his spouse passes on, the remaining registered capital, less income tax, would go to her designated beneficiaries.

The Solution

Under current tax law, Barry is allowed to transfer the commuted value of his registered pension plan to a locked-in RRSP or LIRA. In Barry's case, he can elect to transfer the entire $600,000 commuted value to his LIRA. The LIRA allows Barry's capital to compound on a tax-deferred basis until the end of the year in which he turns age 69. At that time, Barry has to convert his LIRA to a LIF and receive pension income. At age 80, he is then required to convert his LIF to a life annuity.

On the surface, electing to transfer the commuted value of his pension to his own LIRA sounds like a good option. Barry figures that his $600,000 would double to $1.2 million by the time he reaches age 61. He plans to invest the commuted value in a selection of moderately aggressive equity growth mutual funds, which, he hopes, will earn an average annual compound rate of 12 per cent over this six year period. He intends to scale back his consulting business and begin drawing on his LIRA in the form of a LIF at age 62. At a revised eight per cent growth per year, Barry's LIF income would provide anywhere from $42,421.79 and $86,571.83 before tax if he began to draw income at age 62. The projected LIF value at the end of the year in which Barry turned age 79 would amount to a whopping $1,869,890.18 in the first instance and $1,190,683.67 in the second. If Barry took his $45,000 pension indexed at three per cent per year now, it would have grown to $53,732.35 six years later which is far below the maximum income a LIF is allowed to generate. Where Barry elects to take $53,732.35 in LIF income at age 62, its end value at age 79 would still amount to a remarkable $1,787,325.44! This sounds almost too good to be true.

The Plan

If Barry could transfer the entire commuted value of $600,000 to a LIRA, then it would make a great deal of sense to get his cash out of the pension system. Other factors, however, will have to be considered before doing so. First, to commute his accumulated pension amount,

Barry must quit his employer, not retire, prior to age 55. This means that any benefits such as life and disability insurance and extended health coverage will cease. Second, even though Barry can transfer his commuted pension amount to a LIRA, Revenue Canada will be waiting to collect its share. Third, by using mutual funds as the preferred investment for his LIRA proceeds, Barry's anticipated rate of return to age 62 of 12 per cent is not guaranteed. These complicating factors impact on the attractiveness of Barry's proposition.

Replacing lost group insurance benefits could be an expensive proposition. Life insurance has to be purchased and depending on the amount and kind of insurance considered, it could cost at least $3,500 per year for $200,000 coverage. If Barry had a history of poor health he could pay a much higher amount in the form of a risk premium. If Barry had too many health complications, he might not be insurable at all. At age 55, Barry is not insurable under a standard disability policy and, if he were, it would be still difficult to purchase because most insurers require a work history, but Barry would be newly self-employed with no employment or income history. At age 55, premiums could very easily exceed $200 per month. Of course, health coverage, including enhanced hospital benefits, eye care and dental coverage, would probably amount to another $200 per month or more, if he could get them through a private carrier. So, to replace lost extended benefits, Barry could end up paying an additional minimum monthly cost of $691.67 or $8,300 per year.

Depending on how Barry's total severance package is structured, he could pay up to $100,000 in income tax in addition to his regular employment income tax, depending on when in the year Barry receives his entitlement. So, instead of having $600,000 to work with, Barry has only $500,000 to put to work after he quits teaching. Obviously, having 16.7 per cent less capital to invest will have a perceptible effect on how much of a retirement nest egg he will have to draw from at age 62.

Barry has calculated the value of his LIRA using a 12 per cent annual compound rate of return. He believes investing in a selection of good quality common stock mutual funds will provide him with the best opportunity to double the value of his nest egg at the end of six years. Unfortunately, there is no guarantee that his mutual fund portfolio could provide such returns. As a group, moderately aggressive common stock mutual funds have earned a 15-year average annual rate of return of 10.8 per cent. If Barry bought into a stock market at a comparative high point in its growth cycle, he could realize much less growth, even a loss, over such a short time frame as six years.

Taking these *caveats* into consideration, Barry reworks the figures: $500,000 invested for six years, earning just 10.8 per cent per year, will result in a retirement nest egg of $925,142.36.

The value of his retirement nest egg amounts to just $925,142.36, well below the original goal of $1.2 million. When Barry becomes self-employed, he will earn $60,000 per year and will pay about $20,000 income tax each year. Since he already has paid tax of $100,000, Barry may be able to recover a certain percentage of this tax over the next several years by using an existing carry-forward provision. By investing his tax savings each year and earning a more conservative eight per cent, his nest egg will have grown to an additional $146,718.58. His total retirement nest egg now amounts to $1,071,860.94.

The Results

Translated back into a retirement income stream at age 62, Barry could expect to enjoy a maximum annual LIF income of $77,327.47 before tax as shown in Figure 7.3. This exceeds his projected teacher's pension of $53,732.35. This result is based on an semi-annual compound rate of return of eight per cent and partial indexing to age 79. Barry might receive some CPP benefits as well as a small OAS benefit, if government abides by current pension rules.

THE CASE OF JACK AND JILL

Jack and Jill are both age 57, married, and are within three years of Jack's retirement. Their three children are mature and living on their own. As the principal income earner, Jack started full-time work at age 25 and has been with his employer, XYZ Corp., for his entire working life. An Ontario resident, Jack earns $52,000 a year. He belongs to a DCPP and a company-sponsored GRRSP. Jill has never been gainfully employed outside of the home, but she has accumulated RRSPs as a result of Jack's spousal contributions over the years. Jack will be entitled to CPP and OAS benefits, while Jill will receive only OAS benefits at age 65.

Retirement Goals

Now that Jack is just 36 months from full retirement, he is preparing to leave his job after 35 years of service. His retirement goals are to spend as much time with Jill and their children as possible. Once a year, they would like to spend two weeks outside of Canada touring the Caribbean or Mediterranean. Both he and Jill enjoy gardening and spend most of their summers out of doors. Of course, all of these leisure activities require money. Unfortunately, Jack has just been informed by his company that his services are no longer required.

Figure 7.3
Barry's Maximum LIF Income Stream from Age 62

Amount:	$1,071,860.94		**Issue Date:**		Sep 09, 1998	
Freuqency:	Annually		**New Funds After 1992:**		Yes	
Int. Rate: 8.00%	Semi-Annually		**First Payment Date:**		Dec 31, 1999	
Birth Date:	Jan 01, 1937					
Plan Type:	LIF		**Payment: Maximum**			

			Gross Payment	Withholding Tax per	Net Payment	Total Net Annual
Age	Year	Open Value $	per period $	period $	per period $	Payment $
62	1999	1,098,445.33	77,327.47	11,830.68	65,496.79	65,496.79
63	2000	1,110,734.38	78,162.74	11,548.10	66,614.64	66,614.64
64	2001	1,123,190.80	80,209.77	11,583.03	68,626.74	68,626.74
65	2002	1,134,616.16	82,317.84	11,603.63	70,714.21	70,714.21
66	2003	1,144,865.30	84,489.67	11,608.52	72,881.15	72,881.15
67	2004	1,153,778.48	86,728.22	11,596.23	75,131.99	75,131.99
68	2005	1,161,179.98	89,036.74	11,565.20	77,471.54	77,471.54
69	2006	1,166,876.39	91,418.78	11,513.68	79,905.10	79,905.10
70	2007	1,170,655.07	93,878.30	11,439.85	82,438.45	82,438.45
71	2008	1,172,282.04	96,419.70	11,341.68	85,078.02	85,078.02
72	2009	1,171,499.88	99,047.94	2,518.25	96,529.69	96,529.69
73	2010	1,168,025.03	101,768.63	2,880.07	98,888.56	98,888.56
74	2011	1,161,545.36	104,588.17	4,928.06	99,660.11	99,660.11
75	2012	1,151,716.81	107,514.00	5,614.99	101,899.01	101,899.01
76	2013	1,138,159.85	110,554.79	6,362.77	104,192.02	104,192.02
77	2014	1,120,455.13	113,720.81	7,258.94	106,461.87	106,461.87
78	2015	1,098,139.02	117,024.43	8,257.83	108,766.60	108,766.60
79	2016	1,070,697.57	120,480.77	9,387.50	111,093.27	111,093.27

Funds exhausted: n/a

Total payments: $1,858,797.51 $173,520.48 $1,685,277.03

Closing Value: $1,037,559.89

The Query

Once the initial shock was overcome, both Jack and Jill decided to calculate the implications of being severed from work. They are naturally concerned about whether they have enough of a retirement nest egg to last them through their retirement, especially in light of the many leisure activities they would like to pursue. They figure they will need about $35,000 of retirement income for the first year.

The Answer

The answer to their query depends on what financial resources they have and how they access those resources. Jack provided the details of his finances as shown in Figure 7.4, including the "retirement package" he received from his employer.

Figure 7.4
Jack and Jill's Finances at "Early Retirement"

Current Assets (Excludes Mortgage-Free Home)	$
GRRSP	80,000
DCPP	90,000
Spousal RRSP	60,000
Non-Registered Investments	100,000
Cash On Hand	10,000
XYZ Corp. Retirement Package	
Termination Pay	12,000
Severance Amount	26,000
Retirement Allowance	60,000
Health Care Package:	Expired

The Solution

The first step in determining how much money will be available for retirement is to protect Jack's "retirement package" from income tax as much as possible. As his position was terminated at the end of September, Jack received approximately $36,000 of employment income. Coupled with his lump sum termination payment of $12,000, his taxable income amounts to $48,000, which is close to his regular annual salary. His severance pay of $26,000, which represents payment equivalent to 26 weeks of work, can be rolled directly into an RRSP. Jack also received a $60,000 retiring allowance in recognition of his 32 years of service to his company. Under current legislation, Jack is allowed to roll his entire retiring allowance into an RRSP as well.

Jack's company has requested that he transfer the proceeds of his GRRSP to his own plan. He can do this on a tax-free basis using a Government of Canada transfer form called a T2033. He has also been told that he can commute the accumulated value of his DCPP and transfer the proceeds to a LIRA.

Jack and Jill's total retirement resources amount to $426,000, excluding $12,000 of termination pay, which has been used as income to support them through the remaining three months of the year. The $90,000 commuted value of Jack's DCPP is the only capital that has been "locked-in" as required by Ontario law. The last contribution Jack made to Jill's spousal RRSP was three years ago.

If Jack and Jill were to take just 8.22 per cent of their total retirement nest egg of $426,000, they would generate $35,017.20 for their first year. At this stage, there are sufficient funds to achieve their first year income requirement. However, as we know, inflation will reduce the purchasing power of money over time. In their case, Jack and Jill's $35,017.20 first year income will be reduced to just $27,642.90 if inflation prevails at three per cent over the next eight years. To ensure they maintain their long-term purchasing power, Jack and Jill will have to arrange their retirement assets in such a way so that they automatically index their income by three per cent each year.

The Plan

Jack knows that he can elect to receive CPP benefits when he turns age 60, however, he prefers to build up his benefit payment and receive it as of his sixty-fifth birthday. Jack figures he can offset this lost CPP income by keeping income tax as low as he possibly can. To maximize his after-tax income, Jack implemented the following strategy.

First, he and Jill decided to income split as much as they possibly could. They decided to attack their non-registered jointly held investments first. Jack and Jill began a systematic withdrawal plan based on an eight per cent figure. This would provide each of them with $4,000 income per year. Second, since Jack made his last spousal RRSP contribution to Jill's plan three years prior, he knew Jill could elect to receive income from her plan without having the income attributed back to Jack for tax purposes. In this case, Jill would take an additional $4,800 per year from her RRSPs. Jack, on the other hand, would have to make up the income difference of $22,200 from his registered resources. Third, he decided to avoid converting his LIRA to a LIF. This was because the LIF provided him with less flexibility than regular RRSP assets. Jack decided to withdraw $22,200 from his combined RRSP assets of $166,000 instead. Both Jack and Jill figured that they could earn an average annual compound return of 8.0 per cent on their investments. They indexed their $35,000 first year income requirement by three per cent per year to offset the long-term effects of inflation.

The Results

At age 65 the value of Jack and Jill's retirement assets is shown in Figure 7.5.

Figure 7.5

Jack and Jill's Retirement Assets at Age 65	($)
LIRA	166,583.72
Jointly Held Non-Registered Investments	87,884.10
Jack's Combined RRSPs	69,651
Jill's RRSP	57,861.08
Cash On Hand	10,000
Total Value:	391,979.90

This represents a decline in capital value of $34,020.10 or 7.98 per cent.

At age 65, however, Jack hopes to receive full CPP and OAS benefits and Jill will receive OAS. If we assume that today's CPP and OAS benefits are indexed at three per cent, their combined monthly retirement pensions will amount to $1,974.64 or $23,695.68 a year. Their combined retirement income requirement will also have increased to $43,095.64. Based on these figures, they will have to draw only $19,399.96 from their own retirement resources. Jack's income is comprised of $17,506.44 of CPP and OAS benefits and Jill's income is comprised of $6,189.24 in OAS benefits. Jack should roll his RRIF back into an RRSP until the end of the year in which he turns age 69. To make up for his portion of their income shortfall, Jack should elect to convert his LIRA to a LIF and take the maximum payment. At 8.21 per cent, his LIF income would add an additional $13,676.52 ($166,583.72 × 8.21%) to their income stream. Jill should maintain her $400 monthly RRIF withdrawal, following up with just $100 per month from her portion of their non-registered investments. Their finances four years later are outlined in Figure 7.6.

Figure 7.6

Jack and Jill's Retirement Assets at Age 69	($)
LIRA	172,949.81
Jack's RRSPs	94,759.42
Jill's RRSP	51,599.19
Jointly Held Non-Registered Investments	113,066.82
Cash On Hand	10,000
Total Value:	432,375.24

This represents an increase in capital value of $40,395.34 or 10.32% over Jack and Jill's capital value at age 65.

Based on these figures, Jack and Jill will have enough retirement capital to live out their retirement years. It should be noted here, however, that without the addition of CPP and OAS benefits available at age 65, Jack and Jill would have drawn from their retirement nest egg far more by age 69 than what would have been financially prudent.

THE CASE OF SALLY SMITH

Sally Smith has been retired for three years. Sally is age 63 and was widowed early this year. Her husband, Robert, was a retired secondary school teacher and died at age 65. Prior to his death, Robert and Sally lived comfortably in a well-maintained century home located outside of a major urban centre. They had no debts and had a moderate retirement nest egg comprised of some RRSPs and non-registered mutual funds.

Retirement Goals

Prior to Robert's death, both Sally and he had planned to sell their home, move into a condominium project in town, travel when they wanted and enjoy a little golf. Now, things have changed. In addition to a change in lifestyle, Sally's financial circumstances have been altered, too.

The Query

Sally has been informed that Robert's teacher's pension will be reduced to just 60 per cent of what he received while he had been alive. Although Sally and Robert had discussed what might happen to his retirement pension should he decease prematurely, Sally wasn't prepared for Robert's early and sudden departure. Now, she is concerned that she may not have enough assets to live on through her retirement years.

The Answer

Robert and Sally's retirement finances prior to Robert's death are outlined in Figure 7.7.

Figure 7.7

Robert and Sally's Retirement Finances Prior to Robert's Death ($)

Teacher's Pension	42,000 (Gross)
Robert's OAS Benefit	4,885.80 ($407.15 Gross Monthly)
Sally's RRSPs	50,000
Non-Registered Jointly-Held Mutual Funds	100,000
Cash On Hand	15,000
Century Home	250,000
Total Value:	(Excludes Pensions & Personal Affects) $415,000

Their combined annual income needs amounted to $45,000 gross per year and they managed to achieve this income without touching their other retirement assets.

Now that Robert has deceased, everything remains the same except Sally's income has been reduced dramatically. Instead of receiving Robert's full pension, she is entitled to only $25,200 before taxes and has lost Robert's OAS entitlement, leaving her with a retirement income that is 46.3 per cent less than what she enjoyed while Robert was alive. Sally did not want to reduce her income requirement of $45,000 per year.

The Solution

Fortunately, Sally is entitled to benefits under the CPP and she does have adequate financial resources to achieve their goals and to continue to live comfortably through her retirement.

While her survivor's benefit under Robert's pension plan has been reduced to $25,200, Sally is entitled to a widow's pension under the CPP. In 1998, this benefit amounts to $410.70 per month and adds $4,928.40 to her annual income. In addition to this, she receives a one-time lump sum death benefit of $2,500 to assist her with Robert's interment costs.

Still facing a shortfall of $14,871.60, Sally believed she could make this up by converting her investments to generate a suitable income stream.

The Plan

With the help of her financial planner, Sally decided to sell her current home and move into a two-bedroom condominium in town. While she very much enjoyed her rural property, she felt it too big, now that she was living alone. Her condominium cost her $160,000 and she received an additional cash sum of $75,000, net after expenses, from the sale of her century home. She added this extra cash to her non-registered mutual fund portfolio.

To help offset her $14,871.60 cash shortfall, Sally elected to implement a SWP from her investment portfolio. This amounted to about 8.5 per cent of the $175,000 value of her mutual fund assets. While the income level was higher than the maximum recommended eight per cent SWP rate, Sally felt that she would only have to draw this much until her OAS benefit kicked in at age 65. At that point, she would have an additional $431.95 per month or $5,183.35 a year at age 65, reducing her income requirement from her non-registered investments to just $10,593.93 or 6.0 per cent based on her original $175,000 capital investment. In reality, at age 65 Sally's non-registered investment would have been reduced to $171,389.76 if her earnings amounted to only eight per cent per year. Sally had no need to touch her RRSPs and she planned to keep them intact until the end of the year in which she turned age 69.

The Results

All things considered, Sally was now in good shape to carry on with her retirement. She had indexed CPP and OAS benefits, an indexed pension from Robert's teacher's pension, sufficient indexed income from her non-registered investments and tax deferred growth on her RRSPs. Her financial position at age 69 is outlined in Figure 7.8.

Figure 7.8
Sally's Retirement Assets at Age 69 ($)

Teacher's Pension Proceeds (Indexed)	30,090.12
CPP Survivor's Benefit (Indexed)	5,884.80
OAS Payment (Indexed)	5,833.20
Investment Income Indexed at 3%	11,576.27
Investment Value at 8%	179,403.63
RRSP Value Earning 8%	79,343.72
Condominium	160,000
Total Annual Income at age 69:	53,384.39
Total Net Worth at Age 69:	$18,747.35

CHAPTER EIGHT

PLANNING FOR WHEN YOU'RE GONE

No one wants to admit his or her mortality. Twist and turn as we may through life, we cannot avoid the fact that, one day, we won't be here. No matter what our station in life or personal circumstances, no matter what our deeds have been, we all deal, sooner or later, with that common denominator called death.

On the other hand, acknowledgment of our mortality can go a long way to help make living today much more satisfying than if we simply ignored it. This is because prudent retirement planning forces us to acknowledge our mortality. If you've planned your retirement properly you will have confronted and integrated the fact of your mortality into the financial planning equation. Unfortunately about 65 per cent of Canadian adults today will die without having any kind of will or *succession plan* in place.

I have written this chapter to assist those who have yet to put your succession plan into action. A "succession plan" makes clear to your surviving beneficiaries what you want done with your life's accumulated assets. It's hard enough to deal with the death of a loved one. The least you can do is ensure that the disposition and allocation of your assets will be accomplished with minimum cost, effort and frustration.

This chapter is at best a synopsis of just a few of the more important aspects of estate planning. Estate planning is a complex and convoluted field. Before acting on any ideas mentioned in this chapter, be sure to speak with an appropriately qualified estate-planning professional.

WHAT HAPPENS TO YOUR ASSETS AT DEATH

At death, two processes come into play regarding your accumulated assets. The first process is to determine what your assets are, commonly referred to as your *estate*, and to whom you wish your assets to go to upon your passing—your spouse, children, relatives, favourite charity and friends are your potential *beneficiaries*. The second process is to determine the content and size of your estate and how much of its value will be eaten up by estate processing costs and income tax. *The job of estate planning is to ensure that your intended beneficiaries in fact receive as much of your estate as possible.*

Under current tax law, when you die you are considered to have abandoned, or given-up title to, your estate. In other words, you have *disposed* of your assets. This *deemed disposition*, as it is called, is key to understanding the consequences of dying in Canada today. The first consequence is to determine who will receive your assets now that you no longer own them. The second consequence is the amount of income tax that will accrue to your assets. According to Revenue Canada, a deemed disposition means that you have theoretically "liquidated" your estate and converted it to cash. This cash value is declared as income to you in the year of your death and is reported on your final tax return, called your *terminal return*. So, the determined value of your estate assets is added to whatever regular retirement income you earned up until the day of your death and your estate representative or *executor* submits notice of this income to Revenue Canada for tax purposes.

But, as simple as the estate settlement concept is, there are countless items, maneuvers and pitfalls that will complicate the settlement of an estate when the time arrives. The better you prepare for this inevitable challenge now, the easier it will be to protect your surviving spouse or other intended beneficiaries. Following is an outline of some of the major estate planning tools that will help you understand what is involved in estate planning and in thinking through an effective estate plan.

DYING INTESTATE—WITHOUT AN ESTATE PLAN

If you do not have an effective estate plan that can be implemented either now or after you've passed on, you've put your estate at risk. Without a will, your assets will often transfer to a provincially appointed *public trustee* who will manage your assets until disposed of, usually according to the *law of consanguinity*. Since you have not stated what is to be done with your estate assets, the public trustee will allocate and dispose of your assets according to a fixed lineage hierarchy based on blood relations or next of kin. Second, since there is no plan of action to refer to, your life's accumulated assets will be disposed of without any regard for tax planning. The end result, of course, is that someone other than your intended beneficiaries could receive your life's accumulated assets, but only after your estate has paid an inordinate amount of income tax on the proceeds. Sound like fun? It isn't. Your family or friends will have to live with the consequences for the rest of their lives.

REVENUE CANADA TAXATION—THE BOTTOM LINE

The main part of the Canadian *Income Tax Act* (ITA) that deals with taxation at death is found in section 70 and section 72. Sub-sections 70(1) to 70(4) pertain to the computation of earned income to the date of death and sub-section 70(5) onwards provides the rules for the deemed disposition of assets of an individual just prior to death.

According to the ITA, *your executor must include all income earned up until the day of your death on your terminal tax return. Since Revenue Canada asserts that you have "liquidated" all of your assets at death, the term "income" applies to all of your assets in its widest sense.*

Special rules apply to categories of assets such as income designated as periodic payments, amounts receivable (rights and things), resource properties, land inventories, capital property and eligible capital property. Periodic payments include any income that had been accruing but not yet declared or paid to an individual prior to his death. Interest earnings, rental income, royalties, annuities and employment income would qualify as periodic payments. Amounts receivable or rights and things are items that have been declared but not yet received as income. Stock dividends, matured bond interest coupons, inventory of an individual who is using the cash basis of reporting income (e.g., a farmer), vacation leave credits, and work in progress (e.g., income from an accounting, dental, legal, chiropractic, veterinarian or doctor's practice) are examples of amounts receivable or rights and things. Resource properties and land inventories include land value and buildings. Capital property and eligible capital property apply to any item not categorized above. Eligible capital property pertains to property used in the operation of a business, which is now run by a surviving spouse or child beneficiary.

The amount of income tax you pay is based on the assets you hold at death, less regular, allowable deductions as outlined in the ITA. A good estate plan endeavours to enhance and extend those deductions by applying various strategies currently accepted by Revenue Canada.

THE TAXATION OF ASSETS AT DEATH

On your death, your estate is directed to your survivors. There are two possibilities, however, that will determine the amount of income tax your estate will pay. The first situation involves a direct beneficiary such as your surviving spouse. The second situation pertains to indirect beneficiaries, such as parents, brothers, sisters, relatives and friends. Where your estate is directed to your spouse, the tax your estate pays will be minimal, if anything. Significant taxes will accrue, however, should anyone other than your spouse be designated as your estate beneficiary.

Registered Assets, The Taxman and Your Survivor Spouse

Registered assets such as registered pensions, registered annuities, RRSPs, RRIFs, LIRAs, LIFs and registered life insurance policies all have special conditions that come into play at your passing. Where there is a surviving spouse, all of these registered assets can transfer with or without income tax, depending on the election your spouse chooses at the time of your death. In almost all cases, a surviving spouse will elect to defer paying income tax and transfer ownership of these registered assets directly into his or her name. The rules that apply to registered assets and death of the registrant are found in paragraph 60(j), 60 (j.1) and 60(l), subsections 147(19-22) and section 147 of the ITA. Where your spouse survives you, any RRSPs, RRIFs, LIRAs or LIFs can be transferred intact to your spouse tax-free. Neither your estate nor your surviving spouse pays tax where your spouse is named the beneficiary of your plans, and your spouse elects not to convert your plans to cash. Figure 8.1 shows an outline of your available options.

If you are member of a registered pension plan or RPP, things become a little more complicated. Any lump sum payment that is made as a result of your interest in the RPP at death is paid to your spouse, and your spouse, not you, includes this commuted RPP lump sum in his or her income in the year that it is received. Most RPPs, however, arrange to continue to pay regular benefits to your surviving spouse. Tax is paid by your spouse on pension plan income, just as you did while you were alive. The amount of income your spouse receives will depend on the stipulations of your RPP. For example, Ontario teacher pensions are reduced by up to 40 per cent to a surviving spouse, whereas many corporate plans provide a full entitlement.

Registered life annuities often continue to pay the surviving spouse where there is a payment guarantee attached to it. The spouse is designated beneficiary and can often elect to continue receiving regular annuity payments or receive the commuted value of the annuity in the form of a lump sum. Annuity income is taxed in the hands of your recipient spouse.

Registered universal life and whole life insurance policies are treated in exactly the same way as RRSPs. The insurance component is paid to your spouse on a tax-free basis, while any accrued cash value is deemed a registered asset and can be transferred under the same conditions as a regular RRSP.

Non-Registered Assets, Revenue Canada and Your Survivor Spouse

When it comes to non-registered assets, such as your family home, the cottage, bank accounts, GICs, bonds, stocks, mutual funds, business interests, land and moneys lent, your estate and your surviving spouse can avoid paying a lot of income tax because of the *spousal rollover provision* and *spousal trust option*.

The *spousal rollover provision* is found in subsection 70(6) of the ITA. According to this provision, your spouse can receive your estate virtually intact and defer paying income tax until your assets are either sold or deemed disposed of on the death of your recipient spouse.

Figure 8.1
Registered Asset Options for Your Survivor Spouse

Registered Plan Type	Spouse Takes Plan Proceeds As Cash	Spouse Transfers Plan to Own RRSP	Spouse Converts RRSP To Income	Alternative Conversion Transfer Option
RRSP	Taxed in hands of surviving spouse at his/her marginal rate	RRSP in spouse's name	RRIF registered in spouse's name	Registered Life Annuity registered in spouse's name
RRIF	Taxed in hands of surviving spouse at his/her marginal rate	RRIF registered in spouse's name	RRSP registered in spouse's name providing spouse has not yet reached 69th birthday	Registered Life Annuity registered in spouse's name
LIRA/ LRRSP	Taxed in hands of surviving spouse at his/her marginal rate*	Regular (not locked-in) RRSP registered in spouse's name	RRIF registered in spouse's name	Registered Life Annuity registered in spouse's name
LIF	Taxed in hands of surviving spouse at his/her marginal rate*	RRIF registered in spouse's name	RRSP registered in spouse's name providing spouse has not yet reached 69th birthday	Registered Life Annuity registered in spouse's name

* Locked-in plan proceeds become unlocked and revert to an RRSP in the case of a LIRA and LRRSP, and to a RRIF in the case of a LIF.

Revenue Canada ascertains the value of your estate in the form of an adjusted cost base. Your spouse then receives your estate at the same adjusted cost base. Since there is no reported gain or loss for tax purposes, your survivor spouse receives your estate tax-free. This doesn't mean your estate is ultimately tax-free. It simply means that taxes are not payable until your spouse dies in turn. At that point, taxes are due. A similar transfer of your property can occur during your lifetime (ITA 73(1)).

A *spousal trust* is defined in paragraph 104(4)(a) of the ITA. It is essentially a relationship where a person or trustee has legal ownership, control and management of property that is held for the benefit of another person or beneficiary. Accordingly, you can elect to have your assets transferred under a trust agreement to provide an income to your spouse. This can be done at the time of your death and directed through your will—a *testamentary trust*, or, during your lifetime—an *inter vivos trust*. To be designated as a spousal trust it must have been created by a Canadian resident for the benefit of his or her spouse. The spouse must be the sole beneficiary of all the trust income and be the only person who receives either income or capital or both while the transferee spouse is living.

REVENUE CANADA TAXATION AND FINAL ESTATE SETTLEMENTS

The real trouble with taxation begins with the death of both spouses. Unless there are dependent children involved or complicated business issues to resolve, the cumulative value of your estate is taxed at your marginal rate at death, and, depending on the size of your estate, could be taxed at the highest individual marginal tax rate. Where your estate is valued at hundreds of thousands of dollars or more, your tax bill could easily run into hundreds of thousands of dollars as well. If you and your spouse do not mind giving a large portion of your estate to Revenue Canada, you can stop here and proceed to Chapter Nine of this book. But, very few hard working Canadians would allow a major portion of a lifetime of effort and hard work to simply vanish in the form of a gratuitous payment to our federal and provincial governments. This is the thrust of estate planning—capital preservation in the face of excessive income tax. Here are the strategies that Canadians use to help preserve the value of their estates.

The Will

A will is a document that outlines in detail your personal wishes regarding the disposition of your assets at death. It gives, in unmistakable terms, the conditions, direction and circumstances of the disposition of your estate. The will also allows your executors to expedite the estate settlement process at the lowest possible cost. In addition to these issues, your will:

- names a legal guardian for the care of minors, in particular, a child or other non-arm's length dependent
- appoints executors to deal with estate matters
- provides income for your survivors during the estate settlement process
- directs specific legacies such as gifts of property, money, money realized from the sale of property, and gifts from the residual capital after tax and expenses
- makes special provisions for the easy, unencumbered care of children
- minimizes taxes, for example, in the case of the election to establish a spousal trust (a testamentary spousal trust is established through the will)
- can create a provision for disinheritance, where applicable
- can avoid the inconvenience and cost associated with the posting of a performance bond as is required by most provinces to process an intestate estate.

Principal Residence Exemption

Most couples who own a home register it in joint tenancy. On the death of one spouse, his or her interest in the home is transferred to the surviving spouse on a tax-deferred or rollover basis. But, unlike many other kinds of estate assets, if the home is designated a *principal residence,* even though it is deemed disposed of as a result of the death of the surviving spouse, no income tax applies to the proceeds of the disposition.

Care must be given to ensure that your home retains its status as a principal residence. To be denoted a principal residence, a home must be owned and inhabited by the taxpayer and the land on which the house sits must not exceed a certain size. Second, for 1982 and beyond, only one home may be deemed a principal residence. Prior to 1982, both spouses could own a home and designate each as a principal residence.

Joint Ownership of Property

Jointly held property is of two kinds: *joint tenancy* and *tenancy-in-common.* At death, a joint tenant's interests automatically transfers to the survivor. Under a tenancy-in-common agreement, the deceased individual can leave his or her interest in a property to a specified beneficiary other than his or her original tenant-in-common.

Where joint tenancy is between spouses, the interest of a deceased spouse transfers free of tax to the surviving spouse by way of the spousal rollover provision. Since the interests of the deceased spouse bypasses his or her estate, no provincial processing fees or probate is payable on that interest.

It is important to ensure that the property you wish to hold in joint ownership is held equally. This equivalence test can be a valuable ally when dealing with property that is not so easily determined to be held in joint ownership, for example, jointly held bank accounts between a parent and a child.

Gifts, Income Splitting and Loans

Income splitting is often used to shift income earned by a highly taxed spouse to a spouse or child who pays tax at a significantly lower marginal rate. The end result, of course, is a lower tax bill for all taxpayers. Three examples of income splitting are spousal RRSP contributions, split CPP benefits and registered education savings plans (RESPs).

Revenue Canada does not like income splitting. Lower marginal tax rates mean less tax collected. To combat taxpayers' attempts to income split, Revenue Canada instituted special anti-avoidance regulations called *attribution rules*. What these rules do is limit the ability of family members to shift income among themselves. These rules seek to attribute income, and the tax that goes along with it, back to the individual who originally earned the income in question. The mechanics of attribution are summarized below:

- Where an individual has either transferred or loaned property to a spouse, all income, gains and losses generated by that property is attributed back to the transferor or lender.
- Where an individual transfers or lends property to a minor (someone who has yet to reach his or her eighteenth year) and is either not at arm's length or is a niece or nephew of the transferor or lender, all income will be attributed to the transferor or lender. Capital gains and losses are exempt from attribution in this instance.
- Where property is transferred or lent to a designated person named in a family trust, income is attributed back to the transferor or lender. The designated person can be a spouse, a non-arm's length child under age 18 or a niece or nephew of the transferor or lender who has yet to reach his or her eighteenth birthday.
- Attribution rules also apply to transfers and loans of property to corporations, where it can be proven that the intention of the transfer or loan was to reduce taxes payable by the transferor or lender and to benefit a designated person who holds at least 10 per cent of the

issued shares of the corporation concerned. Attribution also applies to a trust that holds at least 10 per cent of a corporation's issued shares and at least one beneficiary of the trust is a spouse, non-arm's length minor, niece or nephew. Attribution is suspended if the corporation involved retains its identity as a small business corporation (SBC). Special care should be exercised when looking at making a transfer of property or a loan to a corporation because of the potential for double taxation.

- Where property is transferred or loaned to adult children or other non-arm's length persons who have reached the age of majority and there is either no interest charged or the rate charged is below the rate prescribed by Revenue Canada at the time the loan was made, attribution of income will flow back to the transferor or lender. All loan interest must be paid within 30 days of the end of each year.

The attribution rules were implemented to thwart income shifts among family members while living. They were also instituted to curb the shifting of assets indiscriminately for estate planning purposes. Imagine if taxpayers could simply gift, transfer or loan property to family members now, without penalty, and then sidestep taxation at death and provincial probate levies. Attribution puts an effective stop to these kinds of evasive maneuvers.

Revenue Canada Taxation, however, does allow a number of good income-splitting techniques that allow you to reduce income tax. I've listed several of the more common income splitting techniques below:

- If an individual runs a business, he or she can hire family members who are old enough to work and pay each a reasonable salary. In this case, the business deducts salaries as an expense and distributes company profits around the family. Family members earn an income and they can contribute portions of their respective salaries to an RRSP. Where the business is an incorporated company, family members can become directors and receive directors fees as well.
- An income split can be achieved where a lower income spouse inherits a tangible asset of value, such as jewelery. The spouse who earns a high income can purchase the tangible asset from the lower income spouse and the latter can invest the proceeds of the sale. The high-income spouse can purchase the item involved with cash saved from earned income or, where there is a dearth of available cash, can give the lower income spouse a promissory note with interest accrual set at Revenue Canada prescribed interest rates to be paid not later than 30 days after year-end. There is no attribution of earnings on the lower income spouse's investments.
- Where capital property is transferred from one spouse to another, outside of the spousal rollover provision, it will trigger the appropriate

amount of gains or losses. These items will be attributed to the transferor spouse, but once attributed, any future gains or losses will be attributed to the spouse to whom the property was transferred. Where there are no accrued gains, as with cash and cash equivalents, no attribution occurs.

- Another way of beating future attribution is for the transferor spouse to pay tax on any interest, dividends or capital gain dividends earned and allocate those after tax earnings to his or her lower income spouse. There is no attribution of subsequent earnings on transferred after-tax earnings.

- Attribution rules do not apply to income generated from a business. If the business is incorporated, however, any income is the product of shares or property held by the corporation. We've noted one exception under the SBC provision.

- Of course, attribution rules do not apply to outright gifts of property to adult children. This is in contrast to loans where earnings are attributed back to the lender.

- Attribution rules do not apply to property that is transferred or loaned to minors by way of a trust and earns capital gains.

- If a grandparent or other relative lives outside of Canada, the non-resident relative can transfer or lend capital to a trust on behalf of minor children or grandchildren without attribution. Attribution rules only apply to Canadian residents.

Charitable Gifts

Charitable gifts are either *inter vivos* or testamentary. If testamentary, it means that the deceased person's estate can make a charitable gift of any amount and can carry-forward the tax credit for up to five years. A gift made in the deceased's will also means that it is a tax-deductible item to be used against the deceased's income in the year of death. Gifts made by the deceased outside of the will, but in the year of death, are deductible against income of the preceding tax year. Subsection 118.1(1) of the ITA states that gifts made by the individual are limited to a maximum of 20 per cent of the individual's earned income, unless such gifts are to the Crown or represent cultural property.

There are 13 ways to gift, today, which will provide various tax savings. They are outlined in Figure 8.2.

Figure 8.2

Charitable Gifts and their Relative Tax Savings

Type of Gift	Benefits to Charity	Benefits to Donor	Acceptable Assets	Qualified Recipients	Market
Cash	Immediate use, liquid, no risk	Tax receipt for full amount	Cash or cash equivalents	Any charity or foundation	Anyone willing to give up principal plus potential earnings
Securities	Immediate use, liquid, no risk	Tax receipt for fair market value, possible avoidance of tax on capital gains	Stocks, bonds and related securities	Any charity or foundation	Anyone willing to give up ownership of securities and the dividends that such securities earn
Real Estate	After property sold, proceeds are available, choice of retaining property	Tax receipt for fair market value, possible avoidance on capital gains	Real estate	Any charitable organization or foundation that can manage real estate	Owners over age 50 who own a principal residence or investment property who don't need the asset or proceeds of sale of such an asset
Certified Cultural Property	Immediately available for display or exhibition	Tax receipt for fair market value (FMV) determined by appraisal, 100% contribution limit, no tax on capital gain	Art works, artifacts and historic structures certified by the Cultural Property Review Board (CPRB)	Universities, museums and other institutions certified by the CPRB	Owners age 50 and above who want to preserve cultural treasures within Canada

Figure 8.2

Charitable Gifts and their Relative Tax Savings (*Continued*)

Type of Gift	Benefits to Charity	Benefits to Donor	Acceptable Assets	Qualified Recipients	Market
Tangible Personal Property	Retained or sold and proceeds used for other purposes	Tax receipt for FMV and possible tax avoidance on capital gains	Art works, furniture, equipment, collections, automobiles and other such objects	Any charitable institution or foundation	Owners age 50 or beyond who no longer intend to use objects in question
Life Insurance (Charity is Owner)	Access to policy cash value, assured of proceeds on death of the insured	Tax receipt for cash value and all premiums paid, smaller current outlay leveraged into larger future gift	Any whole life, universal life or term policy	Any charitable institution or foundation	Individuals aged 30 to 60 who have an older insurance policy that is no longer needed or who want to make a large donation but have limited resources
Life Insurance (Charity Named as Beneficiary but not Owner)	Receives death proceeds unless donor changes beneficiary	Provide a future gift while retaining full control of the policy, tax receipt if donor has death proceeds paid to estate and provides a bequest of an equivalent amount	Any whole life or term policy	Any charitable institution or foundation	Individuals whose personal needs and family situation may be subject to change
Interest-Free Loan	Provides capital for building or investment without interest costs applied	Principal recoverable at any time, interest earned on loaned funds not taxable to donor	Cash	Charitable institutions but not foundations	Individuals who have enough current income but want to preserve capital for their own future security and/or heirs

Figure 8.2

Charitable Gifts and their Relative Tax Savings (*Continued*)

Type of Gift	Benefits to Charity	Benefits to Donor	Acceptable Assets	Qualified Recipients	Market
Charitable Gift Annuity (Self-Insured)	Irrevocable gift of remaining principal after making required payments	Guaranteed life payments, all or most tax-free, possible tax receipt for a portion of the contribution	Cash or marketable securities	Charitable institutions authorized under provincial law to issue gift annuities	Donors who are 65 years or older who want guaranteed income
Charitable Gift Annuity (Reinsured)	Irrevocable gift of that contribution portion retained after purchasing annuity	Guaranteed life payments, all or most tax-free, possible tax receipt for a portion of the contribution	Cash or marketable securities	Any charitable institution or foundation with the capability of administering an annuity program	Donors who are 65 years or older who want guaranteed income
Residual Interest In Real Estate or Works of Art	Irrevocable future gift of property	Ability to continue to use property for life or specific number of years, tax receipt for present value of residual interest, avoidance of tax on a portion of or all of capital gain, property is probate-free	Principal residence, other real estate, and works of art	Any charitable institution or foundation	Individuals age 60 or more who would otherwise give the property in question under their will

Figure 8.2
Charitable Gifts and their Relative Tax Savings (*Continued*)

Type of Gift	Benefits to Charity	Benefits to Donor	Acceptable Assets	Qualified Recipients	Market
Charitable Remainder Trust	Irrevocable future gift of remaining principal	Net income from property for life or specified number of years, tax receipt for present value of remainder interest, avoidance of tax on part or all capital gains, property is probate free	Cash, securities and real estate	Any charitable institution or foundation	Individuals over age 60 who want to make a future gift and obtain present tax relief, but who want to preserve investment income for themselves and/or a survivor
Bequest	Future gift provided the donor's will is not changed	Provides a future gift while retaining full control of property, tax receipt for final income tax return, possible avoidance of tax on a portion or all of capital gain when bequest consists of appreciated property	Cash, securities, real estate, tangible personal property	Any charitable institution or foundation	All individuals, but especially older individuals with few or no heirs

Trusts

A trust has been defined as a *fiduciary relationship between a trustee, who is given property by a settlor on certain conditions, and a beneficiary, in whose favour the property is to be held.* It is a relationship of trust between appointed *trustees* who act in the *capacity* as trustees on behalf of a specified beneficiary. The settlor is the person who provides the property and the rules for the trust; the beneficiary is often a spouse, child or grandchild; while the trustee is appointed to manage the business of the trust relationship relative to the trust rules.

Trusts are created most often to protect the assets and income of a disabled spouse, a disabled child or dependant, and for a spouse or adult child in the event of the death of the settlor.

A simple example of an "informal" trust is the case of a grandparent who gifts $1,000 to a grandchild to help fund his or her university education. There exists the express condition that the money is to be held on behalf of the grandchild until his or her eighteenth birthday, at which time the money becomes the property of the grandchild. In this example, the grandparent is the settlor, the grandchild is the beneficiary, and you, the parent, are the trustee. The grandparent's intent is to provide property, in this instance $1,000, to be held for the educational benefit of the beneficiary. This intent is essentially the reason for the trust and the trust agreement. This would be an example of an *inter vivos trust* or a trust that was established while the settlor is living.

A *testamentary trust* is the most common form of trust because it is established after the death of the settlor and through the settlor's will. The spousal trust is typically a testamentary trust and allows for the rollover of the deceased spouse's assets to his or her surviving spouse on a tax-deferred basis. A testamentary trust also allows a parent to direct and transfer the proceeds of the estate to his or her children.

Generally, trusts allow you to:

- avoid provincial probate levies
- protect the future welfare of a spouse, child or other non-arm's length person
- creditor-proof certain assets or entitlements on behalf of family members
- assure the survival of estate assets beyond the death of the settlor
- have access to professional trust management through a trust company
- protect a business until a decision has been made to include or exclude children as beneficiaries and, ultimately, as owners of the company.

Capital Gains Exemption for Qualifying Small Business Corporations (QSBC)

Under current tax law, a provision is made for qualifying small business corporations to be sold or transferred on a tax-free basis providing the realized capital gain does not exceed $500,000. What Revenue Canada means by "qualifying small business " is convoluted and technical. The upshot of this exemption, however, is that you can save substantial amounts of income tax when selling or transfering the ownership of your QSBC while you are living or upon death. Of course, care must be taken to avoid entangling oneself in the attribution rules.

Capital Gains Exemption for Family Farms

If you are a Canadian resident and own and operate a farm, as defined by the ITA, your property is eligible for a $500,000 capital gains exemption as well. This exemption applies to the sale or transfer of your farm property, shares of a family farm corporation and interests in family farm partnerships. The same caution regarding attribution applies in this case, too.

Special Farm Rollovers

Where the principal business of your property is farming and you depend on the successful operation of the farm to provide the necessities of life, generally speaking, you can make an election to transfer ownership to your children or grandchildren without triggering income tax. This tax-free transfer can be done during your lifetime or at death. There are a number of stringent rules that govern this rollover and the rollover can be revoked later if these rules are transgressed.

The Estate Freeze

Of all of the tax-reducing maneuvers available today, the estate freeze is the most complicated. The estate freeze is a means of freezing future growth on your investments or property and transferring the potential for future growth to other family members. By implementing this maneuver, you know what capital gains you will incur and the taxes your estate will pay at death. The estate freeze gives you advance notice as to how to prepare for any eventual tax liability as well as transfer ownership of certain property to other family members without triggering any immediate tax liability.

An estate freeze might be applied where a parent owns all of the shares of a growing business, while his or her children are also employees of the business. The parent wants to retire in five years, but the business is increasingly profitable and is expanding rapidly. Knowing that his or her children will eventually be taking control of the business, the parent freezes the value of the company's shares now so as to avoid increasing the future tax liability of the firm upon the transition to the children at his or her death. Any future gains made by the business will be deferred in the hands of the children.

Shareholder Agreements

Where you are a shareholder among several shareholders of a private company, you can be party to what are known as shareholder agreements or buy-sell agreements, which deal with the consequences of share ownership at death. Where there is no shareholder agreement, on the death of the shareholder, his or her interest transfers to the surviving spouse or children. Where this is not acceptable, a shareholder agreement is drawn up to determine what is to happen to the deceased's interest in the company. This agreement can be particularly helpful in quickly resolving a deceased's interest in the company, allowing it and the surviving shareholders to continue the operations of the firm. What the deceased or the estate will receive is based on the funding mechanism involved and how income tax is to be dealt with. Corporately sponsored life insurance is one of the most common means of funding the purchase of a deceased shareholder's interest in the company.

Life Insurance

The role of life insurance in estate planning is tough to over-estimate. Adequate amounts of life insurance can fund even the most extreme income tax liabilities. The focus of life insurance is to provide funds to the estate and, eventually, to survivor beneficiaries. Life insurance proceeds can provide immediate cash that can be used to:

- provide adequate cash to cover living expenses for beneficiaries such as a surviving spouse
- cover funeral expenses of the deceased
- pay outstanding debts or indebtedness incurred by the deceased
- pay outstanding property taxes and income tax on estate proceeds
- cover estate settlement costs, including accounting, administration and legal costs and provincial probate fees
- provide specific cash bequests to designated heirs, including charitable institutions and foundations
- provide instant estate liquidity
- fund buy-sell agreements.

Segregated Funds

Segregated investment funds are the latest wrinkle to envelope Canada's mutual fund manufacturers. By investing in these funds, you can avoid provincial probate costs or administrative processing fees normally applied to the net value of your estate. The reason segregated funds can do this is because, as investments, they fall under insurance contracts which normally by-pass the probate fee process. In addition to being able to avoid probate, segregated investment funds offer a capital guarantee of up to 100 per cent of the original invested capital. So, where you invest $25,000 in year one, you are guaranteed to receive at least your $25,000 back should stock markets fail or you die. Many investors buy segregated funds because of this capital guarantee. But, before buying them, read the fine print. Special conditions apply and will sometimes vary dramatically between companies.

Other Items

Other less common, yet important items that can be used to offset taxes at death are *reserves* (applied on the disposition of capital property), *net capital losses, capital loss carry-backs,* and the *preferred beneficiary election.*

Capital reserves are profits that were realized in one year, but were not actually received until the subsequent tax year. You are allowed to set up a capital reserve for the subsequent tax year and, thereby, defer income tax on those profits.

Net capital losses are investment losses that you incurred on an investment, where the amount of capital loss you incurred exceeded your taxable capital gains in that year. When you carry-forward such losses to future years, they are known as net capital losses.

A capital loss carry-back is the same as a net capital loss, except that a taxpayer can carry-back any losses to previous years where a taxable capital gain has been earned. In this instance, capital losses can be carried back for up to three years.

The preferred beneficiary election occurs where an individual is designated the sole recipient of income from an *inter vivos* trust. Under this arrangement, the preferred beneficiary is taxed on trust income, while the trust gets to deduct the income paid for tax purposes.

CHAPTER NINE

THIRTY HINTS FOR RETIREMENT RICHES

A great deal of material has been covered in the first eight chapters of this book. However, no one book could ever hope to encapsulate all of the ideas that could be included under the topic of retirement planning. The field is simply too vast.

The preceding chapters of my book have given you pertinent details of the tactics and techniques that you can use to help get you started on the path to a financially secure retirement.

This ninth and final chapter is an outline of the key steps on which you can focus to help provide order to an otherwise complicated and potentially overwhelming topic.

THIRTY HINTS FOR RETIREMENT RICHES
Step # 1—Don't rely on government-sponsored pensions.

It's time to wake up and recognize the fact that, someday in the not too distant future, government-sponsored pension plans will no longer provide sufficient supplementary retirement income. Most, if not all, financial planners today, refuse to include benefits from CPP, OAS or other supplementary pension income in their retirement income calculations. Neither should you. The fact is government is planning to reduce and eventually eliminate its commitment to long-term pension funding. They will do this through a reduction in benefits, increased taxes and participation restrictions over a 10 to 15 year time frame.

Step # 2—Invest wisely.

Remember the six keys to retirement wealth.
- Allocating your investment assets properly will help make your capital accumulation programme efficient and enjoyable.
- Making regular contributions to your investments will help build a long-term savings and investment habit.
- Having sufficient time to accumulate sufficient amounts of retirement capital will ensure you achieve your retirement goal.
- Remember the corrosive effects of inflation. A dollar earned today is worth much more than the same dollar earned 10 years down the road. You will need more money at retirement to produce an income equivalent to the income you enjoy now.

- Always be prepared to implement measures that reduce the amount of income tax you pay. Like inflation, too much income tax can reduce the size of your retirement nest egg by inhibiting your savings and investment capabilities.
- Be prepared to monitor and maintain your long-term capital accumulation plan. The many circumstances that impact on the power of money can enhance as well as deter your ability to build sufficient retirement capital. Be prepared to alter your plan whenever required.

Step # 3—Understand your risk comfort zone.

Take the time to fully understand the nature of investment risk. Risk means different things to different people. Analyze your present financial situation, how you spend and save, your knowledge of investments and your investment comfort zone. Then, identify those investments with which you are comfortable and examine ways to make the most efficient use of each.

Step # 4—Learn about rates of return.

Like investment risk, take the time to learn which investments have generated the highest investment returns and why. Be particularly vigilant of the fact that investment rates of return will vary from year to year, and the fact that generally, the higher the rate of return earned by an investment, the greater the risk of loss of value of your original invested capital.

Step # 5—Develop your own risk-reward formula.

Relate investment rates of return to your understanding of risk and determine which level of risk and the rate of return with which you are comfortable. Once you have constructed your own formula that accounts for an acceptable amount of risk-reward, discover which investments fit the bill.

Step # 6—Diversify your investments.

When constructing your long-term retirement accumulation portfolio, always choose securities from several asset classes. Each asset class represents securities that can contribute positively to some aspect of your current financial situation. Diversifying your investment capital across different securities provides growth opportunities and reduces the amount of risk you expose your capital to over time.

Step # 7—Use dollar cost averaging to build your portfolio.

Always save and invest on a systematic basis over the long term. Enlist the help of dollar cost averaging to ensure that you average out the purchase cost of securities comprising your investment portfolio. Over the long term, dollar cost averaging can enhance your rate of return by one to two per cent per year, depending on the securities purchased.

Step # 8—Make lump sum investments to build your portfolio faster.

Lump sum investing is an efficient way of building the value of your retirement nest egg. A lump sum of cash will compound much faster than a smaller amount. The more capital you can put to work early in your capital accumulation plan, the faster it will appreciate in value. The long-term effects of a lump sum investment are particularly effective towards the last few years of an investment cycle.

Step # 9—Use other people's money, but carefully!

Borrowing capital to invest or leveraging is one of the more effective ways of building capital over the long term. Providing you are willing to assume the risks associated with using other people's money to make money for you, leveraged investing can be a particularly attractive means of building your retirement nest egg. A large lump sum grows faster than systematic investing. There are numerous tax benefits in the form of deductible loan interest and tax-deferred capital gains.

The downside of leveraged investments, however, sometimes outweighs the benefits. Stock markets can be uncooperative and provide little growth of capital. Your lender could get nervous and call in your loan at the most inopportune time. Losses could occur, which you have to pay for, often over long periods of time at significant expense.

Step # 10—Use the principles of RMT™ to take advantage of fluctuating prices.

Risk Master Technology™ is a risk-averse method of investing at any time during the course of a standard business cycle. It allows investors to apply the best features of the "buy and hold" approach to investing and the best features of "market timing." Both investment methods are combined to allow investors to invest without unnecessary regard for where stock markets are headed and how they perform. In fact, *RMT*™ outperforms in volatile stock markets over flat ones, taking advantage of fluctuating securities prices. The more volatile the index becomes, the more money you make.

Risk Master Technology™ is an ideal solution to those problems inherent in leveraged investments. Under this concept, the chances of a margin call or loan retraction is minimized, the negative impact of excessive volatility is thwarted, and the chances of losing your original invested capital is dramatically reduced.

Step # 11—Calculate your ideal retirement income and how much capital you'll need.

Know how to calculate what capital you will need to generate a sufficient retirement income. To do this, you have to first identify those expenses you have today that you will likely not have when you retire. Add these expenses together and express them as a percentage of your existing budget. Deduct this percentage from 100 per cent and this will give you the approximate percentage of income you will need on retirement. Find what your current income will amount to in today's dollars at retirement based on a long-term inflation rate of three per cent, and work backwards to determine the amount of capital you will need to generate your required income at eight per cent withdrawal per year.

Step # 12—Build flexibility into your retirement plan.

There are three major sources of income from which you can draw at retirement. The first is employer-sponsored pension plans or RPPs. The second is government pensions such as CPP, OAS and GIS. The third and most important is investment assets. RPPs and government pensions provide fixed levels of periodic income, which is usually indexed to inflation. Some flexibility is provided by RPPs through various commutation and transfer options. CPP and OAS benefits provide no flexibility whatsoever. The best source of retirement income comes from your own accumulated investments, be they registered in the form of RRSPs or otherwise. When building your retirement nest egg, focus on building retirement assets outside of RPPs, CPP and OAS—even outside of your home. Two of the biggest concerns you'll have when you retire are capital flexibility and liquidity.

Step # 13—Minimize income tax payable wherever you can.

One of the biggest inhibitors of financial security in Canada is personal income tax. Unfortunately, this problem becomes even more problematic in retirement since retirement income is usually lower and, if mostly pension income, inflexible. Ensure that you enlist the help of every tax saving device available and be prepared to decrease, defer and eliminate taxation whenever possible. Learn how to income split with your spouse or other dependants. Generate tax-preferred and tax-free investment income. Push income tax liabilities into the future. The longer you put off paying tax, the more money you have to spend now. Make use of all available deductions and tax credits. Pay particular attention to capital rollovers. They can save you thousands of tax dollars.

Step # 14—Protect your assets and your family.

Protecting your assets is a key point of every retirement plan. Having an appropriate amount of disability and life insurance while you are working to accumulate retirement capital will protect your spouse and dependants by providing adequate income protection should you become sick, hurt or die prematurely.

Disability income insurance will provide an income equivalent to your after-tax salary, for example, should you be unable to continue performing your regular duties due to accident or sickness. This insurance guarantees your income so that you and your dependants can continue to live without fear of destitution or compromising your long-term retirement capital accumulation programme.

Life insurance will provide readily available cash for your survivors in the event of your premature death. It can also provide a cash lump sum that will help your survivors maintain their lifestyle without interruption. Life insurance can pay all of the costs of settling your estate, such as accounting, administration, legal and probate costs, including federal and provincial income tax. By doing so, you leave your accumulated life assets intact for your spouse and children.

Step # 15—Keep up-to-date on government pension plans.

Always note the particulars of today's rules pertaining to CPP, OAS, GIS and SPA benefits and what they can and cannot do for you. Are you eligible for one or more of these benefits? If so, how much pre-tax income can you expect and when? If married, will your spouse be eligible for such benefits? Will CPP benefits be harmonized with your company pension? If so, how much of a loss will you suffer, if any?

These and related questions will have to be addressed before you can tally what the overall impact of government-sponsored pension income will be.

Step # 16—Understand and take advantage of your company's pension plan.

Make a point of knowing what kind of employer-sponsored pension plan you have and how your benefits are calculated. Before retiring, make sure you know your options regarding pension commutation and transfers of commuted amounts. Determine whether it is in your best interests to leave your company before your compulsory retirement date or whether you should elect to retire and accept your periodic pension.

Pay particular attention to how your plan benefits change when you decease. Will your surviving spouse or other dependant receive your full pension entitlement? If so, will your entitlement continue to flow as a periodic pension to your surviving spouse or will he or she receive a cash lump sum? If your spouse can elect to continue receiving your pension entitlement, is the pension amount reduced? If so, by how much? How will receiving CPP benefits affect receipt of your RPP benefits?

Step # 17—Determine the income tax liabilities of different withdrawal scenarios.

Always determine whether it is good policy to access your registered investments such as RRSPs, LRRSPs and registered deferred annuities before any other non-registered asset. Income tax accrues to proceeds from registered plans and, except for the pension tax credit, can rarely be reduced. Using proceeds from non-registered investments first will often provide you with many different ways of keeping income tax at a minimum. Try different combinations to ensure that you continue to receive adequate amounts of retirement income without paying an inordinate amount of personal income tax.

Step # 18—Investigate annuities.

Sometimes owning either a registered or non-registered annuity can have significant benefits. As a non-registered source of retirement income, tax savings can be achieved by prescribing annuity income. Where annuity interest rates are abnormally high, you can lock into these rates for long periods of time, up to 20 years or for as long as you live.

The drawback of owning an annuity is that it robs you of any control, flexibility or capital liquidity. These can be a high price to pay for the tax savings non-registered annuities offer and the potential for locking-in high interest rates.

Step # 19—Analyze the best non-registered sources of income for you.

Recall that non-registered resources fall into three separate income formats: capital preservation-high income, capital preservation-growth and income, and capital preservation-high growth and tax-preferred income. The first format is designed to give you high pre-tax income and capital preservation. The second format is designed to provide you with high pre-tax income, capital preservation as well as some long-term capital preservation. The third income format is designed to provide you with capital preservation, high growth potential and moderate levels of tax-preferred income. These three categories should be used to pre-classify the kinds of non-registered investments you have and help determine which investment formats best suit your current and future income needs.

Step # 20—Keep both income and growth potential in mind.

When deciding how to generate retirement income from your accumulated retirement assets, you should review the income-generating capacity of each asset. Ascertain the liquidity and flexibility of each asset as well.

Most investments will provide you with income to one degree or another, but only a few assets or securities can provide both income as well as additional long-term growth potential.

A truly superior investment is one that generates a good income level, will offer inflation-protection in the form of future growth potential, and attracts above-average tax savings. This kind of investment is the preferred investment for anyone facing retirement.

Choosing securities from a broad selection of investments provides you with an above-average chance to select the most appropriate investments. It also supplies you with an entire range of investment rates of return from which to choose.

Step # 21—Create a SWP using mutual funds.

Managed investments such as mutual funds offer some of the best non-registered investment income options available. Full and partial lump sum withdrawals provide you with excellent capital liquidity and flexibility. Dividend payments and occasional capital gain distributions provide excellent tax-preferred income. A systematic withdrawal plan (SWP) in the form of a ratio, fixed dollar, and life expectancy withdrawal programme can address inflation, while providing high rates of return, below average investment volatility, capital preservation, tax savings and investment diversification.

Make sure you consider each SWP option to ensure you take advantage of at least one for your retirement income strategy.

Step # 22—Keep the big picture in mind.

Your choice of retirement income options will always depend on the larger context of your lifestyle needs and wants, your familial obligations, your marital status, your health, the health of your spouse and any deemed dependants, your current and future tax liability and the nature of your retirement assets.

Step # 23—Careful estate planning is essential.

It is important to remember that, unless there is a surviving spouse or dependant beneficiary, all of your assets are considered "liquidated" for tax purposes and must be included in income in the year of your death. In many cases, your marginal tax rate will escalate to the maximum allowable and up to 50 per cent of your accumulated retirement assets could head off to government coffers. It is therefore absolutely critical to ensure that appropriate estate planning techniques be applied so as to reduce income tax to the absolute minimum.

It is also necessary to have a proper will in place to ensure that your wishes as to disposition of a direction of assets are made clear to the courts. Otherwise, your estate will be turned over to a government agency and distributed according to accepted standard procedure, without due regard to your family members or to income tax that might otherwise have been avoided.

Step # 24—Defer taxes by naming your spouse as beneficiary.

When dealing with registered assets such as RRSPs, LRRSPs, LIRAs and registered deferred annuities, always name your spouse as the direct beneficiary. By doing so, your registered assets remain intact and avoid going to your estate to be taxed at your highest marginal rate.

The spousal rollover provision would normally protect your registered assets from this kind of occurrence, however, it would require a petition on the part of your surviving spouse to have the estate removed as the beneficiary of your registered assets. Do it right the first time.

Step # 25—Ensure your will is kept up-to-date.

If you do not have a will, get one. If you have a will, be prepared to update its contents whenever there has been a change in financial or personal circumstances that will substantially alter your current or future circumstances.

Step 26—Hold non-registered assets in joint tenancy.

Always hold non-registered assets in joint tenancy. This assures that your interest in the asset will transfer automatically to the surviving joint tenant upon your death. By doing so, you avoid provincial probate costs and potential tax liabilities to the estate.

Step 27—Remember attribution roles when considering a gift, loan or income split.

Be aware of the attribution rules when considering making a gift, a loan, or setting up an income split with a spouse or other non-arm's length person. If you do not understand the attribution rules, any income or gain you might have wished to go to some other family member could be attributed back to you for tax purposes. Where the attributed income is substantial, and you already pay tax at a high marginal rate, the consequences of such attribution could be devastating.

Step 28—Use charitable giving wisely.

Charitable gifts can be used effectively to generate good income, receive a generous tax benefit and retain control of your asset until after you have deceased. Make sure your estate plan has accounted for this important tax-planning item.

Step # 29—Consider the use of trusts, where applicable.

The use of trusts can be a great way to protect your disabled spouse or dependant in the event of your premature death. Trusts also allow you to avoid probate fees, provide creditor proofing to certain assets, preserve the value of your estate beyond your death and protect your business from interlopers and the dispossessed.

Step # 30—Investigate all available tax-saving maneuvers.

Make sure you remember to investigate special capital gain exemptions, farm rollovers, estate freezes and shareholder agreements. The judicious use of these important estate planning maneuvers can save you and your beneficiaries tens of thousands of precious tax dollars.

Now that you have come to the end of this book, I hope you have gained a perspective on how important it is to plan for your eventual retirement, today. Our parents were the first generation of Canadians to be able to retire secure in the knowledge that, if everything else failed, they could depend at least on a minimum income standard based on federal government pension plans. Nowadays, a basic guaranteed income is no longer assured. Unfortunately, for every Canadian, today, the onus to provide adequately for one's retirement is placed squarely on his or her shoulders. To not do so would be a big gamble and, I think, a mistake. The signs are already here that our government is fully prepared to knock down its commitment to public pension funding and to tell you and I that it has no further interest in providing for its citizens upon retirement. This fact is clear. Don't lose out. Make sure you have your retirement capital accumulation plan in place and make sure you follow through so that you, too, can count yourself among those Canadians who will be financially well-prepared for what could truly be the best years of your life.

RETIREMENT PLANNING RESOURCES

The following information has been included to provide you with a readily available set of references to assist those of you who may have already retired or who are in the process of doing so. This list of references is a comprehensive one and covers such important retirement concerns as health, insurance, investment, government & private pensions, and taxation. Every attempt has been made to ensure the accuracy of this material. If for whatever reason you discover that certain references below have changed since the publication of this book, please feel free to contact the author at your earliest convenience.

HEALTH ISSUES
Federal

Canadian Clearing House on Disability Issues
Status of Disabled Persons
Secretariat
Human Resources Development
Canada
Ottawa, Ontario K1A 0M5
1-800-665-9017

Health Canada
Communications
25 St. Clair Avenue East,
4th Floor
Toronto, Ontario M4T 1M2
(416) 954-9021

National Advisory Council on Aging
Third Floor
473 Albert Street
Ottawa, Ontario K1A 0K9
(613) 957-1968

Provincial

Alberta:

Canadian Red Cross Society
Alberta & Northwest Territories
Division
737-13th Avenue Southwest
Calgary, Ontario T2R 1J1
(403) 541-4400

Seniors Policy and Programs
Women's and Seniors' Secretariat
Alberta Community Development
16th Floor, Standard Life Centre
10405 Jasper Avenue
Edmonton, Alberta
T5J 3N4
(403) 427-6358

British Columbia:

Canadian Red Cross Society
British Columbia and Yukon
Division
Room 400, 4710 Kings Way Street
Burnaby, British Columbia
V5H 4M2
(604) 431-4200

**Ministry of Health and
Ministry Responsible for Seniors**
Bag Service 3003
Victoria, British Columbia
V8W 3L4
1-800-665-7108

Office for Seniors
Ministry of Health and
Ministry Responsible for Seniors
6th Floor, 1515 Blanshard Street
Victoria, British Columbia
V8W 3C8
(604) 952-1238

Manitoba:

Canad9ian Red Cross Society
Manitoba Division
236 Osborne Street North
Winnipeg, Manitoba
R3C 1V4
(204) 982-7359

Deaf Centre Manitoba
285 Pembina Highway
Winnipeg, Manitoba R3L 2E1
(204) 284-0802

Manitoba Health
Insured Benefits
599 Empress Street
P.O. Box 925
Winnipeg, Manitoba R3C 2T6
1-800-282-8069

Manitoba Seniors Directorate
Unit 803 – 155 Carleton Street
Winnipeg, Manitoba R3C 3H8
(204) 945-6565

**Income Security Central
Directorate**
301 – 267 Edmonton Street
Winnipeg, Manitoba R3C 1S2
1-800-282-8060

New Brunswick:

Canadian Red Cross Society
New Brunswick Division
405 University Avenue
P.O. Box 39
St. John, New Brunswick
E1C 8R3
(506) 648-5000

Health and Community Services
Family and Community Social
Services
P.O. Box 5001
Moncton, New Brunswick
E1C 8R3
(506) 856-2400

Office for Seniors
Department of Health and
Community Services
P.O. Box 5100
Fredericton, New Brunswick
E3B 5G8
(506) 453-2480

**Pensions and Insured Benefits
Branch**
Department of Finance
P.O. Box 6000
Fredericton, New Brunswick
E3B 5H1
1-800-332-3692

Prescription Drug Program
P.O. Box 690
Moncton, New Brunswick
E1C 8M7
1-800-332-3692

Newfoundland:

Canadian Red Cross Society
7 Wicklow Street
P.O. Box 13156, Station "A"
St. John's, Newfoundland
A1B 4A4
(709) 754-0461

Department of Health
1st Floor, West Block
Confederation Building
P.O. Box 8700
St. John's, Newfoundland
A1B 4J6
1-800-332-3692

Nova Scotia:

Canadian Red Cross Society
1940 Gottingen Street
Halifax, Nova Scotia B3J 3Y2
(902) 423-9181

Disabled Persons Commission
2695 Dutch Village Road, Suite 203
Halifax, Nova Scotia B3L 4T9
1-800-565-8280

The Gerontology Association of Nova Scotia
P.O. Box 952
Halifax Central
Halifax, Nova Scotia B3J 2V9
(902) 465-5578

The Nova Scotia Centre on Aging
Caregiver Resource Library
Suite 310, Tower 1
Halifax Shopping Centre,
P.O. Box 35
7001 Mumford Road
Hailfax, Nova Scotia B3L 4N9
(902) 457-6546

Nova Scotia's Seniors' Information Line
Senior Citizens' Secretariat
1-800-670-0065

Nursing Homes
Homes for the Aged
Department of Health
P.O. Box 488
Halifax, Nova Scotia B3J 2R8
(902) 424-2324

Programs for Seniors
Senior Citizens' Secretariat
4th Floor, Dennis Building
1740 Granville Street
P.O. Box 2065
Halifax, Nova Scotia B3J 2Z1
(902) 424-0065

Ontario:

Canadian Red Cross Society
Ontario Division
Toronto, Ontario M4T 2A1
(416) 480-2500

Ministry of Health
Residential Services Branch
5700 Yonge Street
7th Floor
North York, Ontario M2M 4K5
(416) 482-1111

Prince Edward Island:

Canadian Red Cross Society
Prince Edward Island Division
62 Prince Street
Charlottetown, Prince Edward Island C1A 4R2
(902) 628-6262

Department of Health
Health and Community Services
P.O. Box 2000
Charlottetown, Prince Edward
Island C1A 7N8
(902) 368-6130

Quebec:

Canadian Red Cross Society
Quebec Division
6 Place du Commerce
Ile-des-Soeurs
Montreal, Quebec H3E 1P4
(514) 362-2929

Saskatchewan:

Canadian Red Cross Society
Saskatchewan Division
325-20th Street East
Saskatoon, Saskatchewan
S7K 0A9
(306) 975-8888

Health Insurance Registration
T.C. Douglas Building
3475 Albert Street
Regina, Saskatchewan S4S 6X6
1-800-667-7551

Medical Care Insurance Branch
T.C. Douglas Building
3475 Albert Street
Regina, Saskatchewan S4S 6X6
1-800-667-7581

Drug Plan and Extended Benefits
T.C. Douglas Building
Second Floor
3475 Albert Street
Regina, Saskatchewan S4S 6X6
1-800-667-7581

Saskatchewan Social Services
Income Security Division
T.C. Douglas Building
3475 Albert Street
Regina, Saskatchewan S4S 6X6
1-800-667-7581

Programs Branch
T.C. Douglas Building
3475 Albert Street
Regina, Saskatchewan S4S 6X6
1-800-667-7581

INSURANCE ISSUES

Canadian Life and Health Insurance Association Inc.
(English) 1-800-268-8099
(French) 1-800-361-8070

Toronto
1 Queen Street East
Suite 1700
Toronto, Ontario M5C 2X9
(416) 777-2221

Montreal
1001 Boul. Maisonneuve Ouest
Bureau 630
Montreal, Quebec H3A 3C8
(514) 845-9004

Ottawa
46 Elgin Street
Suite 400
Ottawa, Ontario K1P 5K6
(613) 230-0031

Insurance Bureau of Canada (IBC)
151 Yonge Street, Suite 1800
Toronto, Ontario M5C 2W7
(416) 362-9528

Alberta:
1-800-232-7575

British Columbia:
(604) 684-3635 (can request call-back if out of 604 area)

Manitoba:
1-800-377-6378

Ontario:
(416) 362-2031

Quebec:
1-800-361-5131

Atlantic Provinces:
1-800-565-7189

Liberty Health
(special extended benefits company)
1-800-268-3763

TRAC Insurance Services Limited
(Insurance company rating agency)
133 Richmond Street West, Suite 600
Toronto, Ontario M5H 2L3
(416) 363-8266

FINANCIAL PLANNING & INVESTMENT ISSUES

Canadian Association of Financial Planners
439 University Avenue, Suite 1710
Toronto, Ontario
(416) 943-6907

Canadian Institute of Financial Planning
(Educational Institute for Canadian Financial Planners)
151 Yonge Street, 5th Floor
Toronto, Ontario M5C 2W7
(416) 865-1237

Canadian Securities Institute
(Educational Institute for Canadian Securities Industry)

Calgary
355–4th Avenue S.W.
Suite 2330
Calgary, Alberta T2P 0J1
(403) 262-1791

Montreal
1 Place Ville Marie
Bureau 2840
Montreal, QC H3B 4R4
(514) 878-3591

Toronto
121 King Street West, Suite 1550
P.O. Box 113
Toronto, Ontario M5H 3T9
(416) 364-9130

Vancouver
650 West Georgia Street, Suite 1350
Vancouver, BC V6B 4N8
(604) 683-1338

Investment Dealers Association
(Regulates all member stock brokerages & their brokers)
121 King Street West, Suite 1600
Toronto, Ontario M5H 3T9
(416) 943-6907

Investment Funds Institute of Canada
(Regulates Canadian mutual funds)
151 Yonge Street, 5th Floor
Toronto, Ontario M5C 2W7
(416) 363-2158

PENSIONS

Federal

Human Resources Development Canada
(Contact for all government pension programs)
English 1-800-277-9914
French 1-800-277-9915

Hearing & speech impaired
1-800-255-4786
Internet Address
http://www.hrdc-drhc.gc.ca

Canada Pension Plan
Contact numbers as above

Old Age Security
Contact numbers as above

Guaranteed Income Supplement
Contact numbers as above

Spouse's Allowance
Contact numbers as above

Seniors Benefit
Contact numbers as above

International Social Security Agreements
Contact numbers as above

Veterans Affairs

Ontario Region:
1-800-387-0930 (area code 807)
1-800-387-0919 (all other codes)

Pacific Region:
(604) 666-7942 (Vancouver local)
1-800-663-1931
1-800-253-0239 (Yukon)
1-800-253-1980 (French)

Prairie Region:
(204) 983-7040 (Winnipeg local)
1-800-665-8717

Quebec Region:
(514) 496-2211 (Montreal local)
1-800-361-6867
1-800-361-6868

Atlantic Region:
(902) 426-6448 (Dartmouth local)
1-800-565-1528

Newfoundland (sub-region):
(709) 772-4965 (St. John's local)
1-800-563-9623

Provincial
Pensions and availability vary
from province to province
and you should contact the
appropriate provincial authority
in your area. Some contact numbers are listed under *Health Issues,* outlined earlier in this appendix.

REVENUE CANADA TAXATION & TIPS

NEWFOUNDLAND/ LABRADOR

Newfoundland/Labrador Tax Services Office
165 Duckworth Street
P.O. Box 12075
St. John's NF A1B 4R5
Fax: (709) 754-5928

St. John's Tax Centre
290 Empire Avenue
St. John's NF A1B 3Z1
Fax: (709) 754-3416

PRINCE EDWARD ISLAND

Charlottetown Tax Services Office
94 Euston Street
P.O. Box 8500
Charlottetown PE C1A 8L3
Fax: (902) 368-0248
Tel: 1-800-725-4425

Summerside Tax Centre
275 Pope Road
Summerside PE C1N 5Z7

NOVA SCOTIA

Halifax Tax Services Office
1256 Barrington Street
P.O. Box 638
Halifax NS B3J 2T5
Fax: (902) 426-7170

Sydney Tax Services Office
47 Dorchester Street
P.O. Box 1300
Sydney NS B1P 6K3
Fax (902) 564-3095

NEW BRUNSWICK

Bathurst Tax Services Office
201 St. George Street
Bathurst NB E2A 1B8
Fax: (506) 548-9905

Moncton Tax Services Office
107 - 1600 Main Street
P.O. Box 1070
Moncton NB E1C 8P2
Fax: (506) 851-7018

Saint John Tax Services Office
126 Prince William Street
Saint John NB E2L 4H9
Fax: (506) 636-9658

QUEBEC

Chicoutimi Tax Services Office
211 - 100 Lafontaine Street
Chicoutimi QC G7H 6X2
Fax: (418) 698-5544

Outaouais Tax Services Office
16th floor
15 Eddy Street
Hull QC K1A 1L4
Fax: (819) 994-1103

Jonquière Tax Centre
2251 de la Centrale Blvd.
Jonquière QC G7S 5J1
Fax: (418) 548-0846

Laval Tax Services Office
3131 St-Martin Blvd. W.
Laval QC H7T 2A7
Fax: (514) 956-6915

Montérégie Rive-Sud Tax Services Office
1000 de Sérigny Street
Suite 300
Longueuil QC J4K 5J7
Fax: (514) 928-5900

Montréal Tax Services Office
305 René Lévesque Blvd. W.
Montréal QC H2Z 1A6
Fax: (514) 496-1309

Québec Tax Services Office
165 de la Pointe-aux-Lièvres Street S.
Québec QC G1K 7L3
Fax: (418) 649-6478

Rimouski Tax Services Office
320 St-Germain Road E.
Rimouski QC G5L 1C2
Fax: (418) 722-3027

Rouyn-Noranda Tax Services Office
44 du Lac Avenue
Rouyn-Noranda QC J9X 6Z9
Fax: (819) 797-8366

Shawinigan-Sud Tax Centre
4695 - 12th Avenue
Shawinigan-Sud QC G9N 7S6
Fax: (819) 536-7078

Sherbrooke Tax Services Office
50 Place de la Cité
P.O. Box 1300
Sherbrooke QC J1H 5L8
Fax: (819) 821-8582

Trois-Rivières Tax Services Office
111 - 25 des Forges Street
Trois-Rivières QC G9A 2G4
Fax: (819) 371-2744

ONTARIO

Barrie Tax Services Office
99 Ferris Lane
Barrie ON L4M 2Y2
Fax: (705) 721-0056

Belleville Tax Services Office
11 Station Street
Belleville ON K8N 2S3
Fax: (613) 969-7845

Hamilton Tax Services Office
150 Main Street W.
P.O. Box 2220
Hamilton ON L8N 3E1
Fax: (905) 546-1615

Kingston Tax Services Office
385 Princess Street
Kingston ON K7L 1C1
Fax: (613) 545-3272

Kitchener/Waterloo Tax Services Office
166 Frederick Street
Kitchener ON N2G 4N1
Fax: (519) 579-4532

London Tax Services Office
451 Talbot Street
London ON N6A 5E5
Fax: (519) 645-4029

Toronto West Tax Services Office
77 City Centre Drive
P.O. Box 6000
Mississauga ON L5A 4E9
Fax: (905) 566-6182

North Bay Tax Services Office
180 Shirreff Avenue
P.O. Box 4300
North Bay ON P1B 9B4
Fax: (705) 671-3994

Toronto North Tax Services Office
1000 - 5001 Yonge Street
North York ON M2N 6R9
Fax: (416) 512-2558

Oshawa Tax Services Office
78 Richmond Street W.
Oshawa ON L1G 1E1
Fax: (905) 725-3780

Ottawa Tax Services Office
78 Richmond Street W.
Oshawa ON L1G 1E1
Fax: (905) 725-3780

Ottawa Tax Services Office
333 Laurier Avenue West
Ottawa ON K1A 0L9
Fax: (613) 238-7125

Ottawa Tax Centre
875 Heron Road
Ottawa ON K1A 1A2
Fax: (613) 739-1147

Peterborough Tax Services Office
185 King Street W.
Peterborough ON K9J 8M3
Fax: (705) 876-6422

St. Catharines Tax Services Office
32 Church Street
P.O. Box 3038
St. Catharines ON L2R 3B9
Fax: (905) 688-5996

Sault Ste. Marie Tax Services Office
22 Bay Street, 2nd floor
Sault Ste. Marie ON P6A 5S2
Fax: (705) 671-3994

Toronto East Tax Services Office
200 Town Centre Court
Scarborough ON M1P 4Y3
Fax: (416) 973-5126

Sudbury Tax Services Office
1050 Notre Dame Avenue
Sudbury ON P3A 5C1
Fax: (705) 671-3994

Thunder Bay Tax Services Office
130 South Syndicate Avenue
Thunder Bay ON P7E 1C7
Fax: (807) 622-8512

Toronto Centre Tax Services Office
36 Adelaide Street E.
Toronto ON M5C 1J7
Fax: (416) 954-5961

Windsor Tax Services Office
185 Ouellette Avenue
Windsor ON N9A 5S8
Fax: (519) 973-7188

MANITOBA

Brandon Tax Services Office
1039 Princess Avenue
Brandon MB R7A 4J5
Fax: (204) 726-7836

Winnipeg Tax Services Office
325 Broadway Avenue
Winnipeg MB R3C 4T4
Fax: (204) 943-3928

Winnipeg Tax Centre
66 Stapon Road
Winnipeg MB R3C 3M2
Fax: (204) 661-6989

SASKATCHEWAN

Regina Tax Services Office
1955 Smith Street
Regina SK S4P 2N9
Fax: (306) 757-1412

Saskatoon Tax Services Office
340 - 3rd Avenue N.
Saskatoon SK S7K 0A8
Fax: (306) 652-3211
Tel: 1-800-667-5508

ALBERTA

Calgary Tax Services Office
220 - 4th Avenue SE
Calgary AB T2G 0L1
Fax: (403) 264-5843

Edmonton Tax Services Office
Suite 10, 9700 Jasper Avenue
Edmonton AB T5J 4C8
Fax: (403) 428-1584

Lethbridge Tax Services Office
300 - 704 4th Avenue S.
P.O. Box 3009
Lethbridge AB T1J 4A9
Fax: (403) 382-3052

Red Deer Tax Services Office
4996 - 49th Avenue
Red Deer AB T4N 6X2
Fax: (403) 341-7053

BRITISH COLUMBIA

Burnaby - Fraser Tax Services Office
201 - 4664 Lougheed Highway
Burnaby BC V5C 6C2
Fax: (604) 666-2818

Kelowna Tax Services Office
118 - 1835 Gordon Drive
Kelowna BC V1Y 3H5
Fax: (250) 862-4744

Southern Interior B.C. Tax Services Office
277 Winnipeg Street
Penticton BC V2A 1N6
Fax: (250) 492-8346

Northern B.C. and Yukon Tax Services Office
280 Victoria Street
Prince George BC V2L 4X3
Fax: (250) 561-7869

Surrey Tax Centre
9755 King George Highway
Surrey BC V3T 5E1
Fax: (604) 585-5769

Vancouver Tax Services Office
1166 West Pender Street
Vancouver BC V6E 3H8
Fax: (604) 689-7536

Vancouver Island Tax Services Office
910 Government Street
Victoria BC V8V 1X3
Fax: (250) 363-3726

NORTHWEST TERRITORIES

Yellowknife Tax Services Office
4920 - 52nd Street, Suite 902
Yellowknife NT X1A 3T1

YUKON TERRITORY

Whitehorse Tax Services Office
120 - 300 Main Street
Whitehorse YK Y1A 2B5
Fax: (250) 561-7898

INTERNATIONAL TAX SERVICES OFFICE

International Tax Services Office
2204 Walkley Road
Ottawa ON K1A 1A8
Fax: (613) 941-2505

TAX INFORMATION PHONE SERVICE (T.I.P.S.)

T.I.P.S. is an automated telephone service that provides you with general and personal tax information. T.I.P.S. offers the five services listed below:

1. Telerefund—tells you the status of your 1997 refund. This service is available from February to September.
2. Goods and Services Tax/Harmonized Sales Tax (GST/HST) credit—tells you if you are eligible for the GST/HST credit and the date you can expect to receive your payment. This service is available for five weeks each time GST/HST credit payments are issued.
3. Registered retirement savings plan (RRSP) deduction limit—gives the amount of RRSP contributions you may deduct for 1997 and, if it applies, any undeducted amounts available for you to claim on your 1997 return. This service is available from September to the end of April.
4. Bulletin Board—contains recent information that may be of concern or interest to you.
5. Info-Tax—gives recorded tax information. For a list of topics, see the chart below. This service is available from mid-January to the end of June.

Telerefund, GST/HST credit, and RRSP deduction limit are available:

Weekdays from 7:00 a.m. to 11:00 p.m.
Saturdays from 8:00 a.m. to 4:00 p.m. and
Sundays from 8:00 a.m. to 1:00 p.m.

Bulletin Board and Info-Tax are available:

24 hours a day, 7 days a week.

How to use T.I.P.S.

Call the T.I.P.S. number under "Revenue Canada" in the "Government of Canada" section of your telephone book. Select the language you want to use, either "1" for English or "0" for French. Next, select the service you want to use:

"1" for Telerefund

"2" for GST/HST credit

"3" for RRSP

"4" for Bulletin Board or

"5" for Info-Tax. Once you are in the Info-Tax system, to select the topic you want, use the three-digit number from the chart below.

For **Telerefund, GST/HST credit,** and **RRSP** information, the auto-attendant will ask you to provide your social insurance number, as well as your month and year of birth. It will also ask you to state the total income you entered on line 150 of your return, so be sure to keep your working copy handy. If you call **on or before April 30,** you will need the amount you entered on line **150 of your 1996 return.** If you call **on or after May 1,** you will need the amount you entered on **line 150 of your 1997 return.**

Info-Tax Message Numbers and Topics

999 Main Menu	Table of contents	
121 Interest income	305 Equivalent-to-spouse amount	605 Authorizing representatives
126 Rental income	306 Amounts for infirm dependents age 18 or older	606 Refunds
127 Capital gains	314 Pension income amount	607 TELEFILE
128 Support payments received	316 Disability amount	609 Exchange rates
130 Other income	323 Tuition and education amounts	610 Do you have to file a return?
147 Non-taxable income	324 Transferring tuition and education amounts	611 Missing information
208 RRSP deduction	326 Transferring amounts from your spouse	612 Newcomers to Canada
214 Child care expenses	330 Medical expenses	630 Special services
215 Attendant care expenses	349 Donations and gifts	631 Services for disabled persons
219 Moving expenses	448 GST/HST credit	655 Home Buyers' Plan
220 Support payments	449 Child Tax Benefit	702 Instalment payments
221 Carrying charges or interest expenses	601 Electronic filing (EFILE)	703 Making payment arrangements
229 Other employment expenses	602 Filing or making changes to a previous year's return	705 Interest on unpaid taxes
232 Other deductions	603 Your appeal rights	706 Late-filing penalties

Info-Tax Message Numbers and Topics (*Continued*)

999	Main Menu		Table of contents		
254	Capital gains deduction	604	Voluntary disclosures	707	Interest rate
255	Northern residents deductions			882	Direct deposit
301	Age amount			883	Problem Resolution Program
303	Spousal amount			899	Info-Tax survey

Samples of Important Estate Planning Documents

ESTATE PLANNING WORKSHEET

Prepared on: _____

PERSONAL INFORMATION: An individual preparing a Will should familiarize himself or herself with the personal facts regarding the Testator, including marital status and dependants, if any.

Name: _____

Address: _____

_____, _____ _____

S.I.N.: _____

Telephone: Home: _____

Date of Birth: _____

Place of Birth: _____

Employer: _____

Address: _____

_____, _____ _____

WILL HISTORY:

I do not currently have a Will.

MARITAL STATUS:

I am married.

Name of Spouse: _____

S.I.N: _____

Date of Birth: _____

Business Address: _____

Previous Marriages:

I have been previously married.

Name of former spouse: _____

Obligations owed to former spouse:

_____

CHILDREN:

My children (including adopted children and stepchildren) are:

SAFETY DEPOSIT BOX:

I currently have ____ safety deposit box(es).

     Name of Bank: _____

     Address of Bank: _____

                          _____, _____ _____

     Key Location:

     _____

     _____

     Status of Box: Held jointly with Spouse

VALUE OF THE ESTATE: A valuation of the estate assets is needed to determine whether tax consequences are an important consideration in the preparation of the Will. While there are no estate taxes in Canada as such, there are deemed dispositions of capital property and other tax consequences affecting various assets on death and it may become important to consider more complex estate planning techniques in the case of an estate of significant value or complexity. The manner in which assets are held (for example, "jointly" or "in one name only") is also important in determining who will receive certain property (for example, "joint" property passes outside of the estate to the "surviving" joint tenant regardless of what the Will may provide).

<u>Detailed Listing of Assets and Liabilities</u>
<u>of</u>
<u>Bank Accounts (chequing, savings, GIC's, etc.)</u>

Testator Accounts Totals $ 0
Spouse's Accounts Totals $ 0
Joint Accounts Totals $ 0
Total Bank Accounts $ 0

Retirement or Pension Plans:

Testator Total	$	0
Spouse Total	$	0
Joint Total	$	0
Total Value of Retirement Benefits	$	0

Investments (Brokerage accounts, mutual funds, etc.):

Testator Total	$	0
Spouse Total	$	0
Joint Total	$	0
Total Value of Investment Accounts	$	0

Stocks:

Testator Total	$	0
Spouse Total	$	0
Joint Total	$	0
Total Value of Stocks	$	0

Bonds:

Testator Total	$	0
Spouse Total	$	0
Joint Total	$	0
Total Value of Bonds	$	0

Real Property:

Type of Real Estate	*Owner*	*Amount*	
Testator Total		$	0
Spouse Total		$	0
Joint Total		$	0
Total Value of Real Estate		$	0

Life Insurance:

Testator Total	$	0
Spouse Total	$	0
Joint Total	$	0
Total Value of Life Insurance	$	0

Business Interests:

Type of Business Interest	*Owner*	*Amount*
Testator Total		$ 0
Spouse Total		$ 0
Joint Total		$ 0
Total Business Interests		$ 0

Vehicles:

Registered in the name of the Testator:

Vehicle Year, Make and Model	Registration No:	Amount

Registered in the name of the Spouse:

Vehicle Year, Make and Model	Registration No:	Amount

Registered in the name of the Testator and Spouse:

Vehicle Year, Make and Model	Registration No:	Amount

Testator Total	$	0
Spouse Total	$	0
Joint Total	$	0
Total Vehicles	$	0

Personal Property:

Description	*Owner*	*Amount*

Testator Total		$	0
Spouse Total		$	0
Joint Total		$	0
Total Personal Property		$	0

Liabilities:

Liability	*Person Liable*	*Amount*

Testator Total		$	0
Spouse Total		$	0
Joint Total		$	0
Total Liabilities		$	0

Net Assets:

	Testator	*Spouse*	*Joint*	*Totals*
Assets	$ 0	$ 0	$ 0	$ 0
Liabilities	$ 0	$ 0	$ 0	$ 0
Net Estate	$ 0	$ 0	$ 0	$ 0

DISTRIBUTION OF THE ESTATE ASSETS: The persons or organizations (beneficiaries) who will receive the assets of the estate should be identified.

First Priority:

My first priority is to provide for my Spouse (on the assumption that my Spouse will provide for my children).

Second Priority:

My second priority is to provide for my Children.

Bequests:

I would also like to include the following bequests:

Legacies:

I would also like to include the following legacies:

In general terms, I would like to have the assets of my estate distributed as follows: This summary assumes that the bequests and legacies noted above have already been made.

       Percent   Beneficiary

TRUST FOR MINOR CHILDREN: I wish to include Will provisions that will create a "trust for minor children". This trust should be included only if my spouse does not survive my death. I understand that this type of trust provides that my trustee will manage all or a portion of my assets for the benefit of my children, until each child attains an age specified by me for the outright distribution of the trust assets to that child.

The trust assets should be distributed outright to each of my children in two (2) distributions at the following ages: 0 and 0.

TRUSTEE: A trustee is the person or entity named in a Will who has the responsibility to administer ongoing trusts by managing the trust assets and making distributions as required by the terms of the trust. Often the term "trustee" is used interchangeably with the term "executor" in a Will if the same person is fulfilling both roles.

First Choice:
      Name: _____
      Address: _____
                      _____, _____ _____

GUARDIAN: A guardian is a person named in the Will who has the legal responsibility to take care of minor children until the children reach the age of majority, usually at 18 years. A choice of guardian in a Will is not legally binding but the Court will most frequently give effect to the Testator's wishes unless there is a compelling reason not to do so.

First Choice:
      Name: _____
      Address: _____
                      _____, _____ _____

EXECUTOR: An Executor is the person named in the Will who has the responsibility to carry out the terms of the Will (for example, collect the deceased's assets, pay the debts, distribute the remaining assets to the beneficiaries, and administer ongoing trusts). The term "Executor" is often used interchangeably with "Trustee" when the individual takes on the administration of ongoing trusts as part of his or her responsibility in carrying out the terms of the Will. Where possible, the Testator should choose an Executor who resides in the same Province as him or her to avoid delay in the administration of the estate and the possibility that the Court might require a bond to be posted for an out-of-province Executor.

First Choice:
      Name: _____
      Address: _____
                      _____, _____ _____

WILL

THIS IS THE LAST WILL of _____ , of
_____ , in the Province of _____ .

Part I
Initial Matters

Revocation

1. I REVOKE all former Wills and Codicils.

Executors and Trustees

2. I APPOINT _____ to be the Executor and Trustee
of my Will.

Cremation/Burial

3. I DIRECT that my remains be cremated.

Funeral

4. I DIRECT _____
_____
_____
_____
_____

Guardian

5. If my spouse should predecease me, I APPOINT
_____ to be the guardian of my minor child.

a. I expressly authorize my Trustees at their discretion to provide out of the residue of my estate
any financial assistance my Trustees consider advisable to any person or persons who are acting
as guardians of my minor children for the purpose of assisting such guardian or guardians to

accommodate my minor children or for any other purpose which my Trustees deem to be in the best interests of my minor children. This assistance may be provided in whatever manner my Trustees in their discretion consider advisable, including by way of loan or payment in respect of which there is no obligation for repayment. It is my wish that the resources of my estate be made available for such guardian or guardians so that they are not subjected to financial or physical burden by agreeing to look after my children.

Life Insurance Declaration

6. I DECLARE that all insurance policies on my life shall be paid to my spouse, _____ , if my spouse survives me by thirty (30) days. If my spouse predeceases me or fails to survive me by thirty (30) days, then I DECLARE that the proceeds shall be added to my estate to be dealt with as part of the residue of my estate.

Tax Deferred Assets

7. I DIRECT that my entitlement to any assets that were income tax deferred during my lifetime by virtue of them being deducted from my normal income and taxable as income in the year of my death be paid or transferred over to my spouse, _____ , if my spouse survives me for thirty (30) days, and for my spouse's own use absolutely, and if my spouse does not so survive me, then I DIRECT that all entitlement to any of these assets shall be dealt with as part of the residue of my estate.

Headings

8. I DECLARE that the paragraph headings in my Will are for convenience and shall not be construed to affect the meaning of the paragraphs so headed.

Part II
Disposition of Estate

9. I GIVE AND APPOINT all my property, including any property over which I may have a general power of appointment to my Trustees upon the following trusts:

Debts

I DIRECT my Trustees to pay out of and charge to the capital of my general estate my legally enforceable debts, funeral and testamentary expenses and all estate, inheritance and succession duties or taxes that may be payable as a result of my death.

Legacies

I DIRECT my Trustees to pay the following legacies from my estate:

a. The sum of _____
($0) DOLLARS to _____ if such person survives me.

b. The sum of _____
($0) DOLLARS to _____ if such person survives me.

Bequests

I DIRECT my Trustees to make the following bequests from my estate:

Household and Personal Goods

To transfer all articles of personal and household use or ornament belonging to me at my death to my spouse, _____, if my spouse survives me for a period of thirty (30) days; PROVIDED THAT if my spouse predeceases me or survives me but dies within a period of thirty (30) days following my death, such articles shall form part of the residue of my estate.

Distribution to Spouse

To pay or transfer the residue of my estate to my spouse, _____, for my spouse's own use absolutely, if my spouse survives me for a period of thirty (30) days.

Distribution to Children

If the beneficiary or beneficiaries named above as my first priority to receive the residue of my estate, do not survive me or otherwise do not receive their allotted interest in my estate in accordance with the terms contained in my Will; to pay or transfer the residue of my estate to my children who survive me, in equal shares; PROVIDED THAT if any of my children predecease me leaving issue alive at my death, that issue shall take in equal shares per stirpes the share of residue to which my deceased child would have been entitled if he or she had survived me.

Contingent Beneficiaries

If my spouse predeceases me, or if my spouse survives me but dies within a period of thirty

days, to divide the residue of my estate into two (2) equal parts and to distribute those equal parts as follows: To pay or transfer one (1) of the equal parts to my
_____, if such person(s) survive(s) me; and to pay or transfer the remaining equal part to my spouse's
_____, if such person(s) survive(s) my spouse and me.

Part III
Administration of the Estate

10. TO CARRY OUT the terms of my Will, I give my Trustees the following powers:

Realization

To call in and convert into money the residue of my estate in a manner and upon the terms my Trustees think best, and, in order that the residue of my estate is converted in an advantageous manner, I give my Trustees power to postpone the conversion of any part of my estate with power to retain any part in the form in which it exists at my death (even though it may not be in a form which would constitute an investment authorized for trustees and whether or not any liability attaches to that part of my estate) until an advantageous conversion is obtainable and I declare that my Trustees are not responsible for any loss which occurs to my estate resulting from a properly considered postponement and retention of the residue of my estate.

Trust for Beneficiaries

If any person becomes entitled to any share in my estate before attaining the age of 0 years, the share of that person shall be held and kept invested by my Trustees and the income and capital or so much of the income and capital as my Trustees in their absolute discretion consider necessary or advisable shall be used for the care, maintenance and education of that person until he or she attains the age of 0 years, when the capital of that share or the amount remaining shall be paid to him or her, any income not used in any year shall be added to the capital of that share and shall be dealt with as a part of the capital.

Payments for Minors

To make any payments for any person under the age of majority to a parent or guardian of that person whose receipt of those payments shall be a sufficient discharge to my Trustees.

Distribution in Kind

To make any division of my estate or set aside or pay any share or interest, either wholly or in part of the assets of my estate at the time of the division, setting aside or payment, and my Trustees shall determine the value of my estate or any part of it for the purpose of making that division, setting aside or payment and their determination shall be binding upon all persons concerned notwithstanding that any of my Trustees may be personally interested in the division.

Investment Powers

To invest, and from time to time reinvest, assets of my estate in securities and investments inside or outside Canada, without being limited to those investments to which trustees are otherwise restricted by law.

Borrowing to Facilitate Administration

To raise money on the credit of my estate, either without security or by mortgage or charge, on any part of my estate, for the purpose of facilitating the administration of my estate.

Real Property

If at any time and for so long as any real or leasehold property forms part of my estate, I give my Trustees full power and discretion to sell, mortgage, lease without being limited as to term, exchange, give options on or otherwise dispose of or deal with any real estate held by my Trustees and to repair, alter, improve, add to or remove any buildings thereon, and generally to manage that real estate.

Claims

To release, forgive, compromise, settle or waive any claim or debt which may be owing to me or by me at my death.

Direction to Distribute Estate on Timely Basis

I direct that my Trustee administer my estate and distribute my estate to my beneficiaries as quickly as possible and, wherever possible, to make an interim distribution if a final distribution is being delayed for any reason.

Businesses and Corporations

To carry on any corporate enterprise or business to the full extent permitted by law, including all limited liability corporations controlled by me, and any partnerships or proprietorships carried on by me at the time of my death, during such period or periods as they shall think fit and to join in or take any action with any business and corporate investments or to exercise any rights, powers and privileges which at any time may exist or arise in connection with any such investments to the same extent and as fully as I could do if I were alive and the sole owner of such investments.

Employment of Agents

Instead of acting personally, to employ and pay any other person or persons including a corporation to transact any business or to do any act of any nature in relation to my Will and the trusts contained in my Will, including the receipt and payment of money, without being liable for any loss incurred thereby. And I authorize and empower my Trustees to appoint from time to time upon any terms they think fit any person or persons including a corporation, for the purpose of exercising any of the trusts or powers expressly or impliedly given to my Trustees with respect to any property belonging to me.

Tax Elections and Determinations

To make or not to make any election, determination or designation pursuant to any taxing statute including the "Income Tax Act" and the "Excise Tax Act" which they deem to be in the best interests of my estate and the beneficiaries of my estate.

Charitable Receipts

I declare that any receipt given by the treasurer or other official of each organization benefiting under the terms of this my Will shall be a sufficient discharge to my Trustees.

In witness whereof I have to this my last Will and Testament, written upon this and the ____ preceding pages of paper, subscribed my name this _____ day of _____, ___.

_____

_____

SIGNED by the Testator, _____, in our presence and attested to by us in the Testator's presence and in the presence of each other.

_____
Witness

Name: _____
Address: _____
          _____, _____ _____
Occupation: _____

_____
Witness

Name: _____
Address: _____
          _____, _____ _____
Occupation: _____

AFFIDAVIT OF EXECUTION

CANADA
PROVINCE of _____
TO WIT:

I, _____, of
_____, in the Province of _____,
MAKE OATH AND SAY:

1. I am one of the subscribing witnesses to the Last Will of the testator,

   _____.

2. The Will is dated the _____ day of _____, 199__, and is marked as Exhibit A to this Affidavit.

3. When the testator signed the Will, I believe the testator
   3.1 was 18 years of age or more
   3.2 understood that the document being signed was the testator's Last Will
   3.3 was competent to sign the Will.

4. The testator, myself, and the other witness to the Will,

   _____, were all present together when the witnesses and the testator signed the Will.

( ) 5. That no interlineations, alterations, erasures, or obliterations were made to the Will before the testator and the witnesses signed the Will.

   - OR -

( ) 5. That the following interlineations, alterations, erasures, or obliterations were made to the Will before the testator and the witnesses signed the Will.

   _____

   _____

_____

Witness

_____ SWORN BEFORE ME
_____ AFFIRMED BEFORE ME

in _____, in the Province of
_____, this _____
day of _____, ____.

_____

_____ Commissioner for Oaths
_____ Notary Public

LIVING WILL

TO MY FAMILY, PHYSICIAN AND ALL OTHERS CONCERNED:

I, _____ , being of sound mind, willfully and voluntarily, direct that if the time comes when I can no longer take part in decisions for my own health care, that this statement stand as an expression of my wishes and directions.

If at such a time the situation should arise in which there is no reasonable expectation of my recovery from extreme physical or mental disability, I direct that I be allowed to die and not be kept alive by medications, artificial means or "heroic measures".

I do, however, ask that medication be mercifully administered to me to alleviate suffering even though this may shorten my remaining life.

AND for greater clarification I specifically list the following life sustaining measures either to BE undertaken or NOT be undertaken on my behalf:

YES	NO	
X		Cardiopulmonary Resuscitation (CPR)
X		Ventilation (breathing machine)
X		Dialysis (kidney machine)
X		Life saving surgery
X		Blood transfusion
X		Life saving antibiotics
X		Tube feedings

Additional life sustaining measures are directed as follows:

_____

_____

_____

_____

_____

_____

This statement is made after careful consideration and is in accordance with my strong convictions and beliefs. I want the wishes and directions here expressed carried out to the extent permitted by law. Insofar as they are not legally enforceable, I hope that those to whom this Living Will is addressed will regard themselves as morally bound by these provisions.

DATED at _____, in the Province of _____, this _____ day of _____,___.

_____

_____

_____

Witness Name

_____

Witness Name

GENERAL POWER OF ATTORNEY - LONG

I, _____ , residing at

_____ , _____ , _____ _____ ,

appoint _____ residing at

_____ , _____ , _____ _____ ,

as my attorney in my name and to do on my behalf and for my sole benefit anything that I can lawfully do by an attorney and without limiting the generality of the foregoing, to:

1. Demand and receive from any person all sums of money, securities for money, debts, goods, chattels, effects and things which are owing, payable or belonging to me, or for the principal money and interest in respect of any mortgage or other security, or for the interest or dividends payable to me in respect of any shares, stocks, or interest which I hold in any company or for any money or securities for money which are due in respect of any bond, note, bill of exchange, balance of account, consignment, contract, decree, judgment, order or execution or upon any other account.

2. Upon the receipt of any sum of money, securities for money, debts, goods, chattels, effects or things due, owing, payable or belonging to me, my attorney may sign receipts, releases and acquittances, certificates, conveyances, surrenders, assignments, satisfaction pieces, discharges of judgments, partial discharges of judgments, discharges of liens, partial discharges of liens, discharges of mortgages, partial discharges of mortgages, assignments of mortgages without personal covenants, transfers of mortgages without personal covenants, memorials or other discharges that may be required.

3. Examine, settle, liquidate or adjust any accounts between myself and any person. Sign any cheque or order that may be required for the payment of money, bill of exchange or note in which I am interested. Draw upon any bank, trust company or person for any sum of money that is to my credit and to deposit this money in any bank, trust company or other place and at the discretion of my attorney, to withdraw this money from time to time as I could do.

4. In the case of neglect, refusal or delay on the part of any person to render true and full accounts and payments of debts due to me, to compel him or them to do so, and for that purpose to take any legal action as my attorney shall think fit; also to appear before any of the courts of law, and to sue, plead, answer, defend and reply in all matters and causes concerning the said debts; and also to exercise all powers of sale or foreclosure and all powers vested in me by any mortgage belonging to me as mortgagee; also to execute conveyances under power of sale and transfers under power of sale, and to make applications for foreclosure.

5. In case of any dispute with any person concerning any of the above matters, to submit any

such dispute to arbitration as my attorney may see fit; to accept part in satisfaction for the payment of the whole of any debt or to grant an extension of time for the payment of the same, either with or without taking security, as to my attorney shall appear most expedient.

6.   Take possession of and let, sell, manage and improve my real estate and to appoint any agents in managing the same, and to remove such agents, and appoint others using the same power and discretion as I might do.

7.   Sign all leases and agreements for lease as shall be required or necessary in the care and management of my property and to receive and collect all rents that may be payable to me and in my name to give effectual receipts therefor.

8.   Demand and sue for all rents and profits due in respect of my property and to use all lawful means for recovering the rents and profits and for ejecting from the said property all tenants and occupants who are in default, and for determining the tenancy or occupancy and for obtaining, recovering and retaining possession of all or any of the property held or occupied by such persons so making default.

9.   Sell as my attorney decides is reasonable or expedient, all mortgages and other securities for money, debts, choses in action, stocks, shares, bonds, goods, chattels and all other personal property whatsoever owned by me, and to assign or transfer the above to the purchaser, and to execute such assignments of mortgage, transfers of mortgage, assignments of agreements for sale, transfers of stock, bills of sale, conveyances, transfers and assurances with power to give credit for the whole or any part of the purchase money and to permit the purchase money to remain unpaid for whatever time and upon whatever security my attorney shall think proper.

10.   If or when my attorney decides to sell all my real estate which I own or any interest I have in any real estate, either separately or in parcels and by public auction or private contract as my attorney shall see as reasonable and expedient; my attorney shall execute all agreements for sale, including options to purchase, assignments of agreements for sale, conveyances, assurances, deeds, transfers, withdrawals of caveat and partial withdrawals of caveat, also to execute any plan of subdivision of any properties; with power in connection with the sale of any of the above property to give credit for the whole or any part of the purchase price and to permit the purchase price to remain unpaid for whatever times and upon whatever security, real or personal either including the purchased property or not as my attorney shall think proper.

11.   Mortgage and borrow money upon the security of my property, real or personal wherever situated, and in such sums and upon such terms and conditions as my attorney may see as expedient, and for such purposes to sign all mortgages or other instruments which may be required, which mortgages may contain the usual covenants and powers of sale, and such further covenants, clauses and conditions as the mortgagee may require and my attorney may deem

expedient, and to give such bonds or promissory notes collateral to the mortgage as may be necessary in connection therewith and collateral thereto, and to repay the said mortgage moneys at such times as my attorney may see as expedient.

12. Execute all deeds, assurances, covenants and things as shall be required and as my attorney shall see fit for any of the purposes above, and to sign and give receipts for any sum of money which shall come to his hands by virtue of the powers of this instrument, which receipts whether given in my name or that of my attorney shall exempt the person paying such sum of money from all responsibility of seeing to the application thereof.

13. Execute proxies or other instruments authorizing a person to attend and vote on my behalf at meetings of holders of shares, stocks, bonds, debentures and funds of companies in which I hold shares, stocks, bonds, debentures or funds.

14. Have access to examine, deposit, remove or replace any contents of any safety deposit box I may have in any institution.

I GRANT FULL POWER to my attorney to substitute and appoint one or more attorney or attorneys under my attorney with the same or more limited powers, and in my attorney's discretion to remove such attorneys.

I covenant for my heirs, executors and administrators to ratify whatever my attorney (or his/her substitute) shall do by virtue of this instrument, including whatever shall be done between the time of my death or of the revocation of this instrument, and the time my attorney (or such substitute) becomes aware of my death or the revocation of this instrument.

This power of attorney shall remain in full force until due notice in writing of its revocation shall have been given to _____.

IN WITNESS WHEREOF I have executed this document on the _____ day of _____,
___, in _____, in the Province of _____.

_____

_____

_____
_____
Witness Name

_____
_____
Witness Name

AFFIDAVIT OF EXECUTION

CANADA
PROVINCE OF _____
TO WIT:

I, _____, of
_____, in the Province of _____,
MAKE OATH AND SAY:

1.   That I was personally present and did see _____
referred to in the attached General Power of Attorney, who is personally known to me to be the
person named therein, duly sign and execute the same for the purpose named therein.

2.   The General Power of Attorney was executed in _____, in the Province of
_____, and I am the subscribing witness thereto.

3.   That I know the Donor and the Donor is in my belief, of the full age of Nineteen (19) years.

_____
Witness

___ SWORN BEFORE ME
___ AFFIRMED BEFORE ME

in _____, in the Province of
_____, this _____
day of _____, _____.

_____

___ Commissioner for Oaths
___ Notary Public

in and for the Province of _____

(My Commission expires: _____)

POWER OF ATTORNEY FOR PERSONAL CARE

*(Made in accordance with the Substitute
Decisions Act, 1992)*

1. I, _____ , revoke any previous power of attorney
   for personal care made by me.

2. I APPOINT _____ to be my attorney for
   personal care in accordance with the Substitute Decisions Act, 1992.

3. I give my attorney(s) the AUTHORITY to make any personal care decision for me that I am
   mentally incapable of making for myself, including the giving or refusing of consent to
   treatment to which the Consent to Treatment Act, 1992, applies, subject to the Substitute
   Decisions Act, 1992, and any instructions, conditions, or restrictions contained in this form.

4. The following instructions, conditions, or restrictions apply to this power of attorney for
   personal care:

   _____
   _____
   _____
   _____
   _____
   _____

   Further instructions, conditions, and restrictions in the form of a Living Will are attached to
   this power of attorney for personal care.

5. I AUTHORIZE compensation to my attorney(s) for personal care from my property in
   accordance with the fee scale prescribed by regulation for the compensation of guardians of
   property made pursuant to section 90 of the Substitute Decisions Act, 1992.

_____   _____
                                      Date
_____
Grantor

We have no reason to believe that the grantor is incapable of giving a continuing power of attorney for personal care or making decisions in respect of which instructions are contained in this power of attorney. We have signed this power of attorney in the presence of the person whose name appears above and in the presence of each other.

_____   _____
                                      Date

Witness Name: _____

Address: _____
                   _____
                   _____
                   _____

_____   _____
                                      Date

Witness Name: _____

Address: _____
                   _____
                   _____
                   _____

CONTINUING POWER OF ATTORNEY
FOR PROPERTY

*(Made in accordance with the Substitute
Decisions Act, 1992)*

1. I, _____ , revoke any previous continuing powers
of attorney for property made by me.

2. I APPOINT _____ to be my attorney for property.

3. I AUTHORIZE my attorney(s) for property to do on my behalf anything that I can lawfully
do by an attorney, and specifically anything in respect of property that I could do if capable of
managing property, except make a will, subject to the law and to any conditions or restrictions
contained in this document.

I FURTHER AUTHORIZE my attorney(s) for property to make gifts and loans to my friends
and relatives on my behalf. Any gifts and loans shall be made in accordance with the provisions
of the Substitute Decisions Act, 1992.

I FURTHER AUTHORIZE my attorney(s) for property to make charitable gifts from my
property on my behalf in accordance with the provisions of the Substitute Decisions Act, 1992.

This indicates my intention that this document will be a continuing power of attorney for
property under the Substitute Decisions Act, 1992 and may be used during my incapacity to
manage property.

4. The following conditions and restrictions apply to this continuing power of attorney for
property·

_____

_____

_____

_____

_____

_____

5. This continuing power of attorney will come into effect on the date it is signed and witnessed.

6. I AUTHORIZE my attorney(s) to take annual compensation from my property in accordance
with the fee scale prescribed by regulation for the compensation of guardians of property made
pursuant to the Substitute Decisions Act, 1992.

_____

_____   _____

Grantor   Date

We have no reason to believe that the grantor is incapable of giving a continuing power of attorney for personal care or making decisions in respect of which instructions are contained in this power of attorney. We have signed this power of attorney in the presence of the person whose name appears above and in the presence of each other.

_____   _____

                                                       Date

Witness Name: _____

Address: _____

                     _____

                     _____

                     _____

_____   _____

                                                       Date

Witness Name: _____

Address: _____

                     _____

                     _____

                     _____

SOURCES FOR FURTHER READING

The following titles are books I believe you will enjoy reading. Some of them have bibliographies of their own which you can peruse for further references. With the exception of just a few, I have listed distinctly Canadian titles to ensure that the material is relevant. Too many Canadian bookstores, today, stock foreign sources that are often irrelevant to our Canadian retirement reality.

Carroll, Jim and Rick Broadhead. *Canadian Money Management On-Line.* Scarborough: Prentice Hall Canada Inc., 1996.

Clason, George S. *The Richest Man In Babylon.* New York: Penguin Books USA Inc., 1998.

Croft, Richard and Eric Kirzner. *The Beginner's Guide to Investing.* Toronto: Harper Collins Publishers Ltd., 1997.

Deloitte & Touche. *Canadian Guide to Personal Financial Management.* Scarborough: Prentice Hall Canada Inc., 1997.

Ellmen, Eugene. *The 1998 Canadian Ethical Money Guide.* Toronto: James Lorimer & Company, Publishers, 1997.

Foster, Sandra E. *You Can't Take It with You.* 2nd Edition. Etobicoke: John Wiley & Sons Canada Ltd., 1998.

Gadsden, Stephen. *The Canadian Guide to Investing for Life.* Whitby: McGraw-Hill Ryerson Ltd., 1997.

Gadsden, Stephen. *The Canadian Mutual Funds Handbook.* 3rd Edition. Whitby: McGraw Hill Ryerson Limited, 1998.

Gadsden, Stephen and Philip Gates. *The New Heir's Guide to Managing Your Inheritance.* Whitby: McGraw-Hill Ryerson Limited, 1998.

Graham, Benjamin. *The Intelligent Investor.* 4th Edition. New York: Harper & Row, Publishers, Inc., 1973.

Grant, John. *Handbook of Economic Indicators.* Toronto: University of Toronto Press, 1992.

Gray, Douglas. *The Canadian Snowbird Guide.* Whitby: McGraw-Hill Ryerson Ltd., 1997.

Hartman, George. *Risk Is A Four Letter Word.* Toronto: Stoddart Publishing Company Limited, 1998.

Hill, Napoleon. *Think & Grow Rich.* New York: Ballantine Books, 1983.

Jacks, Evelyn. *Jacks on Tax Savings.* Whitby: McGraw-Hill Ryerson Limited, 1998.

Lynch, Peter. *One Up on Wall Street.* New York: Penguin Books USA Inc., 1990.

McNicol, Barry. *The Severance Package Strategy Book.* Toronto: Stoddart Publishing Company Limited, 1996.

Reid, Angus. *Shakedown.* Toronto: Seal Books, 1997.

Stewart, Walter. *Bank Heist.* Toronto: Harper Collins Publishers, 1997.

HOW TO FIND AN EXCELLENT RETIREMENT ADVISOR

It isn't like it used to be. Twenty or so years ago, if you had a question concerning your finances, you most likely talked to mom or dad or, in a pinch, with your friendly insurance agent. If you needed something really esoteric, such as a car loan or mortgage, you probably talked to your local bank manager. Wow, have times changed!

Now that Canada's financial services industry has been deregulated, banks, trust companies, insurance companies and stock brokerages all openly compete with one another to garner hard-won consumer dollars from every quarter. It's no wonder that many Canadians, today, find the realm of personal finance a confusing welter of different products and services.

Determining whom they should have as their financial resource is no exception. Nowadays, anyone can call himself a financial planner. While there are moves in various provinces to set down specific requirements before a person can use the "financial planner" designation, this aspect of Canada's financial services industry still remains largely unregulated. To help you choose the right person as your financial planner, I have summarized below what you should look for to ensure that the person you decide to work with is the right choice for you.

HOW TO KNOW IF YOU NEED A FINANCIAL PLANNER

Before spending time reading the rest of this appendix, you should determine if you really need the services of a financial professional. Asking yourself the questions below will help you make that decision.

- Do you have time to manage your financial affairs?
- Are you confused about conflicting investment or financial planning advice offered by different sources?
- Do you believe that you are paying too much income tax and do not know how to rectify the problem?
- Are your expenses exceeding your regular income?
- Is your savings and investment plan working to the best of its ability?
- Has there been, or will there be, any change in your lifestyle that will affect your financial future, such as marriage, unemployment, retirement, death or inheritance?
- Are you prepared to take the time to research, comprehend, implement and monitor your own investment plan?

If you've found at least two of these questions relevant, you'd better read on to determine who you're going to hire to help put your financial house in order.

PROFESSIONAL QUALIFICATIONS YOU SHOULD LOOK FOR

There are a number of designations that financial professionals use to distinguish themselves from the more than 35,000 people who comprise today's financial services industry. These designations are the Chartered Financial Consultant (CHFC), Personal Financial Planner (PFP), Certified Financial Planner or Chartered Financial Planner (CFP) and Registered Financial Planner (RFP). If you are going to use the services of a financial professional, he or she should have at least one of these designations. This is your guarantee that the person you hire to assist you will have minimum recognized educational requirements.

The Chartered Financial Consultant is a designation adopted by the insurance industry. It is conferred after completing a rigorous training program. It is one of the best in the industry because the CHFC is granted only after candidates have completed a long study program referred to as the Chartered Life Underwriter Program, leading to the CLU designation. While oriented to insurance products and services, the CHFC represents a top-notch education program. The Personal Financial Planner designation is peculiar to the banking industry and is comprised of a series of courses in a variety of financial areas. The PFP is offered only through the banking industry and is an attempt to compete with the more broadly based CFP program. The Certified Financial Planner designation has been conferred on about 4,800 individuals across Canada as of November 1997. The CFP is comprised of six comprehensive courses that cover everything from personal financial planning to economics, taxation and investment management. Today's CFP designation is an outgrowth of the older Chartered Financial Planner program first offered by the Canadian Institute of Financial Planning. The Financial Planners Standards Council of Canada (FPSCC) is a newly formed organization that hopes to one day bring together all of today's financial designations under the CFP. The Canadian Association of Financial Planners offers the Registered Financial Planner designation. The RFP used to compete directly with the older CFP program and didn't do as well. Today, the president of the CAFP refers to the RFP as an "advanced designation" that "includes a higher set of standards than the CFP and other designations." This claim isn't true and is particularly self-serving.

There is another program that is available to individuals who deal in stocks, bonds and other securities through various stock exchanges in Canada. This program is offered through the Canadian Securities

Institute. The first step that an individual has to complete is a general but intensive course on the Canadian securities industry. The first course to be completed is called the Canadian Securities Course (CSC), followed immediately by the Conduct and Practice Handbook Course (CPH). Once completed, individuals are then encouraged to complete a one-year study program called the Professional Financial Planning program (PFP). The PFP program leads to the Certified Financial Planner designation and should not be confused with the banking industry's PFP program. Individuals who achieve the CSI's PFP designation have the option to take the Canadian Investment Management program or CIM that leads ultimately to the highest conferred title, Fellow of the Canadian Securities Institute (FCSI).

These are the designations that you should look for when hiring a financial professional. Unfortunately, this leaves many good people who are working through the ranks in the cold, so to speak. But to be fair, it's your money and you want to ensure that the person who is helping you make it grow is competent to do so.

OTHER PREFERRED QUALIFICATIONS

Just because an individual has completed a formal educational program doesn't mean that he or she is the right financial planner for you. You have to judge your choice on a number of additional items as well.

I have listed some considerations in point form below:

- The person—appearance, personality, personal and professional integrity
- Experience—minimum five years of direct industry experience
- Expertise—financial planning, investment management, retirement and estate planning
- Professional achievements—articles published, books (not self-published or ghost written), newspaper columns, special industry awards, professional associations
- Services provided—accounting, financial planning services, newsletters, regular reviews, tax preparation
- Community interests—community participant
- Costs—reasonable commission, fee and commission, or fee-only
- Professional references—professional and client-based references.

QUESTIONS TO ASK YOUR FINANCIAL PROFESSIONAL

There are a number of specific questions you should ask individuals whom you are considering to act as your financial advisor. These questions, and the answers you receive, will help further refine your search for the ideal financial advisor. These questions are to be directed to the individual as follows:

- Do you specialize in certain financial disciplines? (not more than three and are they what you need)
- Can you supply me with names and phone numbers of your clients who would be willing to speak with me about your services? (you should be able to get as many names as you feel necessary)
- Do you concentrate on attracting a particular kind of client? (particular net worth, age, professional)
- Will you work directly with me or, with whom and why? (advisor should be prepared to work directly with you, administration is usually handled by an assistant or administration associate)
- How do you build solutions and what resources do you use to articulate my financial plan? (this will vary, ask for and receive illustrations of past financial plans he or she has prepared for current clients)
- How are you compensated? (be direct and ask for details so that there are no surprises).

Index

Aggressive common shares, 67
Aggressive growth portfolio, 59, 62
Aging population, 2
Annuities, 109-111
    non-registered, 134, 135
    registered, 128, 129
    RRIFs, compared, 131, 132
Asset allocation, 56-68
Asset classes, 50
Attitude, 13
Attribution rules, 176-178, 194

Bearer deposit notes (BDNs), 62
Bell Canada Enterprises (BCE), 59
Bond discounting, 139
Bonds, 63, 64. *See also* Government of Canada
    bonds
Borrowing to invest, 77-80, 189
Bre-X, 54, 72
Buy and hold, 70
Buy-sell agreements, 185

Canada education savings grant (CESG), 34
Canada Pension Plan (CPP)
    CPP benefits, 97-99
    income splitting, 90
    pay-as-you-go formula, 3
    pros/cons, 125, 126
    restructuring, 2-4
Canada Savings Bonds (CSBs), 63, 121, 122,
    135-137
Canadian investment management (CIM) pro-
    gram, 239
Canadian Life and Health Compensation
    Corporation (Comp Corp), 111
Canadian Securities Course (CSC), 239
Canadian Securities Institute, 238, 239
Capital accumulation plan
    allocation of assets for investment, 31-36
    inflation management, 40-43
    long-term plan maintenance, 47, 48
    start early, 38-40
    systematic savings and investment, 36-38
    tax management, 43-46
Capital accumulation strategies
    leveraging, 77-80
    lump sum investing, 70-72
    lump sum/systematic investing combined,
        76, 77
    Risk Master Technology, 80-82
    systematic investing, 73-76
Capital gains dividends, 91, 124, 144
Capital gains exemption, 184
Capital loss carry-back, 186
Capital preservation and income portfolio, 57,
    58, 60
Capital preservation-growth and income invest-
    ments, 123

Capital preservation-high growth and tax-pre-
    ferred income investments, 123, 124
Capital preservation-high income investments,
    121-123
Capital reserves, 186
Career average pension plan (CAPP), 101
Case studies, 153-168
    Jack and Jill (married couple), 161-165
    prudent engineer, 153-157
    reluctant teacher, 157-161
    Smith, Sally (retired widow), 166-168
Cash and cash equivalents, 50, 51, 59-63, 88, 89
Cashable annuities, 135
Cashable GICs, 137
Certificates of deposit (CDs), 62
Certified cultural property, 179
Certified financial planner (CFP), 238
CESG, 34
CFP designation, 238
Change, 47
Charitable gift annuity, 181
Charitable gifts, 178-182, 195
Charitable remainder trust, 182
Chartered financial consultant (CHFC), 238
CIM program, 239
Commercial paper, 62
Common shares, 52, 67, 68, 89, 142
Comp Corp, 111
Compound GICs, 137
Conduct and Practice Handbook Course (CPH),
    239
Consumer price index (CPI), 88
Continuing power of attorney for property, 233,
    234
Convertible preferred shares, 66
Corporate debentures, 64
CPI, 88
CPP. *See* Canada Pension Plan (CPP)
CSBs, 63, 121, 122, 135-137

DBPP, 101-103
DCA, 107, 108
DCPP, 103
Death. *See* Estate planning
Debentures, 64
Debt, 29, 30
Deferred annuities, 110
Deferred compensation arrangement (DCA),
    107, 108
Deferred profit sharing plan (DPSP), 105, 106
Defined benefit pension plan (DBPP), 101-103
Defined contribution pension plan (DCPP), 103
Desire, 13
Determination, 13
Diamet Minerals, 59
Disability insurance, 30, 94, 191
Diversification, 56, 71, 188
Dividend income, 91, 124

Dividend tax credit, 124
Dollar cost averaging, 73-75, 189
Dow Jones Industrial Average (past perfor-
   mance), 71
DPSP, 105, 106

Early-in-life investing, 38-40
80 factor, 84
Emergency reserve, 33
Employee profit sharing plan (EPSP), 107
Employment, termination of, 126, 127
EPSP, 107
Equity growth securities, 52, 67, 68, 89
Equity income securities, 51, 52, 65-67, 89,
   123, 124
Estate freeze, 184, 185
Estate planning, 96, 169-186, 193, 194
   capital loss carry-back, 186
   capital reserves, 186
   charitable gifts, 178-182
   continuing power of attorney for property,
      233, 234
   deemed disposition, 169, 170
   documents, 210-234
   estate freeze, 184, 185
   family farms, 184
   general power of attorney, 226-230
   income splitting, 176-178
   ITA provisions, 170, 171
   joint ownership of property, 175, 176
   life insurance, 185
   living will, 224, 225
   net capital losses, 186
   power of attorney for personal care, 231, 232
   preferred beneficiary election, 186
   principal residence, 175
   qualifying small business, 184
   registered assets, 171-173
   segregated funds, 186
   shareholder agreements, 185
   spousal rollover provision, 172, 174
   spousal trust, 174
   terminal return (final tax return), 170
   trusts, 183
   will, 174, 175, 216-223
   worksheet, 210-215

Failure of Canada's pension system, 1, 2, 11, 12
Family farms, 184
FAPP, 101
Farm rollovers, 184
FBPP, 102
FCSI, 239
Fellow of the Canadian Securities Institute
   (FCSI), 239
Final average pension plan (FAPP), 101
Finance paper, 62
Financial goal setting, 55
Financial planners, 237-240
Financial Planners Standards Council of Canada
   (FPSCC), 238
Financial reserve, 33

First mortgage bonds, 64
Fixed dollar withdrawal plan, 146-148
Fixed income securities, 51, 63-65, 89, 123
Fixed period withdrawal plan, 148, 149
Flat benefit pension plan (FBPP), 102
Floating rate preferred shares, 66
Foreign bonds, 64
Future capital expenditures, 34
Future value, 41

General power of attorney, 226-230
GICs, 121, 122, 137, 138
GIS, 100
Gold, 54
Government of Canada bonds, 63, 138-140
Government offices. *See* Retirement planning
   resources
Group registered retirement savings plans
   (GRRSPs), 106, 107
Guaranteed income supplement (GIS), 100
Guaranteed investment certificates (GICs), 121,
   122, 137, 138

Hard assets, 53, 54
HCPP, 105
High growth portfolio, 58, 59, 61
High income portfolio, 58, 60
High yield common shares, 67, 142
High yield preferred shares, 141
Hints (30 key steps), 187-195
Hybrid combination pension plan (HCPP), 105

Income GICs, 137
Income splitting, 90, 176-178, 194
Income taxes
   attribution rules, 176-178
   capital accumulation plan, 43-46
   death, and, 170-174
   deemed disposition at death, 169, 170
   interest income/capital gains/dividends, 124
   retirement finances planning, 90-93
   systematic withdrawal plans, 151, 152
Indexed annuity, 110
Individual pension plan (IPP), 105
Inflation
   capital accumulation plan, 40-43
   retirement finances planning, 84-86
   RRSPs, and, 88
Information Circular 91-1, Guidelines for
   Preparation of T1 Returns, 93
Installment refund annuity, 110
Insurance
   disability, 30, 94, 191
   life, 94-96, 185, 191
   retirement finances planning, 94-96
Insured annuity, 110
Inter vivos trust, 183
Interest income, 91, 124
Interest only withdrawal option, 130
International Business Machines (IBM), 59
Intestacy, 170
Investment characteristics, 56

Investment classes, 50
Investment income, 91
Investment strategies. *See* Capital accumulation
    strategies, Retirement income strategies
Investment suitability, 34, 35
Investor reaction to losses/gains, 35
IPP, 105

Japanese stock market index (Nikkei), 75, 76
Joint life annuity, 109
Joint tenancy, 175, 176

Key steps, outline, 187-195

Last-to-die insurance policy, 95
Law of consanguity, 170
Level withdrawal option, 130
Leveraging, 77-80, 189
LIF, 119, 120, 132-134, 173
Life expectancy, 2, 12
Life expectancy adjusted withdrawal plan, 149,
    150
Life income fund (LIF), 119, 120, 132-134, 173
Life insurance, 30, 94-96, 185, 191
Limited partnerships (LPs), 54
Liquidity, 88-90
LIRA, 117, 173
LIRRSP, 116, 173
Living will, 224, 225
Locked-in registered retirement savings plan
    (LIRRSP), 116, 173
Locked-in retirement account (LIRA), 117, 173
Locked-in retirement income fund (LRIF), 119,
    120, 133, 134
Long-term money accumulation plan. *See*
    Capital accumulation plan
LPs, 54
LRIF, 119, 120, 133, 134
Lump sum investing, 70-72, 189

Macdonald Commission, 1
Margin call, 79
Market risk, 69, 70
Market timing, 70
MBSs, 65
MEPP, 104
Minimum withdrawal option, 129
Moderate growth and income portfolio, 58, 61
Money market securities, 59. *See also* Cash and
    cash equivalents
Money purchase pension plan (MPPP), 103
Mortgage backed securities (MBSs), 65
MPPP, 103
Multi-employer pension plan (MEPP), 104
Municipal debentures, 64
Mutual funds, 68, 69, 143-152

Names/addresses of government offices. *See*
    Retirement planning resources
Net capital losses, 186
Net worth statement, 14-31
Nikkei (Japanese stock market index), 75, 76

Non-registered annuities, 109, 134, 135

Old age security (OAS), 99
Over-the-counter market (OTC), 139

Pension tax credit, 125, 126
Personal financial goals, 55
Personal financial planner (PFP), 238
PFP designation, 238
PFP program, 239
Planning your retirement finances, 83-96
    cash management, 83
    converting accumulated assets to retirement
        income assets, 87, 88
    estate planning, 96
    gross vs. net retirement income, 86
    income taxes, 90-93
    inflation, 84-86
    insurance, 94-96
    liquidity, 88-90
    retirement income needs, 83, 84
Portfolio archetypes, 57-62
Power of attorney for personal care, 231, 232
Preferred beneficiary election, 186
Preferred shares, 51, 52, 65-67, 89, 123, 124,
    140-143
Prescribed annuity, 135
Present value, 41
Principal residence, 175
Private pension plans. *See* Registered pension
    plans (RPPs)
Professional advisors, 237-240
Professional financial planner (PFP) program,
    239
Profit sharing pension plan (PSPP), 104
Provincial bonds, 64
PSPP, 104

Qualifying small business corporation (QSBC),
    184
Questions to ask yourself, 55

Ratio withdrawal plan, 145, 146, 151
RCA, 106
Real estate securities, 52, 53, 68, 90
Real-life investing. *See* Case studies
Registered annuities, 109, 128, 129
Registered financial planner (RFP), 238
Registered pension plans (RPPs)
    death, and, 172
    deferred profit sharing plan, 105, 106
    defined benefit plans, 101-103
    defined contribution plans, 103, 104
    group registered retirement savings plans,
        106, 107
    hybrid combination pension plan, 105
    individual pension plan, 105
    liquidity, 126
    multi-employer pension plan, 104
    profit sharing pension plan, 104
    recent changes, 10, 11
    retirement compensation arrangement, 106

Registered retirement income fund (RRIF), 88, 117-119, 129-132, 173
Registered retirement savings plans. *See* RRSPs
Rental income, 91
RESP, 34
Retirement compensation arrangement (RCA), 106
Retirement finances planning. *See* Planning your retirement finances
Retirement income strategies, 125-152
    annuities/RRIFs, compared, 132
    criteria to watch for, 127
    CSBs, 136, 137
    GICs, 138
    Government of Canada bonds, 140
    LIFs/LRIFs, 134
    mutual funds (systematic withdrawal plan), 151, 152
    non-registered annuities, 135
    preferred shares, 142, 143
    registered annuities, 129
    RRIF withdrawals, 131
    RRSP withdrawal strategy, 128
Retirement planning, 14
Retirement planning resources
    financial planning & investment issues, 201, 202
    health issues, 197-200
    insurance issues, 200, 201
    pensions, 202
Retirement resources. *See* Sources of retirement resources
Retractable preferred shares, 66
Revenue Canada offices, 203-207
RFP designation, 238
Risk, 35, 69
Risk comfort zone, 188
Risk Master Technology (RMT), 80-82, 189, 190
Risk-reward, 35, 49, 62
Risk-reward investment pyramid, 50
Risk tolerance, 35, 55
RMT, 80-82, 189, 190
Royal Trustco, 67
RPPs. *See* Registered pension plans (RPPs)
RRIF, 88, 117-119, 129-132, 173
RRSPs, 127, 128
    advantages, 111-114
    carry-forward provisions, 8
    contribution limits, 7, 115, 116
    death, and, 173
    inflation, and, 88
    maturity (conversion) date, 10
    over-contributions, 8, 115
    overview, 6-10
    rollover of retirement allowance benefits, 9
    spousal, 90, 131
    withdrawal strategy, 128

Saving, 30, 36. *See also* Capital accumulation plan
Segregated investment funds, 186
Seniors Benefit, 5, 6
Serial bond, 64
Severance package, 126

Shareholder agreements, 185
Single life annuity with guarantee, 109
Smoothing withdrawal option, 130
Sources of retirement resources, 97-124
    annuities, 109-111
    Canada Pension Plan, 97-99
    capital preservation-growth and income investments, 123
    capital preservation-high growth and tax-deferred income investments, 123, 124
    capital preservation-high income investments, 121-123
    deferred compensation arrangement, 107, 108
    employee profit sharing plan, 107
    guaranteed income supplement, 100
    life income fund, 119, 120
    locked-in registered retirement savings plan, 116
    locked-in retirement account, 117
    locked-in retirement income fund, 119, 120
    old age security, 99
    private pension plans, 101-107. *See also* Registered pension plans (RPPs)
    RRIFs, 117-119
    RRSPs. *See* RRSPs
    spouse's allowance, 100
SPA, 100
Speculative common shares, 68
Spousal rollover provision, 174, 194
Spousal RRSP, 90, 131
Spouse's allowance (SPA), 100
Starting early, 38-40
Straight preferred shares, 65, 66
Strip bonds, 64
Subordinated debentures, 64
Succession plan, 169. *See also* Estate planning
Summary (30 key steps), 187-195
SWP, 144-152, 193
Systematic investing, 73-76
Systematic savings and investment, 36-38
Systematic withdrawal plan (SWP), 144-152, 193
T-bills, 62, 121, 122
T.I.P.S., 207-209
Tax credits/deductions, 93
Tax information phone service (T.I.P.S.), 207-209
Tax shelter, 92
Taxes. *See* Income taxes
Tenancy-in-common, 175
Term certain to age 90, 110
Term to 100 insurance policy, 95
Term withdrawal option, 130
Termination of employment, 126, 127
Testamentary trust, 183
Treasury bills (T-bills), 62, 121, 122
Trusts, 183, 195. *See also* Spousal trust

Universal life policy, 95

Variable annuity, 110
Variable preferred shares, 66

Will, 174, 175, 194, 216-223

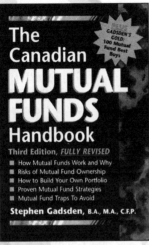

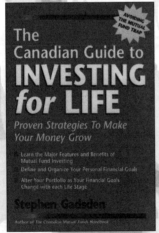

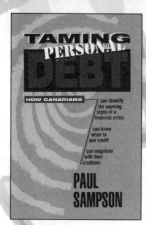

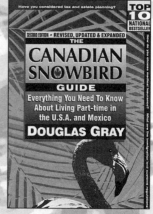
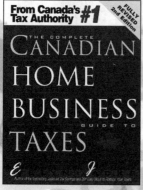